THE GENDER QUESTION IN GLOBALIZATION

Gender in a Global/Local World
Series Editors: Jane Parpart, Pauline Gardiner Barber
and Marianne H. Marchand

Gender in a Global/Local World critically explores the uneven and often contradictory ways in which global processes and local identities come together. Much has been and is being written about globalization and responses to it but rarely from a critical, historical, gendered perspective. Yet, these processes are profoundly gendered albeit in different ways in particular contexts and times. The changes in social, cultural, economic and political institutions and practices alter the conditions under which women and men make and remake their lives. New spaces have been created – economic, political, social – and previously silent voices are being heard.   North-South dichotomies are being undermined as increasing numbers of people and communities are exposed to international processes through migration, travel, and communication, even as marginalization and poverty intensify for many in all parts of the world.   The series features monographs and collections which explore the tensions in a 'global/local world', and includes contributions from all disciplines in recognition that no single approach can capture these complex processes.

Also in the series

Turkey's Engagement with Global Women's Human Rights
Nüket Kardam
ISBN 0 7546 4168 6

(Un)thinking Citizenship
Feminist Debates in Contemporary South Africa
Edited by Amanda Gouws
ISBN 0 7546 3878 2

Vulnerable Bodies
Gender, the UN and the Global Refugee Crisis
Erin K. Baines
ISBN 0 7546 3734 4

Fashioning Inequality
The Multinational Company and Gendered
Employment in a Globalizing World
Juanita Elias
ISBN 0 7546 3698 4

The Gender Question in Globalization

Changing Perspectives and Practices

Edited by

TINE DAVIDS and FRANCIEN VAN DRIEL
Radboud University Nijmegen, The Netherlands

ASHGATE

Published by
Ashgate Publishing Ltd
Gower House
Croft Road
Aldershot
Hants GU11 3HR
England

Ashgate Publishing Company
Suite 420
101 Cherry Street
Burlington, VT 05401-4405
USA

Ashgate website: http://www.ashgate.com

British Library Cataloguing in Publication Data
The gender question in globalization : changing
    perspectives and practices. – (Gender in a global/local
    world)
    1. Women – Social conditions 2. Globalization – Social
    aspects 3. Feminist theory 4. Culture and globalization
    I. Davids, Tine II. Driel, Francien Th. M. van, 1953 –
    305.4'2

Library of Congress Control Number: 2005931415

ISBN-10: 0 7546 3923 1

Cover image design and text formatting by Maarten Slooves.

Printed and bound in Great Britain by MPG Books Ltd. Bodmin, Cornwall.

Contents

Series Editors' Preface

The Gender Question in Globalization: Changing Perspectives and Practices by Tine Davids and Francien van Driel is the 6th title appearing in the Ashgate series 'Gender in a Global/Local World', which saw the publication of its first book three years ago. The consistent high quality titles in the series, mostly single-authored, reflect two distinct trends. First, there has been an interesting turn in feminist and gender studies toward the global. This turn has been the result of increased concerns about the (gendered) impact of globalization and contingent international processes. Second, feminist and gender analyses of globalization are underscoring the importance of studying its multidimensionality, in particular the contingent nature of economic, political, social and cultural processes while simultaneously emphasizing the need to engage in local expressions and articulations of globalization.

The edited collection by Davids and van Driel is a reflection of these important trends in feminist and gender studies. As such it provides a state of the art analysis of feminist scholarship about globalization. The editors have organized the book around themes that highlight the triple dimensions of applying a gender lens: the symbolic, structural and subject dimension. This allows them to question concepts such as global, local, modernity and tradition and the assumptions on which they are constructed.

The first section of the collection focuses on the lived realities of women and men, rejecting discourse which victimizes subalterns. Rather than accepting such a view, the authors of this section emphasize agency in a local context. The second section highlights how globalization produces difference in its articulation at the local. Gender(ed) ideas and ideologies, in particular concerning reproductive issues and sexuality, are important influences on or provide mechanisms for local differentiation. The last section sets out to deconstruct assumed, and often unquestioned, global/modern and local/traditional nexuses. The contributions to this section discuss the construction of identity and (traditional) culture in a transnational context as well as hybridity/modernization in a local (Muslim) setting.

The collection by Davids and van Driel is not only a welcome addition to the Ashgate series, but also provides a synthesis of the aims of the series: to study and understand gendered processes and mechanisms in an increasingly globalized world, while simultaneously focusing on the local articulations and differentiation of such phenomena. In other words, it is a must read for anyone interested in keeping up with the latest feminist and gender scholarship.

Acknowledgements

Gender was high on our research and lecturing agenda long before globalization entered the field of development studies. Once globalization became a buzzword, the relation between gender and globalization puzzled and worried us. In our book proposal to the editors of the Ashgate series, Gender in a Global/Local World, we wrote:

> The central theme of this book is the relation between gender and globalization. Our point of departure is that debates on globalization can be characterized as a normative scientific enterprise. Most positions taken in the debate, in particular within developments studies, range between neo-liberal and anti-liberal modernization lines of thought, focusing mainly on a macro-economical perspective. Once gender enters the stage, the meaning of globalization is taken for granted, which results in an unproblematic relation between gender and globalization.

This book is the result of a process of problematizing this 'taken for granted' link between gender and globalization. We would like to thank the series editors, Pauline Gardiner Barber, Marianne Marchand and Jane Parpart, for giving us this opportunity. Their confidence and support in establishing this academic endeavour gave us a channel to express the ideas that resulted in this book.

However, many more scholars were involved in this process. We would like to thank the Netherlands Association of Gender and Anthropology and Development Studies (LOVA). At their annual conference in 2001 on gender and globalization, we presented our views and appreciate the inspiring reactions. We would also like to thank Marianne Marchand for inviting us to a workshop on gender and globalization at the international annual conference of the European Consortium for Political Research in 2001 in Canterbury, where the idea for this book was born. Moreover, we are grateful to Haleh Afshar, who invited us to the meeting of the Development Studies Association's (DSA) women and development study group in York in 2002.

The stimulating and critical reactions during these meetings and the suggestion of writing a book led us to accept this challenge and to invite a variety of Dutch associate researchers from different specializations and sometimes even different disciplines, ranging from literature studies, development studies and anthropology, to migration and conflict studies, as contributors. During an expert meeting in 2003 at the Radboud University of Nijmegen, the Netherlands, where all authors presented a synopsis of their contributions, this volume gained momentum. The final result is a Dutch academic scientific product and we, as editors, would like to express our gratefulness to Anouka, Annelou, Fenneke, Halleh, Karin, Kathy, Lineke, Lorraine, Mathijs, Marion and Thea for their contributions, their cooperation and great support.

But it was the wonderful assistance of many persons that enabled us to finalize this book. We would especially like to thank Kirstin Howgate at Ashgate Publishing for her wonderful backing, Jerry DeVincent for his English corrections, Gonny van Hal of the University Language Centre, Radboud University, Nijmegen for arranging the corrections. Moreover, we would like to express thanks to Maarten Slooves for the cover design and for making the manuscript camera ready, and Miriam van der Veen for helping with the index. We thank NWO, the Dutch Scientific Foundation, whose financial support made it possible to finalize the book. Our colleagues at the Nijmegen Centre for International Development Issues supported us throughout the process and we thank them for their comments on our introduction.

Tine Davids and Francien van Driel

Nijmegen, May 2005

List of Contributors

Tine Davids is lecturer at the Centre for International Development Issues at the Radboud University Nijmegen, the Netherlands. She is involved in teaching and research on gender, politics, globalization and the link between culture and development. Her regional specialization is on Latin America, where she did research in Mexico on gender and political representation. More recently, she was also involved in research on re-migration and transnationalism.

Kathy Davis is Associate Professor in Women's Studies at Utrecht University, the Netherlands. Born in the United States, she has taught psychology, medical sociology and women's studies at various universities in the Netherlands. She is the author of several books on power, the female body and feminist theories. She is currently working on a cross-cultural history of The Boston Women's Health Book Collective and *Our Bodies, Ourselves*.

Francien van Driel is an assistant professor at the Centre for International Development Issues at the Radboud University Nijmegen, the Netherlands. She has published works on gender theories, globalization and development and female-headed households in Botswana (PhD). For the last 20 years Southern Africa has been her region of specialization and she is currently involved in research on future perspectives and identity construction among young adults in South Africa.

Anouka van Eerdewijk is currently working on PhD research on the gendered construction of pre-marital sexuality of young people in Dakar, Senegal. She is affiliated with the Centre for Gender Studies and the Centre for International Development Studies (CIDIN) at the Radboud University Nijmegen, the Netherlands. Her research interests are sexual and reproductive rights and health, gender and sexuality, and young people.

Halleh Ghorashi is Assistant Professor of Organizational Anthropology in the Department of Culture, Organization, and Management at the Free University of Amsterdam. She was born in Iran and came to the Netherlands in 1988. She has published works on Iranian women exiles in the Netherlands and the USA and on questions of identity, Diaspora, and Iranian women's movement.

Dorothea Hilhorst is an associate professor at Disaster Studies of Wageningen University, the Netherlands, where she specializes in natural disasters, conflict and humanitarian aid in relation to development. Her work focuses on the actors affecting and affected by disasters and aid, and examines their everyday discourses and practices.

Mathijs van Leeuwen is a graduate in Development Sociology and is currently working on PhD research on discourses and practices of civil society peace building and supporting international organizations in the Great Lakes Region of Africa and Guatemala. He is affiliated with Wageningen Disaster Studies, at Wageningen University, the Netherlands.

Lorraine Nencel was born in New York. She has conducted research on prostitution in Lima Peru (PhD). She works as an assistant professor at the Methodology Department of the Free University, Amsterdam, the Netherlands. Her works concentrate on urban, gender and sexuality issues and she has a passion for methodology and epistemology. Her most recent research is on the lives of secretaries and identity construction in Lima, Peru.

Fenneke Reysoo (PhD Anthropology) has conducted research in various countries, among them Morocco, Bangladesh and Mexico, on reproductive rights, women's autonomy and the construction of masculinities. She currently works at the Graduate Institute of Development Studies in Geneva, Switzerland, where she is co-responsible for the annual Colloquium on Gender and Globalization.

Lineke Stobbe is an assistant professor at the Department of Culture, Organization and Management of the Free University, Amsterdam, the Netherlands. She has been doing research on gender and labour in Argentina since 1989. Currently, she is doing research on organizational culture and upward mobility of women, mainly in male dominated organizational contexts.

Marion den Uyl is an assistant professor at the Department of Social and Cultural Anthropology of the Free University, Amsterdam, the Netherlands. She has published works on feminist anthropology and on women and development, especially on Kerala, for which she gained her PhD. She has followed the developments in India for the last two decades. Presently, she is involved in research among immigrants in Amsterdam, the Netherlands.

Karin Willemse is a lecturer at the Department of History of Non-Western Societies at the Erasmus University, Rotterdam, the Netherlands. Since 1999, she has held the Chair of the National Network for Feminist Anthropologists in the Netherlands (LOVA). She has published works on her research in the Sudan. She is currently engaged in organizing research on 'Islam in Africa' for the International Institute for the Study of Islam in the Modern World (ISIM) at Leiden University, the Netherlands.

Annelou Ypeij works at Cedla (Utrecht, the Netherlands). She is involved in research in Cuzco, Peru, on the tourist industry, gender and ethnicity. Formerly she was a senior researcher at the Sociology Department of Erasmus University, Rotterdam, the Netherlands. She has done research on the formal economy in Lima, Peru and on poor single mothers in the Netherlands (the latter in close cooperation with Gerdien Steenbeek).

INTRODUCTION

Chapter 1

Changing Perspectives

Tine Davids and Francien van Driel

Imagine an internet system, linking up computer users. Or a rush of immigrants across national borders. Or capital investments shuttled to varied offshore locations. These world-making 'flows' are not just interconnections but also the re-carving of channels and the remapping of the possibilities of geography. Imagine the landscape nourished by the creek. Yet even beyond the creek's 'flows', there are no stable landscape elements: Trees sprout up, transforming meadows into forests; cattle browse on saplings, spreading meadows past forest edges. Nor are forests and meadows the only ways to divide up the landscape. Consider the perspective of the earthworm, looking for rich soils, or the weed, able to flourish in both meadow and forest, though only when each meets certain conditions. To tell the story of this landscape requires an appreciation not only of changing landscape elements but also of the partial, tentative, and shifting ability of the story teller to identify the elements at all (Anna Tsing, 2000, p. 453).

Introduction

Representing globalization as an ever-changing landscape of ongoing flows and moving structures, shifting borders and different perspectives is a very appealing metaphor. This metaphor addresses precisely those characteristics of globalization we want to explore in this book. The globalization landscape is vast and the constituting elements multiple. However, in this book we do not take an earthworm's perspective to explore the landscape but we put a gender lens in action. In other words, we explore the way gender shapes and curves the globalization landscape and vice versa. By using the gender lens we wish to explore gender constructions at the global/local nexus. We do so by simultaneously looking at how globalization shapes the lives of men and women in a local setting and by looking at men and women as actors in global processes.

Why do we put gender at centre stage? In the steadily growing literature on globalization, a gender perspective is missing; while in the literature on gender and globalization, the phenomenon of globalization is taken for granted and, thus, stays underexposed (see also Fernández-Kelly and Wolf, 2001). Moreover, the analysis of the relation between gender and globalization tends to be restricted to either a global perspective, for example, of neo-liberal economic, social and political restructuring, or a perspective concentrated on local effects of global influences, for example, the so-called feminization of poverty. In this book we not only try to combine the two but also develop a perspective in which we perceive the first as an intrinsic part of the latter and vice versa.

Imagining globalization as a landscape, as Anna Tsing does, implies the challenge of considering globalization as a complicated process in which the global and the local are mediated by each other: the so-called global-local nexus (the landscape). But, what then is meant by the local and the global? Part of the project of this book is to rethink the meaning of both and not to depart from a pre-given meaning of these concepts. We will argue that what one sees tends to shift, not only depending on who describes it but also on what elements are identified as part and parcel of the landscape. This not only holds true for the meaning of the concepts of the global and the local, but also for the meaning of the concept of gender. Different practices, in particular local settings, produce different meanings of gender. Gender therefore seems to be crucial in the production of differences in global/local dynamics. Hence, gender serves as an ethnic, national or other boundary marker, or as a way of fixing the flows, as we will see in this book. However, whatever meaning it is given, the outcome is never predictable. Such a process of giving meaning, i.e. of culture, is at the centre of analysis of the local/global nexus. Consequently it is a challenge to assess the meanings given to this global/local nexus from a gender perspective.

In this book the different authors identify and discuss different elements of the global/local nexus by looking through the gender lens. What all have in common is the objective to deconstruct global orthodoxies (Chant, 1999) in analyzing the relation between gender and globalization. Looking through a gender lens, the authors explore how cultural constructions are being created. In the book we move away from static worldviews and show how the global colours the local and vice versa. Within feminist studies we moved away from static worldviews by replacing the category of women by the concept of gender and so crossing the nature-culture divide. Likewise, in this book, we would like to move away from the global as flux and flow (and ultimately as modern), while the local stands for the receiving end, not able to escape the change (and ultimately for the traditional).

Moreover, we will apply the analytical gender approach to bridge these kinds of divides and dichotomies. The organization of this book rests upon the analytical search concerning the deconstruction of the global/local dichotomy. This search is built upon recent debates on women, gender and globalization and has resulted in an exploration of the many faces that shape the landscape where gender and globalization intertwine. Hence the title of this book: *The Gender Question in Globalization*.

In this introduction we will explain the organization of this book following the different analytical emphasis the authors implement, but not without first mapping the different positions on women, gender and globalization that inspired the overall approach of this book and helped to shape the formulation of our own approach of 'the gender lens'. Consequently, we position ourselves vis-à-vis recent debates on globalization in general and on gender and globalization in particular and seek our own perspective. We realize that we do not honour all the literature, nor can we be exhaustive on this subject, but we use literature mostly in the field of development studies that explicitly addresses globalization to develop our perspective. We do this by reconstructing the journey we made when trying to grasp this link between gender and globalization. After the initial introduction to this theme, which started with writing a paper for a workshop in 1997 and several articles on the subject later, the project expanded by inviting different authors to join in. The mobilization of old and new academic networks shaped the dynamics of this project and, as is the case with all knowledge production, demonstrates the way in which it is situated (Haraway, 1988). Since we consider the scientific perspective to be part and parcel of the globalization landscape, we want to let you as readers in on the current of events and the way our ideas 'travelled'. We will describe how the project and thereby the landscape unfolded, which resulted in this book. We end this introduction by presenting the contributions in this volume and indicate which analytical challenges and questions are taken up by the respective authors to investigate the link between gender and globalization.

Unravelling the Project: The Gender Perspective

The take-off for this project was a workshop on the significance of globalization for development studies at the Radboud University of Nijmegen in the Netherlands in 1997. Challenged to present a paper on gender and globalization during this workshop, we set out to search for literature. A first search for literature taught us that references on women and/or gender and globalization were scarce, in contrast to the enormous variety in literature on globalization itself. It struck us that in this scarcity of literature, globalization appeared mainly as a neo-liberal process that has a rather negative influence on women. An extreme example of such an approach to globalization can be found in Christa Wichterich's book:

> ...['G]lobalized woman' is burnt up as a natural fuel: she is the piece-rate worker in export industries, the worker living abroad who sends back foreign currency, the prostitute or catalogue bride on the international body and marriage markets, and the voluntary worker who helps to absorb the shocks of social cutbacks and structural adjustment... (Wichterich, 2000, p. 167).

In Wichterich's book, entitled *The Globalized Woman* (2000), women feature as victims, while globalization is pictured as a nightmare scenario for most of the world's women. At the same time, women are called upon to resist these developments. Also, in the book *Women Resist Globalization* (Rowbotham and Linkogle, 2001), women are seen as the agents of change. The authors even refer to a new emancipatory trajectory in which millions of poor women with their ingenious forms of resistance and survival must be recognized as part of counter-hegemonic globalization (ibid. 2001, p. 23). Here globalization seems to represent all issues women are mobilizing against, from environmental degradation to reproductive rights and from poverty to racism.

> Many of the movements of poor women around livelihood have arisen in response to the impact of globalization. The version of 'modernization' that puts the stress on

immediate economic efficiency has been forcing groups of women in many parts of the world onto the margins of their societies (ibid. 2001, p. 6).

Although many of these findings about the negative impact of neo-liberal restructuring may be real, this one-dimensional approach of globalization troubled us.

The first limitation of this interpretation of globalization is that globalization only appears as an economic process of restructuring, leaving out questions on social, political and cultural changes. The second limitation is that globalization seems a process beyond the control of women. Women seem victims without being an active part of the changes, but at the same time women are called upon to awaken and resist globalization. This rings a familiar bell from the past: defining women both as problem and as solution to problems that are beyond their control. Besides, it limits gender to women and only the aspect of class is included in the analysis, leaving aside ethnicity, age and religion, among others.

In an attempt to further pinpoint the assumptions beneath these negative approaches to women and globalization, we decided that our next step in this project should consist of a closer look at one of the dominant debates on globalization and women within development studies, which represented a similar economistic approach: the feminization of poverty debate. The feminization of poverty literally refers to the increasing number of women among the poor. In the literature the 'assumed' growth of the number of female-headed households is seen as an indication of this feminization of poverty. The main reasoning of this argument is that globalization has led to an acceleration of the feminization of poverty, mostly reflected in households that are headed by women. The following step – to the claim that households headed by women are poor – is one that is then easily made.

In deconstructing this debate, we were able to demonstrate that these assumptions imply a simplification of both globalization and gender. In this debate the impact of globalization is fixed and sometimes even assumed at the local level. In the process of analyzing along these lines, gender issues are being reduced to poverty issues and gender is substituted by women. The result is that gender analyses disappear almost unnoticed (Davids and van Driel, 2001, pp. 165-167). Furthermore, impoverishment of women becomes a global orthodoxy that is not questioned anymore (Chant, 1999). Starting from these assumptions, a political agenda is formulated that focuses on the impoverishment of women. This representation of globalization does not address the complexities of global restructuring; instead it pictures a homogeneous and one-dimensional process. In doing so it neglects the diversities of women's realities.

Especially troublesome is that women as a category replaces gender and here the theoretical gains of decades seem to be reversed. Starting out as the study of women and development into a study on gender and development, we now seemed to be on the way back to studying women. Moreover, the ways that power relations are portrayed in this debate evoke old paradigms of thinking in dichotomies between oppressors and oppressed, in which globalization replaces (patriarchal) capitalism.

In an article titled 'from women and development to gender and globalization', we explored how, within development studies, a paradigm shift has taken place from women as a category of analysis to gender as an analytical concept (Davids and van Driel, 2002). Simultaneously we discussed how the analysis of gender and power relations has shifted from thinking in dichotomous categories of mainly masculine oppressors and female victims of patriarchy, into analyses with room for multiple processes of gender constructions, for differences and multiple identities (see e.g. Moore, 1994).

In both publications we elaborated upon the gender lens, which will also feature in this book as the main analytical tool. The gender lens, inspired by the work of Sandra Harding (1986), Joan Wallace Scott (1988), C. Hagemann-White (1989) and Rosi Braidotti (1994), consists of three dimensions, which are interconnected. This lens equips us with the analytical apparatus to deconstruct gendered processes such as the above analysis of the feminization of poverty. It is the interconnection of subjects, institutions and practices, ideas and images that shape our special perspective. More importantly, it contains the necessary ingredients to link discourses, with lived realities and vice versa. In other words, the gender lens offers us the methodological tools to observe phenomena from multiple points of view and perspectives. The above-mentioned dimensions of symbols, structures and subjects, which in practice constantly interact, constitute this gender lens.

This approach enables us to study the production of differences but goes beyond thinking in dichotomous categories and includes the analysis of processes (Davids and van Driel, 2001). Processes of gender construction (and processes of globalization) are both historically and culturally variable. Above, we started with the metaphor of the landscape, with its instable landscape features. Additionally, we expressed our uneasiness with persistent stereotypes in some of the literature on women/gender and globalization, i.e. the representation of women as victims of globalization. This stereotyping of both women and globalization is precisely what the symbolic dimension stands for.

This dimension of symbolic order represents symbols, ideas and images that can solidify into very persistent cultural texts and become stereotypes. The male breadwinner paradigm is a clear example of such a stereotype, with implications for the public/private divide. What happens is that differences are articulated as absolute differences, such as differences between *the* man and *the* woman, *the* rich and *the* poor, *the* global and *the* local. This does not mean, however, that the symbolic dimension only holds very clear-cut, opposite differences. In this dimension hierarchies are constructed, but these hierarchies can be contradicting and conflicting as well. Needless to say, at a symbolic dimension, many different ideas or versions of 'the woman' or 'the man' coincide. In our view, as mentioned above, many studies on globalization stop at this point of analysis – hence, the reproduction of stereotypes and, finally, global orthodoxies.

However, these ideas, stereotypes, images, differences and hierarchies not only figure at a symbolic level or dimension, but are also reflected in socially institutionalized practices. Differences get multiplied, reshaped and reinterpreted in different practices such as marriage laws, labour regulations, household statistics and so on. Within this dimension, the structural differences articulated at the symbolic level become institutionalized. For instance, the representation and even ideal of the man as 'breadwinner' is shaped within the context of labour divisions in the labour market and labour legislation, but also through institutions such as marriage systems. This representation also creates its own subject positions and categories. These categories are connected to class, ethnicity, nationality, sexuality, and sexual proclivity, etcetera. Whereas the differences of the symbolic dimension are represented as the differences between 'the woman and the man' or between 'the homosexual and the heterosexual', 'the black and the white woman', etcetera, differences at an institutional dimension get diversified. Categories of class give colour to other categories such as ethnicity and gender and vice versa. At this dimension, we consider these categories as people of flesh and blood and, as such, a homosexual becomes a rich or a poor homosexual and women, poor, rich, black or white, among others. The structural differences get represented as differences between women and men as well as among women and among men, between homosexuals and heterosexuals, but also among homosexuals and among heterosexuals.

How people (or actors) deal with such institutionalized ideas and the meaning attached to them varies, of course, indefinitely. Negotiating the symbolic ground rules not only depends on structural positioning and on identities that are ascribed to people, but also on the individual agency of actors and groups. The third dimension is this dimension of subjectivity, in which individuals shape their own identities. Although the second dimension refers to the differences between specific categories of men and women as well as among men and among women, the third dimension also concerns the differences *within* people. This dimension refers to the process of identification of individuals with the multiple identities or aspects of identities that are handed to them.

By deconstructing hegemonic discourses on femininity and masculinity and at the same time leaving room for subjectivity and agency, gender as an analytical approach gives room for diversity, difference and complex power relations, power relations that looked so simple before (see also Parpart et al., 2002). In the above-cited literature on globalization we see a trend that can be characterized as one step forwards two steps back. Attention for gender and globalization is a welcome contribution to that bulk of literature on globalization that has no attention for gender. However, by portraying globalization only as a monstrous phenomenon in which women reappear as victims, gender becomes this very one-dimensional category (i.e. referring to the category of women) – and, as in days gone by, women should resist their oppressors. Moreover, globalization also appears as a monolithic phenomenon, destructive and negative.

Here we were left with the question of how to apply this analytical tool in studying two complex processes, that of gender and of globalization. During our search of the literature we found in the work of Afshar and Barrientos a confirmation that both globalization and gender should be considered as complex phenomena.

Changes in the global political economy since the 1980s have had a dramatic effect on the lives of women, who have become increasingly integrated as players in the world's production and consumption processes. Women have been affected by globalization in the most diverse aspects of their lives and in the furthest reaches of the world. The effects have been multiple and contradictory, inclusionary and exclusionary (Afshar and Barrientos, 1999, p. 1).

In their work, globalization not only appears as multi-faceted processes that exclude as well as include women but it is also clear that women are players in those processes instead of mere victims. Still, the nature of globalization itself remained implicit, although it is clear that gender should be considered as an integral part of globalization. The global seemed to have an impact on the local, but is this really only a one way street, as it seems to be? As Moore states, the dichotomy between the global and the local is a construction that figures as a truth that is not questioned, let alone theorized and conceptualized (Moore, 2004). Consequently, we had to relate to debates on globalization and to those authors who did address this question, even when gender did not appear in their analysis, in order to problematize the global/local nexus.

Globalization: The Local/Global Nexus

An easy characterization of globalization is not a simple task, given the complicated processes that are simultaneously taking place. Moreover, the scientific views as to what exactly constitutes 'globalization' vary according to the complexity of the process of globalization itself (Schuurman, 2001). Nevertheless, we start from at least one, apparent, common denominator that globalization is, at the very least, about the increasing interconnection of the world through technology, capital flows, commodities and people.

Although some argue this has been the case since the end of the Middle Ages, it has clearly been of an unparalleled scope and impact in recent decades. Modernization seems to be the crucial feature of this shift. What differentiates the pre-modern epoch from the modern epoch is what has become known as the 'time space distanciation' (Giddens, 1984). The modern epoch should not be understood in a narrow sense as the beginning of industrialization or capitalism, but in a broader sense without a specific, marked beginning (Tomlinson 1996; 1999).

Modernity tears time and space away from place. Through modern notions and institutions such as rationalism, standardization of time, statistics, production and surveillance of growing entities of people, the nation states – with their military power, capitalism including industrialization and technological change – complex relations between people, groups, and localities are created across cultures and nations. Regardless of distance, modernity connects people and involves them in complex relations that are no longer restricted to the boundaries of face-to-face relations of a specific locality. It is this myriad of complex connections across geographic distances that characterizes modernity as inherently globalizing.

Coming from an interdisciplinary field of study such as development studies, our perspective is simultaneously an economic, political and cultural one. When we look at all these travelling goods, capital, people and technology, we also notice the scripts attached to them, specific connotations, images and ideas. These scripts represent specific cultural notions that travel over the globe through these networks of complex connectivity, regardless of its local origin. Globalization disconnects culture from a specific locality – also known as the phenomenon of 'deterritorialization' – only to become re-territorialized in another locality or dimension (Appadurai, 1996; 1999). It is not just tangible things and people, but also ideas and images such as democracy, modernity and gender relations that travel.

There is considerable ongoing debate, both in practice and in theory, as to whether this process of 'deterritorialization' results in one global culture. J. Nederveen Pieterse (1996) distinguishes three theoretical perspectives on globalization. The first perspective resembles the one that worried us in the literature on women and globalization. Globalization is conceptualized as a uni-linear, neo-liberal modernization process resulting in a world of sameness that, according to some, will end in a homogenous Coca-Cola culture of consumerism. Nederveen Pieterse calls this the 'convergence' paradigm, of which probably Fukuyama (1992) with his 'End of History' and the anti-globalization movement are the most famous proponents.

The second perspective points to those who think along opposite lines. In their eyes, globalization results in more differences within the parameters of a harmony or conflict model. This is called the divergence paradigm. S. Huntington's theory (1993) is a well-known example of this paradigm. He foresees a clash of civilizations after the disappearance of the iron curtain. The third perspective includes those who think that globalization does not merely result in more sameness or more differences, but produces complex and diverse mixtures of different cultural segments or elements – also known as creolization or hybridization (Hannerz, 1987; Appadurai, 1999). These authors are convinced of the perseverance of local cultures, combining, adapting and transforming different elements, trends and traditions. These mixtures of elements can be old or new, modern or traditional at the same time.

Confronted with these contradictory views on globalization, we were hesitant to choose one of the above perspectives. We opted for a perspective that focuses on the complexity of globalization processes. In our view, globalization cannot be classified either as a straightforward process of convergence, divergence or hybridization, but shows traits of all three. It is obvious from the literature on women and development that globalization as a cultural process has a profound impact on ways of living. Whether globalization presents itself in hybrid forms, in a spread of western-style consumer culture or in some degree of fundamentalist militancy, it directly and profoundly interferes with systems of representation and identification.

These constant flows of people, images and commodities have become a matter of everyday life, influencing what we eat, how we dress, what music we listen to, and so on. It is a process that alters cultural representations, of who we are and what we are, and directly interferes with identity building. The processes of identity building are no longer solely confined to the borders of local communities or nations. Social groups coalesce around a variety of circumstances that form the basis of a sense of shared identity, the most important being the categories of class, gender, sex, ethnicity and nation; but also including a range of other identity markers such as rural/urban, age, religion and region.

Those identity markers do not necessarily originate from the specific locality of such groups. This means that globalization is not a one-directional process of one culture going global, where the global serves as something that influences the local from above. Instead, we see globalization as a dialectical process in which the local is part and parcel of the global and vice versa. This perspective that the global is always articulated with and situated by the local is also called 'glocalization'. Glocalization implies that every process of globalization is always situated in power relations, calling for the need of always accounting for one's positionality (King, 1991). Or in terms of Tsing's metaphor of the landscape, we not only have to identify the different elements that shape the landscape, but we also have to realize that we see different landscapes according to the different perspectives and scripts attached to these different elements.

Hence, we are of the conviction that, to be able to grasp global and local changes and interconnections, we have to dismiss the idea that the world is a collection of fixed and nameable groups (Geschiere and Meyer, 1998). The landscape is constantly changing. Identities are not as exclusive, cohesive and fixed as imagined, but turn out to be in process and multiple. By 'in process and multiple' we mean that we are breaking away from very set dichotomies within western thinking. Said (1978), Hall (1991) and Escobar (1995) have deconstructed this western thinking and its result, the artificial creation of the cultural other. Culture is intrinsic to how we look at the world. This means that culture and political and economic changes intersect and that neither can be understood without the other, placing identity building and cultural differences permanently at the centre. Hence, whatever travels around the world, it is in specific localities only that meanings are attached to it. In our view, this is what makes culture so central to globalization, without disregarding that globalization exists simultaneously as an economic, social, political or technological process.

Consequently, the local and the global are not two separate spheres that are unconnected. A locality gets its characteristics on the one hand through the meanings that are ascribed to it. On the other hand, it is people in specific localities that attach meanings to phenomena, notions that can come from all over the globe. Hence, the local becomes the *glocal* and has to be specified and analyzed in order to pinpoint the scripts attached to it. And here the gender lens comes in as a helpful analytical tool to do so.

Mapping Gendered Visions

Out of the above-discussed ingredients of looking at globalization and the global/local nexus we wrote a paper in which we argued for addressing the link between gender and globalization from the analytical gender perspective, including the symbolic, structural and subject dimension. In this perspective we tried to depict globalization as a multidimensional phenomenon, both negative and positive at the same time, and intrinsically linked with the local. We presented this paper at the annual conference of the Netherlands Association of Gender and Anthropology and Development Studies (LOVA) in 2001, on the theme gender and globalization. We explained our uneasiness with the dominant views on women/gender and globalization. The inspiring reactions stimulated us to take this project beyond deconstructing ongoing debates on women/gender and globalization.

Later that same year we presented these ideas in another forum. This was at a workshop on gender and globalization at the international annual conference of European Consortium for Political Research in 2001 in Canterbury. Apart from receiving constructive feedback and criticism, we were confirmed in our mission. Especially our plea to re-humanize the debate on gender and globalization was felt and shared. Here for the first time the idea to dedicate a book to this theme arose on the instigation of Marianne Marchand, one of the editors of the series 'Gender in a Global/Local World' in which this book is a volume.

In her own book, edited with Anne Sisson Runyan (2000), entitled *Gender and Global Restructuring*, Marchand and Runyan secure a central place for gender. They search for a way to reinstate the link between the global and the local in which women's agency and room to act play a crucial role. The inclination of their contribution is that the processes of global restructuring are neo-liberal and masculine or feminine. Hence, an important starting point for feminist academics, women's networks and NGOs to counteract this (neo)-liberal and patriarchal restructuring is, according to them, to reveal how all these processes are gendered (Marchand and Runyan, 2000, p. 21).

Here we see an approach in which globalization is more than economic restructuring and in which a gender analysis is used. Nonetheless, in our view, the link between gender and globalization still leaves room for discussion. Although they recognize that not all processes of global restructuring are negative for women, the main focus is on the masculine character of these processes. According to the authors, specific masculine spaces, agents and sectors are privileged over 'feminized' spaces, agents and sectors, such as finance capital over manufacturing, finance ministries over social welfare ministries, the market over the state, the global over the local, and consumers over citizens (ibid. 2000, p. 13).

They locate these processes at three dimensions, at the level of thinking, sites of analysis and practice of resistance. Hence the subtitle of the book: *sightings, sites and resistance*. They also refer to multiple subject positions of both women and men and stress that the hegemonic masculine character of changes is not that stable and can be resisted and is changed in the process of restructuring. But they also state that:

Much more work remains to further track trends in global restructuring and its relationship to gender in a variety of local and global contexts. We offer here a way to organize that work by encouraging attention to at least three dimensions of that relationship. Without addressing all three, neither global restructuring nor gender as highly complex (re)organizing systems can be adequately understood (Marchand and Runyan, 2000, p. 229).

What we see is that on the one hand global restructuring is characterized as masculinized and, thus, pre-given, while on the other hand the restructuring is multiple and changeable. Interesting is that a process of fixing and a process of fluidity seems to take place at the same time. What kept on puzzling us was how these authors envisaged the integration of these processes. Is it possible to envision global hegemonic gender discourses, without adhering to the convergence perspective as formulated above? Are we supposed to analyse the process of fixing at the global level and is the entire fluidity taking place at the local level, or is it the other way around?

Other authors also seem to situate the changes and fluidity at the local level at which the outcome of globalization is gendered.

> Globalization cannot be viewed only as a nightmare scenario. It is neither theoretically helpful nor does it promote political action for women to turn into frightened rabbits when confronting the 'snake' of globalization. Undeniably, economic globalization has constrained the political scope of nation-states and narrowed the capacity of citizens to claim gender-neutral social rights from the state. However, one has also to recall that the reconfiguration of the Fordist gender order also offers an opportunity for women to develop new concepts and strategies to achieve gender equality on a global scale (Young 2001, pp. 46-47).

And with the Fordist gender order, Brigitte Young refers to the male breadwinner paradigm as a project of modernization. In the same volume on *Gender, Globalization and Democratization*, Bayes, Hawkesworth and Kelly (2001, p. 3) are of the opinion that globalization fundamentally challenges the public/private divide, and that women are confronted with contradicting gender ideologies locally. Their point of view is that global processes of change have local consequences and people can mediate these changes.

These points of view come closer to the approach we were looking for, as changes in the public/private divide are recurrent issues and demand attention, but the global/local nexus is still underexposed. In the field of women, gender and development since the late nineteen sixties, this divide already played a central role in theorizing and deconstructing gender relations. What is happening with these relations due to changes in the modern notion of the male breadwinner paradigm? Are these discourses really as hegemonic as they seem to be? It is important to deconstruct whether so-called global trends such as feminization of labour and of poverty reflect local interpretations of modern gender notions.

We found an elaborated discussion on gender, globalization and modernity in Dorothy L. Hodgson (2001). She also sees globalization in terms of modernization, which entails interconnected political, cultural and economic processes. More importantly, she states that modernization has many different varieties.

> In other words, although Modernity is a dominant and pervasive mode of imagining and ordering the world, other forms of modernity exist, premised on sometimes radically different ideologies and ideals, such as communal sharing rather than individual profit, or gender complementarity rather than gender hierarchy... ...it is foolish to presume (rather than prove) that these 'other modernities' are all merely reactive to Modernity, rather than grounded in recognizably distinct historical processes (Hodgson, 2001, p. 7).

Here we reached a point where we had to address globalization as the representation of multiple modernities. Travelling images and ideas of what is modern take on different local meanings, as we argued above. However, the pervasiveness of certain issues, such as on the public/private divide and the recurring appeals on family values in which women are blamed for the disorder caused by the decline of the breadwinner paradigm, demands an analysis in which these persistent and crucial gender issues are deconstructed in the light of multiple modernities.

A third presentation of our analysis took place at the meeting of the Development Studies Association's (DSA) women and development study group in York in 2002. Our approach triggered a lively debate in which doubts were uttered as to why an economic approach would be wrong if such an approach demonstrated the exploitive nature of globalization for women. In other words, a political question entered the stage. Is it politically 'correct' to assume that women can also benefit from apparently oppressive and exploitative circumstances? After all, what all diverse points of view have in common is the attempt to address gender inequalities and support feminist political projects. But how is that possible with so many confusing and even contradicting views? Especially, Chandra Mohanty's (2002) position in the debate is outspoken. In a revision of her well-known essay on ethnocentrism within Western feminism in the mid 1980s she states:

> ...[W]hile girls and women are central to the labor of global capital, antiglobalization work does not seem to draw on feminist analysis and strategies. Thus while I have argued that feminism needs to be anticapitalist, I would now argue that anti-globalization activists need to be feminists (Mohanty 2002, pp. 528-529).

Mohanty takes this stand since, according to her, it is mainly black women who are the victims of masculine globalization. She speaks about racialized gender and about (corporate) globalization in terms of capitalism that depends on racist, patriarchal and heterosexual relations of rule. The reorganization of gender is part of the global strategy of capitalism, according to Mohanty (2002, p. 525), and this gender reorganizing is racialized. But she also argues to complicate the monolithic globalized representations of women, as images of victimized women and empowered womanhood negate each other (ibid, 2002, p. 528). If, as Mohanty suggests, we have to overcome the monolithic view on women as victims, how then can we have a political project that addresses apparent negative consequences of globalization? Is globalization as represented by Mohanty not too narrowly interpreted from a divergence perspective, as described above? How to deal with this uneasiness that once again especially women appear as victims in a globalizing world, a globalizing world reflected as a nightmare scenario for humankind?

Challenging Gender and Globalization

Confronted with the challenge to make the complex dynamics of gender and globalization comprehensible, we realized that we needed a more interdisciplinary approach than only an orientation on development studies. As indicated above, we already encountered in LOVA a fruitful platform for debate on the link between gender and globalization. This platform connects a variety of researchers from different specializations and sometimes even different disciplines, ranging from literature studies, development studies and anthropology to migration and conflict studies. What they have in common is a feminist perspective on science that acknowledges that all knowledge (production) is situated. They share an approach that starts its analysis from the experience of women and men as actors in their own right, in their own environments and everyday life situations. This was our reason for inviting several of them to write a chapter in this book. They accepted the challenge of incorporating their approach into the analysis of globalization and gender.

We organized an expert meeting to discuss the first drafts of all chapters. We presented our understanding of the literature on women/gender and globalization and listed the questions that emerged from our journey so far. During this meeting, the contours of a shared vision on globalization became tangible. The outcome of this collective process is an approach towards globalization and gender that considers the global and local to be intrinsically linked. Although we consider modernization to be inherently globalizing, this does not mean that globalization entails only a Westernized process of modernization travelling from the west to the rest, linear in its direction and only neo-liberal in its characterization. The complex interconnections require an intellectual exercise that goes beyond viewing globalization as a homogeneous, linear and macro-process. Moreover, it is the centrality of modernities that are pervasively global and deeply local – and modernities are highly gendered. Hence we needed to broaden the analysis and include issues of meaning into research on globalization.

Since all authors are familiar with the analytical gender approach, they all use this gender lens to focus attention on material conditions, belief systems and ideologies at the same time. Experiences and visions of women and men themselves are incorporated into their analyses. In the chapters of the book, local realities are central in the analysis of the global/local nexus. It is by analyzing historical specific, situated or daily life experiences that abstract ideals and entities take on a variety of meanings. Consequently, as we have tried to demonstrate above in describing our own process, the link between globalization and gender is not given but situated and coloured. It is all about representation, both in knowledge production and in daily practice. The chapters of this book all contribute to an analysis of how this process of giving meaning to gender in different realities takes shape.

Challenging Gender and Globalization: Organization of the Book

As Tsing narrates in her description of the landscape of globalization, there are many different elements and entities to be identified in this landscape. Elements as different as worms and weeds or creeks and meadows, or soil and forests, all, in a mutual exchange, are contributing to a restructuring of the landscape. Accordingly, globalization cannot be understood as mere flows of capital or capitalist expansion, only analyzed from an economic perspective. Nor can it be understood only from the perspective of one issue, be this migration, economics, politics or multiculturalism.

Hence, this book is composed of very different elements that constitute the landscape of gender and globalization. The different authors involved address issues as varied as international labour restructuring, sexuality, national identities, masculinity as well as femininity and international feminism. They all look through the gender lens and analyze specific symbols, ideas and images, connected to certain institutions or structures, and focus on the diversity of identity constructions at the subject level. However, the analytical emphasis chosen as a strategy to deconstruct global orthodoxies differs as well as the locality that is taken as the object of analysis.

We have organized the book in such a way that the different analytical accents in the chapters are grouped accordingly. Different questions are highlighted in these clusters of chapters. In the first cluster, the local lived realities of people are central. Here the agency of people instead of victimization is emphasized by analyzing views 'on the ground'. In the second cluster, the production of differences and unexpected outcomes are central. Because gender (femininities and masculinities, institutional and personal identities) as a global/local nexus is constantly being remodelled and reconstructed, globalization produces unexpected differences (for those married to orthodoxies) identities, processes and outcomes. In the final cluster of chapters, globalized identities are the focal point, in which the modern/traditional divide is abandoned and multiple modernities are central. The local/global lens is rethought by presenting cases of multiple/parallel or alternative modernities.

Local Lived Realities: Agency Instead of Victimization

Local lived realities may look similar from the outside, especially when we consider specific groups of people as victims of certain developments. But in this first cluster of chapters, we will see that these local lived realities differ substantially. When looking through the gender lens and focusing on what constitutes these realities, we see that actors with agency behave and respond in rather diverse ways when confronted with changes.

In chapter 2, Lineke Stobbe portrays the gendered impact of a new production and management system of Japanese origin in the Argentine car components industry. While the general opinion about the effects of neo-liberal labour restructuring is very negative for women and gender relations, Stobbe presents an analysis that this is not necessarily the case everywhere. Making us look at this issue at two local plants results in different patterns of inclusion and exclusion of women. Women on the shop floors both accept and reject new opportunities offered to them, based on contradicting identities to relate to. As a result, women's agency plays an important role in this process of inclusion and exclusion, in a context where the perception of women not suitable for this kind of work, the 'nimble fingers' rhetoric and the notion of women as 'agents of change' compete.

The light that Lorraine Nencel sheds in chapter 3 on the lived realities of secretaries in Peru and changing contents and images of their occupation reveals an interesting exposé of how these women create their working identities. This chapter deals with the dynamics between global discourses on professionalization and local realities in which secretaries continue to be sexualised and kept in place in gendered bureaucracies. Although on the work floor there is a tendency for women to behave 'decently' and, thus, erase any possibility of being accused of living up to the stereotypes, the sexualized stereotype is still central in their identity construction and, for example, reflected in a 'dress code of decency'. It is from this angle of identity construction that Nencel studies secretaries as actors on the work floor, where Peruvian gender discourses mix with so-called neutral global discourses on modernization of bureaucracies. She shows how the daily reality of secretaries sharply contrasts with this new organizational order and how they construct an 'adjusted' professional identity through exclusion of the non-professional, sexualized other.

In the chapter by Anouka van Eerdewijk on being a man in Dakar, contradicting local and global interpretations of tradition and modernity manifest themselves at the subject level. In chapter 4, she unravels the different discourses on sexuality with which a young Senegalese adolescent struggles, while constructing his own masculine identity and dealing with sexual practices. These different discourses are informed by specific constructions of insiders' and outsiders' notions of tradition and modernity in the fight against HIV/AIDS. This results in ambiguous connotations of masculinity from which young men have to construct their sexuality. In illuminating this process of negotiating discourses from an actor oriented view, Van Eerdewijk contradicts the thesis of Connell that globalization leads to standardization of hegemonic masculinity. As such, she emphasizes the importance of the local as the setting where global discourses intermingle with local ones and result in confusing identity formations and practices that informs (un)safe sex behaviour in the Aids Era.

Unexpected Outcomes: Globalization and the Production of Difference

That the acknowledgement of agency as part and parcel of the gender lens contradicts orthodoxies and produces an eye for diversity and difference becomes even clearer in the next four chapters. In chapter 5 Kathy Davis discusses the transnational journey of a famous and influential feminist book from the US, *Our Bodies, Ourselves*. This book not only had a decisive impact on how generations of American women felt about their bodies, their sexuality and their health, but it was also translated and adapted in 20 languages. In studying the way in which this book was translated and adapted, especially in so-called non-western countries, Davis explores the possibilities and the pitfalls of the globalization of feminist knowledge. She questions whether this globalization of feminist knowledge necessarily follows the path of 'feminism as cultural imperialism'. Her chapter is a search into the empowering potential of transnational feminist alliances in the field of the body politic. In her description of how different groups of women gave their own interpretation, meaning and significance to this book, Davis makes clear that this feminist export product cannot be regarded as a reflection of cultural imperialism, which would have been 'a mission impossible', according to her. On the contrary, she deconstructs how the journey of this cultural artefact (or actually the method of how the book was written) represents a process of struggling translators and adapters to develop a book that would address the needs of women in their local contexts. The end products so far are a great variety of re-articulated and re-contextualized books as a result of the unpredictable, ongoing journey of the original.

Another example of unexpected outcomes is central in chapter 6 by Dorothea Hilhorst and Mathijs van Leeuwen. Involved with issues of conflict and peace, Hilhorst and Van Leeuwen study local women's organizations as peace builders in southern Sudan. Recent global discourses on peace building envision women as peace builders par excellence. The chapter describes the emergence of a global discourse on the feminization of peace that was particularly marked during the Beijing women's conference in 1995. The core of the chapter addresses the question of how this global discourse works in local peace-building practices. These practices of peace building are far more complex then the global discourse would have us believe. The deconstruction of this global discourse from a local perspective teaches us that the local meaning of peace can be rather surprising and simple. Sophisticated projects and programmes to support women's peace organizations in southern Sudan, funded by international donor organizations with seemingly congruent intentions, failed, due to requirements of project implementation, accountability, effectiveness and so on. Local realities on both sides took over and, in terms of project implementation, the outcome was disappointing. However, in daily practice in southern Sudan, initiatives for mutual support and unity from the home became translations of peace building. Hence, the authors warn for too-easily accepted global truths. Only in local practices does global discourse derive meaning and this meaning can be diverse and surprising.

Annelou Ypeij shows us that questions of migration and multiculturalism cannot be understood only within the borders of the receiving country. Ypeij illustrates this in chapter 7 with her study on single Surinamese, Antillean and Moroccan mothers in the Netherlands. She demonstrates how matrifocal or patriarchal gender notions from the home country are redefined, remodelled and reinterpreted due to the opportunities and ambiguities in Dutch gender discourses. In contrast with what one would expect on the basis of the feminization of poverty thesis, a large part of (especially) the Suriname women, although belonging to the relatively poor, are able to build a life in the Netherlands by combining motherhood with labour market participation or depending on welfare. Transnational female kin networks play an important part in this. They make use of the combination of the support that these transnational networks offer and of the Dutch practices of migration and welfare policies to create new lives. For Moroccan women, depending on age and marital status, the story is rather different, but the same possibilities offer them an opportunity to challenge traditional gender relations and develop lives of their own. Such migration processes should be understood from this global/local nexus, in particular the different ways in which these women are able to negotiate intersecting discourses on motherhood.

Fenneke Reysoo came across opposite practices of pregnancy discrimination in Free Trade Zones in Mexico and Morocco. Her chapter 8 entails a comparative study of these two cases, where companies and production relations are on the move as part of a neo-liberal economic development policy. Reysoo explores the question of why the practice of pregnancy testing and the dismissal of pregnant women is present in Mexico but not in Morocco, while both industries in the free trade zones are part and parcel of the same neo-liberal economic labour relations and ethics. This chapter intends to trace where global capitalism transgresses social and reproductive rights of their female employees and how women deal with and resist pregnancy testing and screening. The local differences that are produced as an outcome of this process are located at the level of dominant gender ideals and laws.

Glocalized Gender Identities: Tradition and Modernity Deconstructed

How re-invention of traditions and multiple modernities intermingle in identity construction is reflected in the last clusters of chapter. The authors challenge the orthodoxies of modernity in globalization discourses, as if modernity produces sameness and travels from the west to the rest.

In chapter 9, Marion den Uyl deconstructs the spread of dowry in India that is prohibited by law as a 'modern monstrosity', but socially sanctioned among its perpetrators and beneficiaries, as much as among its victims and losers. The spread of dowry, a bridal gift of the girl's parents to the groom's family, leads to the increasing neglect of the girl child, female infanticide and bride burning, among others, reflected in an increasingly skewed sex-ratio. She studies the changes that cultural practices of dowry underwent during colonization, decolonization and modernization of India. By unravelling the multiple facets, practices and meanings of contemporary dowry, den Uyl addresses the question of whether the changes in a traditional custom can be considered as a process of hybridization or creolization of modern and traditional influences. She comes to the conclusion that a transformed and remodelled custom has become a many-faced standard of dominant Hindu nationalist and patriarchal discourse, which represents a conservative process of creolization, despite its many faces with modern and traditional ingredients.

Karin Willemse analyzes how a project of 'purifying' Islamic beliefs and practices in the context of Islamization of North Sudan serves to cover up a crisis in masculinity and seems to be targeted at restoring male dominance. In chapter 10, she asks herself whether the ideal of the male breadwinner is an ideal that needs to be considered as part and parcel of a Euro colonial world or can be considered as a Sudanese form of modernity. In deconstructing (or re-constructing) how this ideal figures in constituting a Sudanese national identity and is intertwined with fundamentalist trends, Willemse provides grounds for thinking about globalization in multiple or alternative modernities. She analyzes how the breadwinner-cum-housewife ideal has become represented as an 'original' traditional Islamic notion of family values. However she demonstrates that this so-called traditional notion is more complex and hybrid than dominant discourse presents it to be. In demonstrating its multiple heritage of being both modern in a Sudanese, regional manner, as well as part and parcel of Islamic discourses, Willemse offers a way out of the dichotomy of considering modernization as solely European or Western, and tradition as a native, local answer to foreign modernization.

In a similar stream of thought, in chapter 11, Tine Davids analyzes how the image of motherhood figures as a gender identity in processes of political modernization and democratization in Mexico. For women active in politics, in particular women of right wing political parties, motherhood can be a strong identity marker in legitimizing their entrance in the political arena. Motherhood generates political and professional opportunities as well as the possibility of reconciling the contradictions of being both good wives and mothers and professional politicians at the same time. Davids analyzes how the image of motherhood serves to include as well as exclude women from the political arena at particular historical moments of democratization in Mexico. Motherhood seems to serve different masters simultaneously. As such, the identification with the image of motherhood is not only paramount in creating a modern Mexican national identity but shares a common history and features with other Latin American countries, characterizing them as parallel modernities.

Halleh Ghorashi depicts how a new community of Iranian immigrants in the United States of America is able to create a new home: 'Irangeles'. Reinvention of tradition constitutes a large part of the new home, though not for all. In chapter 12, Ghorashi gives an insight in how Iranian female political exiles, although part of that new (imagined) community, are able to reinvent some of their traditions of political militancy, as they knew it after the fall of the shah of Persia. They are able to do so through their own (political) organizations and through engaging in and identifying with North American feminist organizations and gatherings. Hence, they create gender identities out of a new mix of Iranian and American elements in which both modernity as well as tradition are transgressed. These women travelled from the rest to the west, but it was a specific revolutionary 'rest' that no longer exists in contemporary Islamist Iran. They took with them their ways of surviving, ideas, revolutionary élan and cultural patterns and developed a sense of belonging in a new hybrid positioning of being at the same time Iranian and American.

In the final chapter, we get back to the local lived realities, the unexpected outcomes and the glocalized gender identities. We use the contributions in this book to exemplify the gendered global/local nexus. The different perspectives, the rich material and the varying localities help us to clarify this interconnection. The globalization landscape we see is curved and shaped by gender and also, at the same time, gendered. Hence the title of the final chapter, 'Gender and Globalization: An Analytical Alliance'.

References

Afshar, Haleh and Barrientos, Stephanie (1999), 'Introduction: Women, Globalization and Fragmentation', in Afshar, Haleh and Barrientos, Stephanie (eds.) *Women, Globalization and Fragmentation in the Developing World*, MacMillan, London, pp. 1-17.

Appadurai, Arjun (1999), 'Disjuncture and Difference in the Global Cultural Economy', in Featherstone, Mike (ed.), *Global Culture: Nationalism, Globalization and Modernity*, Sage, London, pp. 295-310.

Appadurai, Arjun (1996), *Modernity at Large: Cultural Dimensions of Globalization*, University of Minnesota Press, Minneapolis.

Bayes, Jane H., Hawkesworth, Mary E. and Kelly, Rita Mae (2001), 'Globalization, Democratization and Gender Regimes', in Kelly, Rita Mae, Bayes, Jane H., Hawkesworth, Mary E., Young, Brigitte (eds.), *Gender, Globalization and Democratization*, Rowman and Littlefield, Boulder, pp. 1-14.

Braidotti, R. (1994), *Nomadic Subjects. Embodiment and Sexual Difference in Contemporary Feminist Thought*, New York, Columbia University Press.

Chant Sylvia (1999), 'Women-headed Households: Global Orthodoxies and Grassroots Realities', in Afshar, Haleh and Barrientos, Stephanie (ed.) *Women, Globalization and Fragmentation in the Developing World*, MacMillan, London, pp. 91-130.

Davids, T. and van Driel, F. (2001), 'Globalization and Gender: beyond dichotomies', in Schuurman, F.J. (ed.) *Globalization and Development Studies, Challenges for the 21st Century*, Thela, Amsterdam, Sage, London, pp. 153-177.

Davids, T. and van Driel, F. (2002), Van vrouwen en ontwikkeling naar gender en globalisering, in Arts, Bas, Hebinck, Paul, van Naerssen, Ton (eds.) *Voorheen de Derde Wereld, Ontwikkeling anders gedacht*, Amsterdam, Jan Metz, pp. 60-85.

Escobar, A. (1995), *Encountering Development. The Making and Unmaking of the Third World*, Princeton, NJ: Princeton University Press.

Fernández-Kelly, P. and Wolf, D. (2001), 'A Dialogue on Globalization', *Signs: Journal of Women, Culture and Society*, vol. 26, no. 4, pp. 1243-1249.

Fukuyama, Francis, (1992), *The End of History and of Last Man*, London, Verso.

Geschiere, P. and Meyer, B. (1998), 'Globalization and Identity: Dialectics of Flows and Closures, Introduction', *Development and Change*, Vol. 29, no. 4, pp. 601-615.

Giddens, A. (1990), *The Consequences of Modernity*, Polity Press, London.

Giddens, A. (1984), *The Constitution of Society. Outline of the Theory of Structuration*, Cambridge, Polity Press.

Hagemann-White, C. (1989), Geslacht en Gedrag, *Socialistisch-Feministische Teksten* 11, pp. 33-48.

Hall, S. (1991), 'Old and New Identities, Old and New Ethnicities', in King, A.D. (ed), *Culture Globalization and the Worldsystem*, London and Binghamton, Macmillan Education Ltd and University of New York at Binghamton, pp. 41-68.

Hannerz, U. (1987), 'The World in Creolization', *Africa*, Vol. 57, no. 4, pp. 546-559.

Harding, Sandra (1986) *The Science Question in Feminism*, London, Cornell University Press.

Haraway, Donna, (1988), 'Situated Knowledges. The Science Question in Feminism and the Privilege of Partial Perspective', *Feminist Studies*, Vol. 14, no. 3, pp. 575-599.

Hodgson, Dorothy L. (2001), 'Of Modernity/Modernities, Gender, and Ethnography', in Hodgson, Dorothy L. (ed.), *Gendered Modernities and Ethnographic Perspectives*, Palgrave, New York, pp. 1-23.

Huntington, S. (1993), 'The Clash of Civilisations', *Foreign Affairs*, Vol. 72, no. 3, pp. 22-49.

King, Anthony D. (1991), 'Spaces of Culture, Spaces of Knowledge, Introduction', in King, A.D. (ed.) *Culture, Globalization and the World-System*, Macmillan, London, pp. 1-18.

Marchand, Marianne H. and Runyan, Anne Sisson (2000), 'Introduction, Feminist Insights of Global Restructuring: Conceptualizations and Reconceptualizations', in Marchand, M. and Runyan, A.S. (eds.) *Gender and Global Restructuring, Sightings, Sites and Resistances*, Routledge, London, pp. 1-22.

Mohanty, Chandra Talpade (2002), '"Under Western Eyes" Revisited: Feminist Solidarity through Anticapitalist Struggles', *Signs*, Vol. 28, no. 2, pp. 499-535.

Moore, Hernrietta, L. (2004), 'Global Anxieties', *Anthropological Theory*, vol. 4, no. 1, pp. 71-88.

Moore, Henrietta L. (1994), *A Passion for Difference*, Cambridge, Polity Press.

Nederveen Pieterse, J. (1996), 'Globalization and Culture. Three paradigms', *Economic and Political Weekly*, Vol. XXXI, no. 23, pp. 1389-1393.

Parpart, Jane, L., Rai, Shirin M. and Staudt, Kathleen (eds.) (2002), *Rethinking Empowerment, Gender and development in a global/local world*, Routledge, London and New York.

Rowbotham, Sheila and Linkogle, Stephanie, (2001), 'Introduction' in Rowbotham, Sheila and Linkogle, Stephanie (eds.), *Women Resist Globalization*, Zed Books, London, pp. 1-12.

Said, E.W. (1978), *Orientalism*, New York, Vintage Books.

Schuurman F.J. (2001), 'The Nation-State, Emancipatory Spaces and Development', in F.J. Schuurman (ed.) *Globalization and Development Studies, Challenges for the 21st Century*, Sage, London, pp. 61-76.

Scott, Joan Wallace (1988), 'Gender: a Useful Category for Historical Analysis', in Scot, J.W. (ed.), *Feminism and History*, Oxford, Oxford University Press, pp. 152-183.

Tomlinson, John (1999), *Globalization and Culture*, Polity Press, Cambridge.

Tomlinson, John (1996), 'Cultural Globalisation: Placing and Displacing in the West', *European Journal of Development Research*, vol. 8, no. 2, pp. 22-36.

Tsing, Anna (2000), 'The Global Situation', *Cultural Anthropology*, Vol. 15, no. 3, pp. 327-360.

Wichterich, Christa (2000), *The Globalized Woman, Reports from a Future of Inequality*, Zed Books, London.

Young, Brigitte (2001), 'Globalization and Gender: A European Perspective', in Kelly, Rita Mae, Bayes, Jane H., Hawkesworth, Mary E., Young, Brigitte (eds.), *Gender, Globalization and Democratization*, Rowman and Littlefield, Boulder, pp. 27-47.

LOCAL LIVED REALITIES: AGENCY INSTEAD OF VICTIMIZATION

Chapter 2

The Gendered Reconstruction of the Argentine Auto Components Industry

Lineke Stobbe

Introduction

This chapter tells the story of the Argentine auto components industry in the 1990s and, more specifically, the story of the women and men working at two auto components firms, López Autopartes and Autoparts Worldwide[1]. The 1990s were characterized by a rigorous restructuring process that greatly affected the ability to stay in business of many Argentine components producers. Many firms closed down and many workers lost their jobs. This was also what happened to the men and women of López Autopartes and Autoparts Worldwide. Both firms closed down and almost two hundred men and more then one hundred women became unemployed. The gendered consequences of this rigorous restructuring process were, however, more ambiguous. At the level of the industry, we see masculinization of labour. At the level of the two firms, we observe feminization of labour.

This chapter focuses its analysis on the possibilities women workers have in accessing jobs and skills during restructuring processes, as well as the constraints acting on them. The restructuring of the Argentine components industry has to be understood within the larger frame of economic globalization and neo-liberal policies. During the 1990s the Argentinean government implemented a harsh Structural Adjustment Programme, liberalized trade and deregulated the labour market. Another essential factor of the restructuring process was the introduction of a global production and management system, also known as lean production. I have chosen to use the term lean production because this was the term most frequently used by my respondents. This system had become the international standard for the car sector during the 1980s.

Lean production gives a central place to flexibility of production and labour, and to product quality (total quality management – TQM); it involves new types of relationships between workers (teamwork), between workers and management (involvement), and between firms and their buyers and suppliers (global and modular sourcing and outsourcing). For workers, TQM, teamwork and involvement means that they undertake a wider range of skills and tasks (functional flexibility), that they do the quality control themselves (self-inspection), and that they are responsible for the output and productivity of the whole team (management of machinery and equipment, expenditures, etc., team-based bonuses). Apart from functional flexibility and flexible remuneration, labour flexibility is also achieved through the hiring of workers on a temporary basis and the introduction of more flexible working patterns (numerical flexibility). In other words, lean production is 'an interrelated set of production, organizational, and human resource practices that, when implemented together, constitute a more flexible system of work and production than the traditional mass production system it seeks to replace' (Kochan et al., 1997, pp. 304-305).

Lean production was originally developed and implemented in Japan and enabled that country to become a world leader in the car sector in the 1980s. A number of studies published in the late 1980s and early 1990s discuss the transferability of lean production to other countries, including developing countries (see e.g. Elger and Smith, 1994; Humphrey, 1993; Kaplinsky, 1994). These studies show that the implementation of lean production varies considerably according to the local situation, producing hybrid forms of lean production. The firms discussed here represent two typical restructuring trajectories in the Argentinean context, namely that of a national firm, López Autopartes, and of a global firm, Autoparts Worldwide. In the next section, I will discuss the Argentinean context in more detail and I will identify the dimensions of the restructuring process that generated gendered consequences.

The gendered consequences can, however, not be understood without insight into the gender regime of the Argentine components industry (Bayes et al., 2001). The dominant ideas about women workers in this industry encompass a very strong tendency to exclude women. As I will discuss in section two, this explains why masculinization occurred at industry level. Nevertheless, the two case studies will present a more complex picture of the interaction between economic globalization and local ideas about gender. The two stories presented in sections three and four will not just reveal differences between women and men; differences among women will be highlighted as well.

Reviewing the literature on gender and industrial restructuring, we see that part of this literature has a rather pessimistic view of the outcomes of restructuring processes for women workers (Elson and Pearson, 1981; Standing, 1989; Walby, 1989). These studies argue that women are increasingly included in the work force because they comply with worse labour conditions then men do and stress the link between flexibilization and feminization of labour. Several studies that pay attention to the implications for women of restructuring towards lean production argue that new gender segmentations are primarily based on the division between male core workers with multi-skilled jobs and female periphery workers, who simply have to do more of the same (multi-tasking) (Jenson, 1989; Roldán, 1993, 1994; Sayer, 1986). The feminization of labour thesis bears much resemblance to the feminization of poverty thesis discussed by Davids and van Driel (2001). They argue that the dominant discourse on gender and globalization pictures a straightforward and homogeneous impact on women. Women are portrayed as victims of globalization; they are the ones that suffer most from the various globalization processes (see e.g. Wichterich, 2000; Pearson, 2000). Davids and van

Driel rightfully argue that these studies are seriously troublesome because they portray women as human beings without agency.

I therefore examine the auto components companies through a structuration 'lens', which means that the (re)production of the sexual division of labour must be understood as an active process founded in the duality of agency and structure (Giddens, 1984). Men and women do gender (West and Zimmerman, 1987), but different rules and recourses enable and constrain them in numerous and complex ways. Moreover, the outcome of industrial restructuring processes for (individual) women workers is dependent on actions (and rules and resources) at other levels, for example, the world or national levels. Therefore, the purpose of this study is to show that gendered industrial restructuring is the result of structuration at different yet interrelated levels. The concluding section of this chapter will compare and discuss the findings and evaluate their implications for the debate on industrial restructuring and gender.

Setting the Scene

During a long period, from the 1950s until the 1990s, the Argentine industry, and in particular the car sector, was protected by high tariff barriers and State subsidies. The result was a relatively small number of produced cars, high prices, low quality, and efficiency figures far below international standards (Kosacoff et al., 1991). From 1990 onwards, the Argentine auto components industry experienced important changes in the rules of the game; foreign trade was liberalized, internal markets were deregulated, Industrial Promotion Plans abolished and subsidies reduced. These changes were part of the neo-liberal policies of the Menem administration, which came to power in 1989. The general aim of these policies was to integrate Argentina into the global economy.

The changes in the rules of the game forced Argentine auto components producers to become globally competitive for the first time ever and a series of regional and national agreements were signed and measures were taken to enhance the competitiveness of the Argentine car sector. During the first years of the 1990s, these new rules appeared to be successful. Several global car manufacturers installed production facilities in Argentina and the production of cars grew. This positive trend was interrupted, however, in 1995. In that year, production volume dropped 30 per cent because of the financial crisis in Mexico. In 1998, the market recovered. Nevertheless, in 1999 a new crisis hit the sector due to the devaluation of the Brazilian currency in January 1999. It became clear that the Argentine producers depended heavily on the Brazilian market and economic instability in the region automatically led to problems for the sector.

In the meantime, car manufacturers started looking for suppliers that met the international quality standards and were capable of producing modules (i.e. a complete door). We see that car manufacturers used the new rules to enlarge imports of components, especially from Brazil, and to strengthen their relationships with global components producers. National firms in particular had a hard time staying in business because they did not possess the necessary finances, scale and technological capabilities to meet the new standards. Their main strategy was to find an international partner or buyer. Global components producers profited from the new regime. They opened new labour-extensive facilities in Argentina and relocated other, labour-intensive, facilities to Brazil. The two case studies will exemplify both strategies.

National and global firms also differed in the nature and level of implementation of lean production. National firms introduced limited changes mainly aimed at the improvement of product quality, whereas global firms tried to transform their plants into lean production sites. These differences had consequences for access to jobs by – and the skills of – women in both firms, as we will see below.

Apart from the introduction and implementation of lean production, other developments need to be taken into consideration as well. One such development was the high level of unemployment and the deregulation of the labour market that started in 1995. In 1995, unemployment reached a historical high of almost 20 per cent and the government used this development to deregulate the labour market. The Argentine working class had always been the most protected on the continent (collective labour agreements, a generous social security system, good labour conditions and the presence of the trade union on the shop floor). In 1995, measures were taken to make the contractual conditions flexible, which made it easier to hire personnel on a temporary basis. Both the high level of unemployment and the flexibility of contractual conditions had consequences for access to jobs by – and the skills of – women workers, as we will see below.

The second development that needs to be considered is the withdrawal of the Argentine State from collective bargaining. This retreat demolished the pillars of the system of collective bargaining that had evolved in Argentina from the 1950s onward. This system can be characterized as highly regulated by the State, highly centralized and highly institutionalized, making trade unions very powerful bureaucracies in Argentine society. The Metal Workers Union, the union that represents workers in the components sector, was a typical example of such a bureaucracy. Decision-making power was concentrated at the top and a central collective labour agreement set the framework (i.e. the job ranking system) for all industrial sectors involved. The legally binding agreement during the 1990s dated from 1975. This agreement was still valid because of the ultra-activity clause that provided for the prolongation of the collective labour agreement in the absence of any new agreement. The outdated agreement did not include the job category, for example, of team leader, which was introduced with lean production. As we will see below, this had a negative effect on the income of women.

In sum, we have come across different dimensions of the restructuring process that will have gendered implications. The first one is access to jobs and skills under lean production. The second one is the high level of unemployment. The third one is the flexibilization of contractual conditions. The last one is the outdated collective labour agreement. In sections three and four, I will show the gendered implications at the level of the shop floor of the two case-study firms.

First, I will discuss the dominant ideas on women workers present in this industry and show why masculinization occurred in the industry as a whole.

An Industry Dominated by Men

The Argentine car sector is known as a male sector. My two surveys (Stobbe, 2000) show that women accounted for 10-12 per cent of the workforce on the shop floor of components companies. Three quarters of the companies surveyed employed no women workers whatsoever, which indicates that the companies that did employ women had relatively many female workers on their shop floors (an average of almost 40 per cent). The two firms discussed in this chapter confirm this. López Autopartes employed 28 per cent and Autoparts Worldwide, 71 per cent women on their shop floors in 1995.

My data show that the gender regime of the auto components industry included three dominant discourses about women workers. These discourses were dominant because both sexes consented to them; they took them for granted and routinely drew upon these discourses in selection decisions. This means that human resource managers, who were almost all men, were likely to select male workers, but women were not likely to look for a job in this industry either. One discourse they drew upon was that women were not suitable for work in this industry because it was heavy, dirty and technical. It was stated that women needed protection from heavy, dirty work and it was claimed that men were better suited for supervisory and managerial functions. In companies with many female workers, their innate 'nimble fingers' was the most important argument.

Another dominant discourse was that women were less available because they have children or will have them in the future. It was considered a woman's primary purpose to be a wife and mother, and then a worker. The opposite applied to men. In other words, men were supposed to be the breadwinners, whereas women worked for extra money. The fact that women had children also implied that they were considered to be more expensive because of maternity and breast-feeding leaves and absenteeism. The last discourse was that women are problematic workers because they compete with each other while men are mates. The presence of women on the shop floor was perceived as problematic for two reasons. One was that it led to romantic encounters between male and female employees. The second was the quarrels and rivalry between female employees. These reasons were related to the 'inevitable' heterosexual attraction between men and women and the competition between women over men. The discourse that women were problematic and more expensive workers is interesting, since the literature on industrial restructuring often suggests that women are hired because they are less expensive and more docile workers (Elson and Pearson, 1981; Standing, 1989; Walby, 1989).

These three dominant discourses on women workers constituted the gender regime of the auto components industry[2]. The data show that these discourses were reproduced with the introduction of lean production. I will exemplify this with the competencies of the 'lean' worker, which can be described as involved, motivated, responsible, flexible and a real team player. These competencies were linked to the above-mentioned discourses about women workers in such a way that men were considered better 'lean' workers than women. The data show that responsibility was linked to the breadwinner principle (men are the breadwinners, women work for extra money), and flexibility to availability (women are less flexible because they are less available). Moreover, women could never be real team players because they were not able to perform every task (some are too heavy, dirty or technical) and because they competed with each other. The data show that between 1992 and 1997 the number of female employees and workers decreased relatively more than the number of male employees and workers, 27 and 29 per cent as against 21 and 18 per cent, respectively. Data gathered during the summer of 2002 confirm this trend. These data demonstrate that, for the industry as a whole, the participation of women decreased and, therefore, it can be concluded that restructuring leads to the exclusion of women. The analysis of the two companies in the next sections will show, however, that women have access to training and new jobs.

Lopéz Autopartes

López Autopartes was founded as a family business in 1955. Twenty years later, in 1975, a group of seven Argentinean stakeholders, all men connected with the firm, took over because of imminent bankruptcy. Most of them were still running the firm in 1995 when I first visited López Autopartes. The firm was located in Greater Buenos Aires, in a neighbourhood where there had traditionally been much metallurgical activity. The products manufactured by López Autopartes were window lifts and door locks (interior equipment).

López Autopartes employed 96 men and 25 women in 1995. The vast majority of the women were employed at the shop floor and did assembly jobs. Like most other firms, López Autopartes did not have any female supervisors or managers in 1995. The firm had experienced an increase in production during the first years of the 1990s and had employed new personnel. The 1995 crisis led, however, to the first layoffs at Lopéz Autopartes and this trend continued during the second half of the 1990s.

The restructuring trajectory of Lopéz Autopartes consisted of two interrelated strategies. First, they tried to find an international partner, which could buy them out and save the company from bankruptcy. In the meantime, the owners tried to enhance the quality of the product. They employed a quality manager who had worked at a respected international components firm and they introduced several lean production techniques, which aimed at improving the flow of production (layout changes) and achieving quality control by the workers (health and safety and visual control programmes). However, the problem was that the firm did not have the technology to produce a qualitatively good product. Their machinery was obsolete and the owners did not invest in new equipment.

The second strategy was that the owners defined assembly as their core business. They wanted to specialize in the assembly of car locks because they thought that this value-adding activity would give them a greater chance of finding an international partner. This decision had important consequences for the sexual division of labour. Firstly, during the first years of the nineties, 18 women were hired to work in the assembly department. This implied a tenfold increase in female shop-floor personnel, since only two women had been working on the shop floor in 1990. Secondly, although the dismissal of personnel started in 1995 and continued (in 1997 only 50 people were left), women were affected less than men (an increase from 28 to 35 per cent of women on the shop floor). The owners used the typical type of work arguments to hire women or dismiss men. Because of better manual and visual competencies, women were considered better assembly-line workers and better quality controllers. Although the training programme was very limited, all women had access to in-company training, and two women even got promoted; one to a supporting staff function at the quality control department and the other one, a technical engineer, to supervisor of the plastic injection department. In other words, women in general, and some women in particular, profited from the restructuring process. These findings do not coincide with the studies discussed in the introduction that concludes that women are excluded from multi-skilled jobs and assigned to the periphery (Jenson, 1989; Roldán, 1993, 1994; Sayer, 1986).

Not every man at the company welcomed these changes. The supervisor of the assembly department, for example, had very clear ideas about this. In his view, the major problem with women was that they did not have enough strength to perform every job in the department. He tried several times to let women do the heavier jobs, but they always ended up crying. He was in fact quite infamous for the way he treated the women. This supervisor openly opposed the decision of his bosses to hire women for assembly-line work. The bosses did not change their minds, however, but they did not replace him either. In fact, López Autopartes did not introduce teamwork and did not replace supervisors with team leaders. As we will see in the next case, these changes would have been a much greater challenge to the traditional ideas about women workers.

The three male workers of the plastic injection department were more successful in their opposition. They had difficulties with a woman giving them orders and the owners decided to replace her with a male colleague. Although the woman did not agree, she had no other choice than to acquiesce in the decision of her boss. Another job would have been very hard (if not impossible) to find and she needed the job very badly (she was single and responsible for her parents). In 1997, she was doing secretarial work.

As we already know, the story has an unhappy ending for everyone. Despite the efforts, the company was unable to obtain new contracts with car manufacturers and to find a buyer. In 1997, the only products they continued to manufacture were for old and obsolete car models and production continued to decline in 1998 and 1999. In 1999, the quality manager was made redundant and only a few senior workers continued at the plant. In June 2000, the company closed down indefinitely for reasons that had nothing to do with the gendered division of labour.

Autoparts Worldwide

The story of Autoparts Worldwide is a different story because of the global strategy of the Autoparts Worldwide Group. The plant involved in the study was the only production facility of the Group in Argentina in 1995. The plant was situated in a village, Campo Grande, in the Province of Buenos Aires, 140 kilometres from the city of Buenos Aires. In the first half of the 1970s, the company had moved its production facilities from the city to Campo Grande, becoming the first factory in the village. The National Economic Census of 1994 shows that Campo Grande had 56 industrial sites employing 368 people. With 250 employees in 1994, Autoparts Worldwide was definitely the main industrial employer. It was also the main employer of women workers. Around 75 per cent of the shop-floor personnel were female.

Autoparts Worldwide was originally founded in Argentina by a European multinational. The company was taken over by the Autoparts Worldwide Group in 1987. In 1996, the Autoparts Worldwide Group had 25,000 employees, of whom 8 per cent were employed in South America (Argentina, Brazil and Mexico). The product lines manufactured in Campo Grande in 1995 were control panels and starter switches. In 1997, two more products were manufactured at the plant in Campo Grande, namely side mirrors and fuel suppliers. The latter were actually manufactured by a different company, Autoworld, a joint venture of Autoparts Worldwide and another European components producer. The Autoparts Worldwide Group was also part of a larger international business group whose main activity was car manufacturing. In short, Autoparts Worldwide was a real global player in the industry.

In November 1992, a new European director and a new female Argentine human resource manager initiated the reorganization towards lean production. A year later, another European, who took over as the head of the quality control department, joined them. These new managers were committed to changing this production facility into a 'lean' factory. This particular site was one of the last to implement the system. When I visited Autoparts Worldwide for the first time in 1995, the company employed 84 men and 91 women. Women were mainly employed on the shop floor, in assembly and screen-printing activities. The proportion of women workers had always been very high at Autoparts Worldwide and the reasons for hiring them were the same as at all other firms (nimble fingers, see section two). Moreover, the director explained that women did this kind of work at every factory operated by the Group.

The restructuring of Autoparts Worldwide towards lean production started with the introduction of a new organizational structure, which involved the creation of three production units and the replacement of supervisors by team leaders. The new organizational structure enabled the management team to replace personnel that did not fit into the new structure and lean philosophy with young, talented engineers (as line managers) and women workers (as team leaders). Moreover, all personnel had access to training activities, to a greater or lesser extent. The female team leaders and the men working with the plastic injection machines received relatively more training than the rest of the workers. The company also invested in layout changes, in enlargement of the factory, in new computer-controlled equipment and machinery, and in an integrated production management system (a database to manage production flows).

The company benefited from the rise in production in the first years of the 1990s and continued to do so after the crisis of 1995. Their market share grew and a large part of the production was exported to Brazil, a smaller part to Europe through assemblers. The production volume fluctuated though and a flexible labour force proved to be an important management tool in coping with these fluctuations. In 1993, the company had already started hiring personnel on a temporary basis (three-month contracts). In May 1995, almost 50 temporary workers were (temporarily) dismissed, due to the crisis. In October 1997, 67 workers had temporary contracts (27 per cent of the total work force). Apart from fluctuations in production, another reason for not renewing a contract was pregnancy. Pregnant women were considered expensive (the company had to pay for their maternity leave, etc.) and problematic (higher absenteeism). The Argentine labour legislation still protected pregnant women with permanent contracts, but the use of temporary contracts created a loophole in the protective legislation. The high level of unemployment also had a negative impact on the employment of women. It was socially more acceptable to dismiss women than men. Although most respondents knew that women had to work because one salary was not enough or the husband was out of a job, men were still supposed to be the breadwinners. Additionally, male managers argued that, when dismissed, women always had their housekeeping work, while men would be out of a job.

A positive outcome for women workers was the new promotion opportunity, as female team leaders replaced almost every male supervisor. This was a revolutionary change for women because, although 75 per cent of the shop-floor personnel were female, it was the first time in the history of Autoparts Worldwide that women workers were promoted to jobs other than those of secretaries. It was also revolutionary because several of the replaced male supervisors came from the old assembly school where strictness was very important. They were in fact very brutish with women workers (they made women cry to make them work harder), just like the supervisor we encountered at López Autopartes.

The shift from male supervisors to female team leaders had been made possible by the new management team. They could decide to select women for this new position; they could confront the Argentine male managers and other opponents because of their positions in the organizational hierarchy. The ideas of the foreign managers about the capacities and capabilities of women workers were less traditional than those of their Argentine colleagues. Additionally, the female human resource manager was a mentor and a role model for these women. The women were labelled 'agents of change' as I will explain in more detail below.

This does not mean that this shift took place easily. Most women working at Autoparts Worldwide said that they did not want to become team leaders. They explained that they did not want to give orders to their (female) colleagues or that they did not want any trouble. The women that had become team leaders expressed more or less the same feelings. They were afraid of being disliked by their colleagues and they always wanted to make it very clear that they treated every team member equally. The general perception was that men had to be in charge because men engender more respect and women do not have enough authority to dominate other women. Lack of technical skills was another important argument to explain why women were not suitable for the job of team leader. Especially men argued that the male supervisors had the technical knowledge to do the job and that this knowledge was lost when women were appointed as team leaders. Moreover, several women, who had an opportunity to become a team leader, argued that it would be difficult to combine being a team leader with being a mother. They preferred not to work after three o'clock or work on Saturdays and, in order to be a good team leader, you had to be available. In other words, women had different reasons for not becoming team leaders.

Education and skills were important selection criteria for the job of team leader. The majority of the women chosen had finished high school and they all had occupied a special place on the assembly line (testing the assembled component at the end of each line). Additionally, an analysis of the selection process of the female team leaders shows that much attention was paid to work attitudes. The line manager, who did the selection, had looked for a predisposition to learn, willingness to talk to the managers, and women with *la camiseta puesta* (the company shirt on). The European quality manager and the female human resource manager stressed their commitment and drive, and labelled them 'agents of change'. They represented the 'lean' principles these managers wanted to achieve. Several of the 'chosen ones' were very proud of being selected and were quite ambitious in their new jobs. One of them was seriously considering obtaining an engineering degree.

The analysis of this important change shows that the restructuring process had different outcomes for different groups of women and not just because they were treated differently by the management. Women had different ideas about the role that paid work played in their lives. Interestingly enough, the role that paid work played in their lives was not related to differences in life cycles. However, women for whom paid work played an important role differed in their ideas about gender roles and their awareness of gender inequalities in the company and in society as a whole. It shows that women can be true agents of change in industrial restructuring processes (Fernández-Kelly and Wolf, 2001).

There was also a more negative side to this change. The fact that the job of team leader did not exist in the Collective Labour Agreement of 1975 had important consequences for the salaries of these women. The new female team leaders earned the same as their team members, whereas the ex-supervisors (men who became team leaders) earned much more, because they continued to receive their supervisor's salary, including extra payments mainly based on seniority. The predominantly male shop stewards did not question the much-distorted salary relationship (we are talking of a difference of at least 750 US dollars), but neither did the team leaders. We see that the 'agents of change' discourse and the discourse that women work for 'the extra money' conflict.

So far the restructuring of Autoparts Worldwide seems quite successful and highlights positive as well as negative outcomes for women workers. Why then does this story also have an unhappy ending? Three important events show how international business groups, like Autoparts Worldwide, operate and explain the unhappy ending for the workers in Campo Grande. The first one was the establishment of two production sites in Cordoba (the second major 'car city' in Argentina) by other divisions of the Autoparts Worldwide Group. The second event was that Autoparts Worldwide sold the starter switch production line to Autocomponents, another European Group of components producers, in November 1997. This transfer involved a quarter of the total work force of the company (about 50 women and 10 men). The final event was the transfer of the production of the control panel with the highest production volume to an Autoparts Worldwide production facility in Brazil in 1996. The extension of activities in Argentina made it possible for the holding corporation to redefine the counterbalanced trade between Argentina and Brazil. In other words, the Autoparts Worldwide Group decided to transfer the labour-intensive part of the production to Brazil and install labour-extensive production in Argentina. By the end of 1998, the management of Autoparts Worldwide informed the personnel that they would transfer the entire production of control panels to Brazil. Subsequently, Autocomponents bought the building and took over around 100 employees, whereas 70 employees were dismissed. In other words, Autoparts Worldwide left Campo Grande, because it was more profitable to relocate this (labour-intensive) division to Brazil. The two remaining divisions in Cordoba enabled the holding corporation to get maximum benefit from counterbalanced trade. Unfortunately, the story does not end here. In March 2002, most workers lost their jobs and on 16 May 2003, the plant in Campo Grande closed its doors permanently.

These events show that global firms do indeed have global strategies. Local managers can try very hard to restructure a factory and enlarge its market share, but headquarters can decide to close the facility down anyway. Situating these events within the context of a little town where this factory had been the main employer and within the larger context of Argentina with high levels of unemployment, prospects for these workers, men and women alike are not very hopeful. A survey among the workers that were dismissed between December 1998 and June 2002, who were still living in Campo Grande, shows that 56 out of 134 have not yet found new jobs. Moreover, many of the 78 workers that were working were doing so under very precarious conditions.

Comparison and Conclusion

This chapter discussed the gendered outcomes of the restructuring of the Argentine components industry during the 1990s. This decade was characterized by the implementation of neo-liberal policies that, among others, engendered more flexible contractual conditions, an outdated collective labour agreement and high levels of unemployment. Components producers were confronted with rigorous changes in the rules of the game and had to introduce a global system of production and management, lean production. The analysis focused on access to jobs by – and the skills of – women workers during restructuring processes. The data show that the dominant discourses about women workers in this industry – women are not suitable, less available and problematic – were reproduced with the introduction of lean production. Men were considered better 'lean' workers because they had always been better workers. Consequently, a further masculinization of labour in the industry took place. Looking more specifically at two components companies, we see more contradictory outcomes for women workers. The restructuring trajectories of national and global components firms differed significantly, as exemplified by the two case studies discussed in this chapter. The hybrid forms of restructuring of the Argentine components industry, motivated by global developments, interacted in different ways with local ideas about gender roles and relations.

The case of López Autopartes shows that the labour force was feminized during the restructuring process, because the company chose assembly as its core competence. The reasons for hiring women did not differ from the traditional nimble-fingers argument, but it did challenge the ideas about women workers held by some men at the company. However, these men were not replaced. In addition, the restructuring trajectory of López Autopartes was characterized by limited changes to enhance the quality of the product. The company did not hire any workers on a temporary basis, nor did they change anything that would conflict with the outdated collective labour agreement of 1975. In other words, much remained the same and, although women profited from the restructuring process, the dominant ideas about women workers did not really change at this company.

At Autoparts Worldwide more important changes took place in this respect. The replacement of male supervisors by female team leaders was very significant because it challenged and changed the dominant ideas about the work that men and women were supposed to do on the shop floor. Women obtained new career opportunities and men from the old school of assembly were replaced. The importance of the arrival of the new management team (two European men and a woman) has to be highlighted as well, because they set the scene for changes in the established gender regime. This case is also a very good example of the potential implications of a confrontation between a new global system of production and an old local system of labour relations. The story of Autoparts Worldwide also shows that the outcomes for individual women differ. They were enabled and constrained in different ways. Some had more education than others. Some had temporary contracts and others, permanent ones. Some just worked out of necessity; whereas for others work occupied a central place in their lives. These differences were not just the result of decisions by the management. The women themselves decided whether they would become team leaders. Some argued that they did not want to give orders; others that they could not combine it with being mothers; and some were very proud of being selected and saw it as an important career opportunity.

This study, like other recent studies, shows that industrial restructuring produces different and contradictory outcomes for women. Feminization and masculinization are both possible outcomes of global industrial restructuring processes (Afshar and Barrientos, 1999; Bradley, 1999; Crompton et al., 1996; Ryan, 1993; Yates, 1998). Moreover, the study also shows that women are active participants in industrial restructuring; they are also agents of change (Fernández-Kelly and Wolf, 2001). Different rules and resources enable and constrain women workers as well as other actors in shaping the industrial restructuring on the shop floor of Argentine component firms. Rules and resources, for example, such as legislation, discourses about women workers, one's education, and position within the company, generate different outcomes in terms of access to jobs and skills for individuals and groups. These outcomes also depend on actions (and rules and resources) at other levels, including flexibilization of contractual conditions. The story in this chapter shows that access to jobs by – and the skills of – women workers is the outcome of developments at different interrelated levels. Discourses about women workers, legal rules, an outdated collective labour agreement, a high level of unemployment, decisions taken at European headquarters, etcetera, are out of the sphere of influence of the individual agency of women workers, but they have an important bearing on the possible outcomes of industrial restructuring. The idea of structuration at different interacting levels permits a more dynamic conceptualization of access to jobs by – and skills of – women workers. It allows for an analysis of the relation between global industrial restructuring and local ideas about gender, which includes women as active agents and shows the different and contradictory ways women are involved in globalization processes.

Notes

1   The data were taken from a longitudinal study into the restructuring of the Argentine auto components industry in the 1990s (Stobbe, 2000). Different qualitative and quantitative data collection techniques were used at different levels, including literature review and secondary data analysis, two visits to Sao Paulo, Brazil, three surveys among auto components producers, interviews with human resource managers, and (participant) observation, formal, informal and group interviews at two firms. The data were gathered during three different periods, from July 1995 to March 1996, from August to December 1997 and in August 2002. Moreover, contacts with key informants have been maintained over the past eight years.

2   The gender regime of the auto components industry was linked to the hegemonic gender order of machismo in the Argentine society. The respondents referred repeatedly to machismo to explain and justify the sexual division of labour in the industry. It is beyond the scope of this chapter to give more details about the relation between gender order and gender regime. See Stobbe forthcoming, for an exposé of how they are linked.

References

Ashfar, H. and Barrientos, S. (1999). 'Introduction: Women, Globalization and Fragmentation', in H. Ashfar and S. Barientos (eds.) *Women, Globalization and Fragmentation in the Developing World*, Macmillan, London, pp. 1-17.

Bayes, J., Hawkesworth, M. and Kelly, R. (2001). 'Globalization, Democratization and Gender Regimes', in R. Kelly, J. Bayes, M. Hawkesworth and B. Young (eds.), *Gender, Globalization and Democratization*, Rowman and Littlefield, Boulder, pp. 1-14.

Bradley, H. (1999). *Gender and Power in the Workplace: Analysing the Impact of Economic Change*, Macmillan, Houndsmills.

Crompton, R., Gallie, D. and Purcell, K. (eds.) (1996). *Changing Forms of Employment. Organizations, Skills and Gender*, Routledge, London.

Davids, T. and van Driel, F. (2001). 'Globalisation and Gender: beyond dichotomies', in F.J. Schuurman (ed.) *Globalization and Development Studies: Challenges for the 21st Century*, Thela, Amsterdam, Sage, London, pp. 153-177.

Elger, T and Smith, C. (1994). 'Introduction', in T. Elger and C. Smith (eds.), *Global Japanization? The Transnational Transformation of the Labour Process*, Routledge, London, pp. 1-24.

Elson, D. and Pearson, R. (1981). 'The Subordination of Women in the Internationalisation of Factory Production', in K. Young, C. Wolkowitz and R. McCullagh (eds.) *Of Marriage and the Market: Women's Subordination in International Perspective*, CSE Books, London, pp. 144-166.

Fernández-Kelly, P. and Wolf, D. (2001). 'A Dialogue on Globalization', *Signs: Journal of Women, Culture and Society*, vol. 26, no. 4, pp. 1243-1249.

Giddens, A. (1984). *The Constitution of Society: Outline of the Theory of Structuration*, Polity Press, Cambridge.

Humphrey, J. (ed.) (1993). Quality and Productivity in Industry. New Strategies in Developing Countries, *IDS-Bulletin* (special issue), vol. 24, no. 2.

INDEC (1995). *Censo Nacional Económico 1994. Avance de resultados. Informe Nº3 Industria Manufacturera. Parte 1: Total País (resultados provisorios)*, INDEC, Buenos Aires.

Jenson, J. (1989). 'The Talents of Women, the Skills of Men: Flexible Specialization and Women', in S. Wood (ed.), *The Transformation of Work*, Routledge, London, pp. 141-155.

Kaplinsky, R. (with A. Posthuma) (1994). *Easternisation: The Spread of Management Techniques to Developing Countries*, Frank Cass, Ilford.

Kosacoff, B., Todesca, J. and Vispo, A. (1991). *La Transformación de la Industria Automotriz Argentina. Su integración con Brasil*, Documento de Trabajo no. 40, CEPAL, Buenos Aires.

Kochan, T., Lansburry, R. and MacDuffie, J. (eds.). (1997). *After Lean Production: Evolving Employment Practices in the World Auto Industry*, Cornell University Press, Ithaca, London.

Pearson, R. (2000). 'Moving the Goalpost: Gender and Globalisation in the Twenty-First Century', *Gender and Development*, vol. 18, no. 1, pp. 10-19.

Roldán, M. (1993). 'Industrial Restructuring, Deregulation and New JIT Labour Processes in Argentina: Towards a Gender-Aware Perspective?', *IDS Bulletin*, vol. 24, no. 2, pp. 42-52.

Roldán, M. (1994). *Flexible Specialization, Technology and Employment in Argentina: Critical Just-in-Time Restructuring in a Cluster Context*, Working Paper ILO, Geneva.

Ryan, R. (1993). *'Japanisation' or a 'New Zealand Way'? Five Years on at Nissan New Zealand*, Working Paper 5/93, ISSN 0113-1788, Industrial Relations Centre, Victoria University of Wellington.

Sayer, A. (1986). 'New Developments in Manufacturing: The Just-in-Time System', *Capital and Class*, no. 30, pp. 43-72.

Standing, G. (1989). 'Global Feminization through Flexible Labor', *World Development*, vol. 17, no. 7, pp. 1077-1095.

Stobbe, L. (2000). *Inclusion and Exclusion in the Argentine Auto Components Industry: A Study of Industrial Restructuring, Gender and Power*, Verlag für Entwicklungspolitik Breitenbach, Saarbrücken.

Stobbe, L. (forthcoming). 'Doing Machismo: Legitimating Speech Acts as a Selection Discourse', *Gender, Work and Organization*.

Walby, S. (1989). 'Flexibility and the Changing Sexual Division of Labour', in S. Wood (ed.), *The Transformation of Work?* Routledge, London, pp. 127-140.

West, C. and D.H. Zimmerman (1987). 'Doing Gender', *Gender and Society*, vol. 1, no. 1, pp. 125-51.

Wichterich, C. (2000). *The Globalized Woman: Reports from a Future of Inequality*, Zed Books, London.

Yates, C. (1998). *Work Reorganization and Women in Auto: Contradictory Trends*, Unpublished paper presented at the International Labour Process Conference, Manchester, England.

Chapter 3

Professionalization, Sexualization: When Global Meets Local in the Working Identities of Secretaries in Lima, Peru

Lorraine Nencel

Introduction

This chapter concerns a group of working women in Latin America who are rarely present in gender studies on development, work or identity. It concerns secretaries and, more specifically, secretaries working in public administration[1]. Unlike in the West where secretaries have made substantial gains in changing the contents and image of their occupation, resounding in titles such as office manager or administrative assistant, secretaries in societies such as Peru have so far been unable to claim the same. Like many of their Latin American colleagues, Peruvian secretaries are continually sexualized, epitomized as sex bombs or as their antithesis. Hence, locally, their working identities are highly informed by a process of sexualization that objectifies them as both victim and seducer. That secretaries reject this imposed version of femininity is clearly embodied in their self-definitions and the norms and values by which they judge themselves and their colleagues. Secretaries are fervently challenging the traditional contents of their occupation by being involved in occupational associations, attending training courses, conferences and courses aimed at professionalization.

The chapter begins by presenting a description of the workings of the bureaucracy. The material and procedural conditions encountered in the ministries form the foundation on which both processes of professionalization and sexualization take place. This will be followed by a section that dissects different strands of the process of professionalization. It will analyze documents used in training given to secretaries to prepare them to take on the challenges of the globalized world. It is in this domain that global discourse of neo-liberal organization theory enters into the women's working experiences. These theories promote a 'global work ethic' characterized by its optimistic and uncritical stance towards the New Economic Order. Catchwords such as 'vision', 'innovation', 'empowerment' and 'mission' are defined as necessary personal attributes to succeed in the new organization. In addition, we will examine the secretarial organization's issues and interests in regard to the subject of professionalization.

This will be followed by a discussion of another powerful discourse that contributes to their working identities, namely the discourse of sexualization. The chapter will take as its point of departure a local event that occurred in 1998 when two members of Congress proposed a bill to prohibit the use of the miniskirt at public and private working establishments. A few excerpts of the proposal will be analyzed to give insight into the different meanings contained within the discourse of sexualization. Finally, we will enter the workplace to present the reactions of the women to these norms and values embedded in sexualization. In conclusion, it will be argued that the global and local discursive dynamics at work in practice currently affect the process of professionalization in varying degrees and, consequently, they inform the construction of the working identities of secretaries. In addition, both discourses reflect broader social processes. The global discourse on organizations is nearly a carbon copy of Western modernization theory and developments, while the process of sexualization comprises a double-edged discourse that simultaneously desexualizes and thus professionalizes and sexualizes their identities. This process reflects and reinforces broader social discourses of femininity and sexuality that support the existing gender order.

The Local Context: The Workings of – and Working in – a Bureaucracy

There are certain idiosyncratic features associated with working at a Peruvian ministry. In the first place, many positions are 'political'. This implies that when there is a change of government there is a change of guard. It is feasible that a whole department will be transferred, including the secretary. The new department heads will bring their 'own' staff or secretaries. This might be a result of political favours or a desire to continue working with the people from their previous positions. But every time a change is announced, many rumours circulate as to who is in line to be transferred. It is a restless period. Even within an election term, if the minister is changed, all persons in political positions are likely to be dismissed or transferred. However, it is also quite common that the secretary is one of the few people that provides continuity to the office culture and serves as the office's store of knowledge. Many secretaries see department heads come and go. To survive, a secretary needs to be in possession of a large measure of resilience since bosses' personalities and working styles change on a regular basis, but procedures do not.

For women in tenured positions (*nombradas*), it is nearly impossible to be fired. They can be transferred at the bosses' whims, or they can be degraded from being in the office of the minister (Directorate) to an office with a lower status, but it is difficult to dismiss them. The secretaries have a built-in view of their work that nothing is permanent – neither the office in which they work nor their superior for whom they work. Although rarely put into practice, the inverse is also the case. A woman can put in for a transfer if she finds it difficult to work with certain colleagues or bosses. Transfers are rarely explained in detail. The person being transferred is usually left with several unanswered questions.

Women with job tenure enjoy other secondary benefits, such as uniforms, optional free lunches or the equivalent in money or paid holiday. At some ministries they receive supplementary payments; in others, they can choose between a monthly package of staple goods or an equivalent sum of money. It is difficult to know whether these are benefits or compensation for their low salaries. Those working on temporary contracts do not receive such benefits, but they do receive more money. However, they complain that for fear of losing their jobs they always stay late when asked to work overtime. Temporary contracts are renewed every three to six months. I met women who have been working on temporary contracts for the last 15 years. During this entire period they had not received health insurance, accrued social security benefits for retirement or taken days of holiday since they had started working. Both the tenured and temporary employees acknowledge that they generally get along. Nonetheless, a tension exists between them. The tenured find it unfair that the temporaries earn more, and the temporaries are jealous of the secondary benefits and the *nombradas'* job security.

Bureaucracies are also renowned for the high degree of paper pushing from one desk to another and back again (*tramites*). It is interesting to note that not many people criticized the amount of *tramites* required. They felt it was a requirement to guarantee accountability. It was always possible to trace the department in which or the desk at which some request stagnated. But nonetheless, they all agreed it took a great deal of their time. The pace of work varies from department to department, but in general much time is spent in registering or tracing documents, placing paper in the printer, answering e-mail messages, questions and the telephone. The following excerpt from my fieldwork notes gives an idea of the rhythm of work:

Mariella told me that it was quieter than normal because the head of the department – la doctora – was out of town. However, she worked at a quick pace. She took her time, was patient with everyone and treated everyone kindly. She made some copies and then we went to dispatch some documents. We got to the third floor to dispatch some documents to the chief administrator. First they had to pass the assistant – a man who was talking on the phone. We waited until he finished. I asked her if he could be difficult and she said, 'Put him under pressure and he will not budge, but if you treat him nicely he will do everything for you. A few days ago I had a document dated the day before. I had to talk very gently and explain what happened so that he would accept it'. I inquired, 'Why wouldn't he accept a document from the day before?' She replied, 'Because he could be held responsible for the delay in processing'.

Everything has to do with control. Every time a document passes a desk it receives a stamp of entrance. So if it gets stuck somewhere it is easy to trace. You cannot be blamed if it gets lost once it leaves your desk and was received by the following day.

Telephone. Mariella stops what she is doing, answers the phone and calls a person to come to the phone. (There are no extensions.) She takes a message for the doctora. She has a book in which she writes down messages and things she has to do immediately. She runs to the phone. Time for a toffee, mmm. She has to finish something quickly. She begins and is interrupted by someone who enters. She is typing and giving orders at the same time, looks in the register of received documents to find another document that was lost. Sonia asks for a rubber band. She stores office supplies in a cardboard box under her desk. She returns to the document she was typing. Another phone call, this time from the minister's office. She still hasn't been able to register the first document. Mariella highlights what has to be read and fills in the summary, thinking carefully about each word she uses. Then it goes to the director and comes back to her to be dispatched. If a document is routine, it can wait a day before it is registered but, if it requires an urgent action, it has to be registered the same day. Intranet message: 'What is the name of the head of logistics?' She answers quickly. Mariella makes labels out of paper, prints them, cuts them and pastes them on the envelope. They do not use prefab labels for anything. She prints out contracts and organizes them to be signed. 'I can't dispatch them until the deputy director signs them and she is not here.' Stella says, 'There is no toner for the printer', Mariella replies, 'There is one in the storage room.' She calls and then puts in an official written request. She waits for her boss to leave for lunch and says, 'I do not go to lunch before my boss leaves. If I went earlier, I would be worried that she might need something and could not find it. I would not be able to think of anything else during my lunch, so I prefer to wait.'

The women working at the ministries are extremely dedicated to their work and do their jobs properly. Their work demands a great deal of stamina, not only because of the fast tempo but also because of the inadequate infrastructure in which they work. There is one telephone for a whole office, thirty desks in one room; one printer for everyone, in which no paper is stored to avoid theft and misuse. Official requests have to be made for everything.

This brief sketch illustrates the material and procedural conditions of a bureaucracy. Peruvian ministries are ailing bureaucracies functioning in a country with a chronic economic crisis. Inherently, this system continually results in insecurity that affects the quality of work and work relations. Paradoxically, secretaries working under these bureaucratic conditions do not object to the paperwork it entails or to the document control system. They may consider it a nuisance but it does not cause any serious complaints and there is a general acceptance and respect for the hierarchy embedded in this system. What was generally echoed in their descriptions of their work was a work ethic that emphasized their desire to be efficient and thorough, and to be regarded highly by their superiors. In this sense, the bureaucratic conditions may be a sign of the inefficient functioning of Peruvian organizational modernity, but it did not diminish the secretaries' desire to work as professionals and be considered as such by others.

The Quest for Professionalization

In this new world a girl with brains will earn more than a woman with a body but without brains. There is no liposuction for the brain (Speaker at the FIAS conference, 2000, Lima).

The quest for professionalization is not one being fought on all fronts or by the majority of secretaries, but it is occurring in the name of them all. It receives its impulse from different occupational associations, for example, on sector level – the National Association of Secretaries in the Health sector (ANASSES) or sector-wide, the National Confederation of Associations of Peruvian Secretaries (CONAPSE), and also internationally, by the Inter-American Federation of Associations of Secretaries (FIAS). These different organizations share the common goal of defending the rights of secretaries as well as fighting feverishly for the modernization of their occupation. To obtain these goals, the associations have put much effort into negotiating the development of a university-accredited study of Secretarial Sciences. The CONAPSE has fought for this goal since the 1970s. In 2000, the Peruvian president of the FIAS explained the importance of obtaining this recognition and talked about progress made throughout Latin America. In Peru, it was now possible for secretaries to receive their Bachelor's degrees (long-distance courses) from a university in Arequipa in the south of Peru.

Another tool used in this struggle is that of conferences and seminars. Titles such as 'Seminar for Secretarial Leaders: the challenge of 2000' (1998), 'The Managerial Assistant in the Next Millennium' (1999), 'The Inter-American Congress of Secretaries: creativity and the administrative assistant and her integration in the global enterprise' (2000) infer notions of change and progress in and towards a modern world. It is through these conferences and seminars that secretaries receive the knowledge and messages of the new organizational discourse.

Global Lessons

In analyzing the lectures given and training material used, certain tendencies surface. Globalization is depicted as an inevitable process that has arrived in Peru, rapidly bringing unavoidable changes, which will be felt in every inch of society. Consequently, 'the World in which we were formed will cease to exist' (Espinoza Sanchez, 1999). This tendency to describe change as such mimics the Western neo-liberal, organizational and theoretical development, which has been described by Courpasson and Reed (2004, p. 5) as an 'apocalyptic vision and "discourse of endings"... Revolutionary change, sweeping away outmoded values and obsolete institutions, rather than piecemeal social engineering and incremental organizational reform, became the defining feature of our time and condition'. Within this new world vision, in which the 'demise of bureaucracy' was announced, secretaries need new knowledge to be able to continue in the new economic social order.

In the Peruvian context, the lecturers profess these American Neo-Liberal organizational theories without taking into account the one-directional position of Peru in the global market. Peru is at the receiving end of global capitalism, knowledge and culture (Banerjee and Linstead, 2001). Moreover, their lectures do not reflect the Peruvian organizational reality. In a recent article, Du Gay (2004) criticizes unproblematic application of the new organizational theories in bureaucracy, particularly state bureaucracies. He shows how certain features necessary for governing are considered outdated and replaced by new entrepreneurial theories, causing distinct problems in relation to governing. Peruvian experts seem to be appropriating this modernized approach, intending to implement it as was done in the North with swift brush strokes that do away with all organizational structures of the past.

The discourse of global organizational change brings with it a new work ethic. The individual is less important; working in a team is emphasized. The emphasis on team building can, in the future, have far reaching consequences for secretaries. Contemporarily, their working relations are based on hierarchical authority. Future reorganizations will potentially be orientated towards creating structures of teamwork. This infers a more horizontal relation between the secretary and other members of the team. This shift can create an unintentionally positive change in the working conditions and thus in the working identities of secretaries.

Moreover, the global discourse of organizational changes is apparently devoid of all identity markers. Gender, class or ethnic descriptions are virtually absent from the literature. Equally lacking are any overt references to sexuality. This is particularly noteworthy because, in the actual situation, secretaries continually receive messages concerning their sexuality. Whether it is in lessons on grooming and appearance that teach them to play down their sexuality and heighten their femininity, or in assertions such as the quote presented above, the image of the secretary is sexually laden. Cautiously, I suggest that the absence of sexuality in the neo-liberal organizational theories is an intentional silence. The absence of all identity markers suggests a (pseudo) neutrality-promoting opportunity for everyone. Anyone can become a new and significant (team) player in the new order.

Organizational changes such as 'flexibility' are described as a positive consequence of globalization. In a lecture entitled 'The Professional Profile and Challenges for the Managerial Assistant' the new organizational order was described as follows:

> Today the competitive reality imposes new paradigms in the person-institution relation.
>
> 1 As we are living in a global environment, highly competitive, moving fast and uncertain, we need to be *flexible* (author's emphasis) to rapidly accommodate to the changes.
> 2 ...
> 3 ....
> 4 During the time you are here, it is not sufficient that you do what is necessary. You must look for other ways to be valuable for the institution. To continue with us you must be a contributor to the team not just a player.
> 5 To continue being a contributor you must grow and develop. You must convert to being a 'studious person' just as the institution will be a 'studious organization'. Although we will give opportunities, you must be in charge of your own development.
> ...

9 Tenured positions are no longer the norm. The day will come when you will want to leave us. Also it is probable that the day might come that we want you to go, without your having done anything wrong. In both cases, the benefit is no longer mutual.

(Benedetti Venturo, 1999, no page numbers)

The new paradigms being offered in these presentations challenge elements inherent in Peruvian organizational modernity, attacking, for example, the virtue of tenured positions, inferring that they are the means to an easy life. The presenters praise the 'new' flexible employer-employee relationship as if they only recently became familiar with the idea, while in reality the Peruvian economy, like all Latin American economies, is characterized by its employment 'flexibility'. The majority of citizens earn their incomes by working informally. Underemployment and unemployment is the rule rather than the exception; temporary work contracts are in abundance and permanent work is only set aside for a select few. To sum up, the so-called restructuring being opted for by Peruvian labour experts is an excellent example of what was described at the beginning of this section, of how the Latin American countries mimic the organizational developments of North America and how the transference of knowledge from the north to the south is one directional.

In the new global order a lot of demands are being placed on the secretary. Being flexible, accepting any and all types of change is essential. In this new profile much emphasis has been placed on obtaining knowledge and new skills. Her responsibilities and contents of her work are envisioned as changing and expanding. She is portrayed as an invaluable asset for the new organizational order. As the quote below illustrates, there is a shift occurring, with less emphasis placed on personal qualities and more on acquirable skills:

The secretary of yesterday, whose sweet image and perseverance still keeps her bright and shiny in our memory, has converted to the secretary of today, professional, scientifically prepared, with full control of the technologies and with a solid ethical formation. The secretary of tomorrow, the secretary of the third millennium whose profile we clearly intuit as a great leader will be the culmination of the ideal professional women, where the alchemy of the traditional and the modern consolidate in a personality enriched with new knowledge, skills and abilities of modern technologies and cyber languages, imperishable values and human attitudes (Robles Morales, nd, p. 11).

This discourse has also been appropriated by the secretaries – in a commendable initiative to strengthen and consolidate secretaries in the health sector. The National Association of Secretaries in the Health Sector (ANASSES) publishes a magazine called 'New Image'[2]. A brief analysis of the different articles provides insight into the secretary's new image. The new image is a secretary who is well informed and is familiar with the changes and developments taking place in the health sector. She physically takes care of her image with tips on make-up, hairstyles and dress. She is a modern worker who is striving for the professionalization of her occupation through redefining the nature of her duties. In an introductory article written by the president of the association, the managerial assistant was described as followed:

> The managerial assistant has converted into the primary articulator between the conductor of the institution and the personnel under him…
>
> It is also our mission, to impregnate the organization in which we move with the necessity to believe in us, to renovate ourselves, learning day by day, and to convince the others that we are capable of placing high objectives upon ourselves, reinforcing our sense of achievement. In this way we will be able to make our bosses change the way that we want them to.
>
> (Meza Camargo, 2000, p. 4)

Thus, the secretary's position as managerial assistant gives her more domains of responsibility, gives her more horizontal lines of communication in the organizational structure with the potential to influence the configuration of power relations to her benefit. Nonetheless, the majority of the secretaries who participated in this study are working in situations that do not show any signs of change. They are cogs in a bureaucracy with few opportunities.

Their daily reality contrasts sharply with what is proposed in the new organizational order. For example, one woman explained that it might be an asset to take the time necessary to think about how to be more creative and innovative, but when her boss sees her sitting there doing 'nothing' he immediately looks for something else for her to do. In the Ministry of Development, I heard complaints concerning the limitations put on them in regard to developing new skills. One woman complained that she was not given permission to follow an English course, even though the demand to communicate in English had increased in her department. She was told that it was not included in the job description. Several women complained that they were not given an opportunity to participate in their department's substantive training courses on gender and development. It was put down to a practicality, 'Who would attend to the office if everyone was taking the training course?' Although their superiors never said that they felt their participation in this training was unnecessary, the secretaries assumed this was the primary reason for their absence from such training.

The ideas constituting the global discourse on organizational change are gaining in popularity. However, their implementation locally is far from being a fact. For example, the director of the Human Resource Institute of the Ministry of Health acknowledges the difficulties he faces in changing the organizational mentality, suggesting that it is a slow process requiring several steps before those involved will be willing to accept change (personal communication, 11, 2003).

Not only do secretaries have to deal with new sources of knowledge that threaten to change the context and content of their work drastically, but they are also confronted with old, antiquated imagery that links their occupation to their sexuality. This relationship is popularly accepted and recurrently reinvented.

Although not all secretaries are exposed to the innuendoes and insinuations daily, they are latently present and the women are (un)consciously aware of the power they have in defining their occupational identity. Portrayals of secretaries in the Peruvian context focus on their bodies, play up their sexuality, eroticize their images, infer their availability and play down their responsibilities. The following section will present one moment when a futile attempt was made to institutionalize the sexualized image of the secretary.

Local Talk: Sexualizing of Secretaries

The Peruvian gender order is one with a high sexual rationale in which sexual notions inform gender labels and identities (Nencel, 1996). In this gender system, men's masculinity is in part defined through their sexuality. This in turn is defined as aggressive, nearly instinctual and uncontrollable (Nencel, 1996; Fuller, 2001). Women's sexuality is defined in juxtaposition. Girls learn from a very early age to contain themselves, because any outward expression of their sexuality would put them in an undesirable category of femininity. Thus, ideally, masculine sexuality manifests itself in its expression and feminine sexuality in its repression. Taking this into consideration, the sexualization of the secretary reflects this sexualized gendered order. Secretaries are situated close to the 'bad girl' category, legitimizing men's sexual overtures. One incident that illustrates excellently the dynamics of the sexualized gendered system and simultaneously exemplifies the process of sexualization in action is the unsuccessful attempt made by two congressmen to ban the miniskirt in the private and public sectors. Early in 1998 two congressmen who were members of the official government party, Cambio 90-Nueva Mayoria, proposed a bill with the unpretentious title 'The Use of Uniforms in Public and Private Centres of Work' No. 3376. Soon after the proposed law was launched, it caused an explosion in the press, unofficially renamed the 'law against the miniskirt'.

The bill's initiators formulated the problem as follows: 'Women's respect and dignity, accorded to all citizens by the Constitution, was being violated'. The perpetrators were their bosses, male colleagues and clients. It was achieved in different ways: 'lecherous looks, dishonest proposals, sexual blackmail, vulgar actions'. One of the causes of this problem is '... the use of a small garment (the miniskirt that permits women to show their female charm) that solicits provocations and induces lecherous conduct that denaturalizes the feminine quality of women, perturbing the normal development at work'. Further on they state 'the solution is not to sanction but rather to provide norms that could create a formal working environment by wearing modest garments, soberly and modestly adorned....' Their fundamentalist conviction was reflected in the passages cited from the Bible concerning proper dress. The justifications were presented in the second part of the bill:

> That, it cannot be denied that individuals have the right to use a suggestive garment (miniskirt) in an outing or celebration because this would impede or deprive them of their universal right.

That the use of the miniskirt is destined to call attention, directly or indirectly, awaking admiration for feminine beauty ... creating provocation. Thus, provocation is the insinuation that initiates hounding or harassment.

That all women have the right to individually develop their customs, taste and ways to dress, like the use of a certain desired piece of clothing (the miniskirts) established by fashion or the season, but this does not justify its use in centres of work... They will be the objects of indiscrete looks appeasing to masculine morbidity, exciting men to act incorrectly, proposing dishonest adjectives. Women's dignity is being blemished by their bosses, male colleagues, through different ways ... We must understand that women's use of the miniskirt is because they have an attribute they directly or indirectly desire to show...

That the way to prevent sexual harassment in its multiple facets is to avoid giving reasons, by not wearing garments (miniskirts) that lend themselves to insinuations and make one lose control of their prudence and conduct...

Hence it can be said that the responsibility is not only the one who commits the offence but also the one who induces or provokes it.

(Proyecto No.3376, Uniforme Formal-Centros Publicos/Privados – Suo De...)

To reach this goal, they suggest the use of uniforms in the office. As one of the initiators said in an interview, 'it is easier to control this aspect than men's mentalities'.

The proposed bill never reached congress. Nonetheless, it exemplifies the process of sexual objectification rooted in the discourse of sexuality. On the one hand, women are the victims, offended by men because men are transgressing gender norms with their inappropriate behaviour. However, women wearing miniskirts at their places of work are also guilty of transgressing gendered norms of sexual decency and thus, provoke men to release their sexuality, which they incessantly try to contain in the workplace. From this perspective, women cause men's sexual restlessness and need to be controlled.

The process of sexualization is symbolized by wearing miniskirts. As we will see below, the sexual connotations imbued in the miniskirt are not just a male issue but many of the secretaries acknowledge this sexual power. Thus, this discourse has been appropriated by the women. However, the way it manifests itself in daily practice is far more complicated than the initiators of the bill thought.

Sex and Secretaries: A Likely Combination?

If one walks into a department of the ministry, one will not see overt signs of sexualization. Women's attire is business-like; many of the women wear uniforms[3]. All the women considered proper appearance and dress essential for fulfilling their occupations adequately. As I was told by several persons, 'secretaries represent the office image; they are the first persons that visitors see when they arrive'. They upheld strict norms concerning what is appropriate work attire. I have called this a dress code of decency. That is to say, the women worked at being presentable and feminine, not calling too much attention to themselves. Miniskirts were out of the question. Tight pants and too much make-up all belonged to the don'ts in their dress codes. Calling attention to your appearance is synonymous with actively constructing your sexuality. They rejected all the symbols that were stereotypically associated with the popular image of the secretary and, at the same time, recognized the sexual power they contained. Women were against the use of (extremely short) miniskirts at work. Some even considered the 'law against the miniskirt' a reasonable solution to the problem.

One of the secretaries' associations has written a Code of Ethics (CONAPSE). Different articles in this code emphasize the ethical qualities required of secretaries to perform their jobs: honesty, discretion, dignity. In addition, the code constantly reminds them not to misuse their organizational position. They should rise above the temptations and bribes, and not practice nepotism. One article warns secretaries not to use their qualities and position to move up through the organization.

> No secretary should take advantage of her influence over her superiors, nor appeal to amicable relations or recommendations to achieve un-deserved promotions and consequently better remuneration than what corresponds to the work she fulfils, obstructing the promotion of others who deserve the promotion more because of their experience, knowledge and years of service (Codigo Deontologico de las Secretarias, n.d.).

A code of ethics is one of the building blocks of a professional identity (Mills, 2003). In this case, the dos and don'ts make inferences to attributes normally considered to belong to a particular type of secretary – the stereotypical sexualized secretary. For example, prohibiting the use of amicable relationships for one's own (undeserved) gains alludes to secretaries who use their talents to climb the career ladder. This is one of the most popular stereotypes concerning secretaries and it is laden with sexual insinuations. Here, again, we see the double-edged knife at work. By dictating correct behaviour, the Association formulates criteria of professionalism and, by doing so, unintentionally reinforces the existence of the sexualized secretary.

Does this overtly sexual secretary really exist? Personally, I never met a woman who fitted the description. Nonetheless, whether she is a figment of the imagination, a mythical personality or a fully-fledged woman is less important for my argument than the fact that it is believed that she does exist. In the talks I had with the participants, a distinction was often made between how they presented themselves and how they described other secretaries. The sexualized image was at times an inferred reference point with which they contrasted their own identity. One of the dividing principles between themselves and others was expressed in the name they had for certain secretaries – 'secretaries for adornment'. They distinguished themselves from those secretaries by identifying themselves as belonging to a different group, 'professional/career secretaries'. According to the definitions, the first group was good looking, more often than not blonde, fair skinned, 'empty headed' and useless. The career women knew these women would not last more than six months, either because they were incapable of doing the job or they were there for the boss's amusement. When he was tired of them, they would be dismissed. The secretaries who came along with their bosses to new positions would be scrutinized to see to which category they belonged. By sexualizing certain women (who are in the minority), they ultimately desexualised themselves and contributed to the professionalization of their identities. This double-edged discourse is continually at work, simultaneously constructing juxtaposed meanings in the construction of their working identities.

The provocative, seductive secretary pops up again in the women's discussions of sexual harassment. Dress has great significance in their depictions:

L: I heard that in the public sector there aren't that many incidents of sexual harassment. Could this be a result of the fact that since we are not that young anymore it is now happening to others?

Juana: No. I think it depends on the boss. Because if the boss is all hands (manosón), he is going to try to harass or annoy the youngest or the middle aged and that is what happened with one director. This director was older, but he would invite all the young girls to get into his car. Some accepted.

L: What happened to them?

Juana: To keep their jobs, some young girls accepted the director's request because they wanted easy money.

L: Do they receive money?

Charo: No, they receive the favour that they can stay in their jobs because they have temporary contracts.

Juana: The same thing happens with the tenured secretaries...

Charo: Because the boss comes with different intentions and finds a way to apply pressure.

Miriam: Today, there are secretaries 18, 19, 20 years old, you see them, ... nowadays, the world today is very liberal. It is also exaggerated. You see a lot of bosses with their secretaries as something normal. It is not a general tendency but you see it a lot.

L: So what is sexual harassment?

Juana: Sometimes the secretary looks for it. I was working in the secretariat and there was a secretary when we left who arrived at 7 in her miniskirt and you could see everything. At 7 in the evening, when everyone should be leaving, she would come and stay there, waiting to see the director. Why would she be looking for him at this hour?

Charo: So, harassment is not only men to women but also women to man.

L: But what is sexual harassment?

Charo: Sexual harassment. Well, anytime I heard about it, it concerned the inverse.

L: But what is your definition?

Charo: In the working environment. To keep your job you have to accept the pressure from your boss and give in to his demands.

Juana: When a boss wants something from a secretary and he blackmails her – sometimes.

Charo: He could be a real harasser but, if he sees a person who is strong, it doesn't work because you can defend yourself.

(Focus Group September, 2000)

The position allotted to women in the conversations concerning sexual harassment constantly shifted between the victim and seducer. Other moments it was confused with a consensual relationship with a superior. If she was wearing a miniskirt, she was more likely to be considered the provocateur than the victim, or in any case making herself available for men's indecent behaviour.

A consensus exists about male sexual behaviour and it is nearly identical with the conceptualization presented in the proposed legislation against the miniskirt. Given that all women know 'what men are like' it is a woman's own responsibility to make sure that she does not get herself into unpleasant situations and, if she does, the women interviewed adamantly agreed on what should be done. They felt it must be reported to some authority, either within or outside the working environment. Women should be prepared to lose their jobs. In an article in the FIAS magazine (2000) entitled 'Harassment at work?', several tips were given as advice for victims of sexual harassment: talk to the harasser and make your standpoint clear; contact the Human Resources Department and, finally, some things the secretary should take into consideration:

Begin with the way you dress. It should be adequate for work. If you like to wear tight miniskirts, black stockings and low-cut blouses, it should not surprise you if men say something offensive. After all, you choose your wardrobe and therefore, you have to accept the consequences.

Within their construction of femininity, they assigned dynamic roles to themselves and expected the same of their occupational group in general. Those women who related incidents of sexual harassment during our interviews told me that it occurred when they were younger and all had the same type of reaction: they not only rejected the proposal but made their opinions strongly known, either by throwing a chair or screaming that they would not have it – and then left the room. None of the women interviewed considered getting involved with their bosses an option for career mobility. In fact, they were of the opinion that getting involved would be detrimental to their careers.

Here, again, we see the double-edged discourse at work in constructing identity. Desexualizing the sexualized, creating standards of proper behaviour by identifying women who behave inappropriately, supports and rejects the process of sexualization, simultaneously. Additionally, it is a lucid example of how they construct their professional identities through exclusion. The processes of exclusion and inclusion are an integral component of identity construction (Hall, 1996).

Conclusions

In this chapter, I have shown that different discourses are at play in constructing the working identities of secretaries. First, there are the secretaries' efforts to improve the content of their work, applying terms such as managerial assistant and holding up the discourse of self-improvement through education. This has manifested itself in negotiations for the inclusion of secretarial studies at university. In the bureaucratic system in which they work, the women possess a work ethic that emphasizes efficiency, discretion, duty and devotion and plays down the insecurity and temporality inherent in the system.

The global discourse introduced from the north also acknowledges the importance of self-improvement. Its introduction has not penetrated all levels of practice. The bureaucracy has as yet not undergone any reform. When we look closer at the workplace, it has not influenced women's work directly or the way they talk about their work. Terms such as mission, vision and empowerment are not integrated in their vocabularies. Whereas the global discourse envisions the secretaries' positions as being part of a team, the women themselves uphold values (i.e. discretion and duty) that reinforce their one-to-one hierarchical relationships with their bosses. Needless to say, the global discourse on organizational change has made its entrance and is most likely here to stay. It is being presented as *the* solution to organizational problems and is highly visible in learning institutions as the new alternative. It contains new elements of professionalization. Discursively, it has made an impact but has not trickled down to all levels of practice; still its potential impact should not be underestimated.

Although it is impossible to predict the future, as the above suggests, a paradoxical situation may arise with the incorporation of neo-liberal organizational theory in the Peruvian context. That is to say, despite its shortcomings, certain elements may contribute positively to women's striving for professionalization. Equally, its claim to neutrality has the potential to further the process of desexualization and strengthen their professional identities, since the new worker is apparently not predefined by any identity markers. However, let's not get over zealous in our praise. As Acker (1990, p. 139) rightfully asserts, '... organizational structure is not gender neutral; on the contrary, assumptions about gender underlie the documents and contracts used to construct organizations and to provide the common sense ground for theorizing about them. Their gendered nature is partly masked through obscuring the embodied nature of work.... This worker is actually a man; men's bodies, sexuality and relationships to procreation and paid work are subsumed in the image of the worker. Images of men's bodies and masculinity pervade organizational processes, marginalizing women and contributing to the maintenance of gender segregation in organizations'. In Acker's undoing of gender neutrality in organizations, she considers the embodiment of gender an important signifier in the construction of identity. For the sake of our argument, this is limited to the embodiment of femininity in the workplace and particularly through dress.

As the previous section illustrates, clothing – whether it be the miniskirt or the dress code of decency – is a locus of meaning. The failed attempt to ban the miniskirt in the workplace and its symbolic significance in incidences of sexual harassment illustrates that the miniskirt is a morally-laden garment that reproduces the existing Peruvian gender order. Dress is a material expression of the double-edged discourse. On the one hand, the acceptance of the miniskirt as a sexual symbol contributes to the process of sexualization. Whereas the miniskirt symbolizes women's uncontrolled sexuality, the dress code of decency constrains their sexuality and simultaneously makes a positive contribution to their professional identities. However, both symbols are at play in women's daily experiences. Entwistle is correct in asserting that the 'discourse and practices of dress operate to discipline the body' (2000, p. 20).

In the quest for professionalization and the turmoil surrounding sexualization, it becomes clear that these processes are not isolated but are situated within locally-embedded social relations of gender and sexuality. Secretaries' embodiment of decency and their rejection – and thus the acceptance of the existence of a sexualized secretary – are expressions of the existing gender order that proscribes two scripts of gender, juxtaposed to each other. Within the Peruvian context, the choices that women can make regarding their agency in the construction of their identities are narrowly defined and are highly informed by this gender discourse in which women's sexuality is highly visible. By enacting and embodying notions of decency women are actively attempting to live up to the script of the good woman, an undertaking not confined to secretaries but one that is a daily task for the majority of all women. In an earlier study (Nencel, 2001; 1999) on women who prostitute themselves, the women were constantly creating ways to show that they were not as promiscuous as they were continually told they were. The phrase 'a job like any other', which first appears to be a statement concerning their recognition of their income-generating activity as a profession, is rather a way of expressing their decency.

In sum, this study has shown how local gender and sexual meanings are reproduced in Peruvian bureaucratic modernity. These processes reproduce the conditions needed for continuity and maintenance, rather than encourage change. The global neo-liberal organizational theory, in making its entrance, attempts to erase all traces of the traditional Peruvian bureaucracy and demands change in all areas. Despite its insensitivity to historical and contextual specificities and in its potential in the long run to change things even further for the worse – institutionalizing even further the insecure situation of individuals working in the Peruvian labour market – it is constituted by elements that can have a positive effect on the working situations of women, promoting their professionalization.

Notes

1   See Calvacanti (2002) for an example of a review article on gender and labour in Latin America in which white-collar occupations are not discussed. In a recent review article on workplace ethnographies, only 2.3% were ethnographies written about South America (Hodson, 2004).
2   Unfortunately, due to funding issues, the magazine only appeared once.
3   Uniforms are not garments with official colours or badges. The women receive two outfits annually, one for the winter and one for the summer. If a woman works there for a long time, she will acquire a diversified wardrobe.

References

Acker, J. (1990), 'Hierarchies, Jobs, Bodies: A Theory of Gendered Organizations', *Gender and Society*, vol. 4, pp. 139-158.
Banerjee, S.B. and Linstead, S. (2001), 'Globalization, Multiculturalism and Other Fictions: Colonialism for the New Millennium?', *Organization*, vol. 8, pp. 683-722.
Cavalcanti, H.B. (2002), 'Sociology of Work in Latin America', *Work and Occupations*, vol. 29, pp. 5-31.
Courpasson. D. and .Reed, M. (2004), 'Introduction: Bureaucracy in the Age of Enterprise', *Organization*, vol. 1, no. 1, pp. 5-12.
Entwistle, J. (2000), *The Fashioned Body. Fashion, Dress and Modern Social Theory*, Cambridge: Polity Press.
FIAS (2000), 'Acoso en el trabajo?', Numero 9 enero – junio, p. 5.
Fuller, N. (2001), *Masculinidades. Cambios y permanencies*, Lima: PUC Fondo Editorial.
du Gay, P. (2004), 'Against "Enterprise" (but not against "enterprise" for that would make no sense)', *Organization*, vol. 11, pp. 37-57.
Hall, S. (1996), 'Introduction: Who Needs "Identity"', in S. Hall and P. du Gay (ed.) *Questions of Cultural Identity*, London: Sage Publications, pp. 1-17.
Hodson, R. (2004), 'A Meta-Analysis of Workplace Ethnographies. Race, Gender and Employee Attitudes and Behaviors', *Journal of Contemporary Ethnography*, vol. 33 pp. 4-38.
Meza Camargo, G. (2000), 'De Secretaria a Asistente de Gerencia. El Porque de la Evolucion', *Nueva Imagen*, Numero 1, Julio, pp. 4-5.
Mills, D. (2003), '"Like a Horse in Blinkers"?: A Political History of Anthropology's Research Ethics', in P. Caplan (ed) *The Ethics of Anthropology: Debates and Dilemmas*, London: Routledge, pp. 37-54.
Nencel, L. (2001), *Ethnography and Prostitution in Peru*, London: Pluto Press.
Nencel, L. (1999), 'Ongezegd, Onverteld, Onuitgesproken: Gestalte Gegeven aan gender in een veldwerk-praktijk', *Tijdschrift voor Genderstudies* ('*Unsaid, Untold and*

Unspoken: Feeling Gender Speak in Fieldwork Practice', *Special Issue: Feminist Anthropology, Knowledge and Representation*), vol. 2, pp. 15-26.

Nencel, L. (1996), 'Pacharacas, Putas and Chicas de su Casa: Labelling, Femininity and Men's Sexual Selves in Lima, Peru', in M. Melhuus and K.A. Stølen (eds), *Machos, Mistresses and Madonnas*, London: Verso, pp. 56-82.

Robles Morales, M. (n.d.), '*Poder Femenino. Su proceso historico*', *Imagen Secretarial* APSE – Ucayali, p.11.

Documents

Benedetti Venturo, N. (1999), 'Perfil Profesional y Retos de la Asistente de Gerencia', Presentation at I Congreso Nacional de Secretarias de Sector Salud 'La Asistente de Gedrencia del Proximo Milenio'.

Codigo Deontologico de las Secretarias.

Espinoza Sanchez, G.N. (1999), 'Globalizacion y La Asistente de Gerencia en el Proximo Milenio', Presentation at I Congreso Nacional De Secretarias Del Sector Salud, 'La Asistente de Gerencia del Proximo Milenio'.

Proyecto Ley No.3376, Uniforme Formal-Centros Publicos/Privados – Suo De..., http://www.congreso.gob.pe/ccd/proyectos/pr9802/00337695.html, downloaded 5/11/01 2:32 PM.

Chapter 4

Being a Man:
Young Masculinities and
Safe Sex in Dakar

Anouka van Eerdewijk

Introduction

Given women's higher vulnerability to HIV infection, in both biological and social terms[1], AIDS prevention has mainly focused on women's sexual behaviour and skills to negotiate safe sex. The male position has only rarely been addressed as a gendered one in its own right (e.g. UNAIDS, 2000). In AIDS prevention, but also more generally in feminist thought, masculinity is often addressed in so far as it is problematic to women and allows men to exercise power over women. The concern is then with hegemonic masculinity, but not with men as subjects (Whitehead, 2002). Without dismissing the need for gender equity and women's empowerment, and without downplaying the role men play in achieving this, I think questions on men and masculinity should not only be addressed from the perspective of women's issues. It is therefore of great importance to explore how hegemonic masculinity is problematic to men themselves (Horrocks, 1997).

In this chapter I will address men's construction of masculinities. I will explore how Malick, a 20-year-old boy living in Dakar (Senegal), shapes his sexuality by negotiating multiple masculinities. I consider both gender and sexuality as social constructs, in the sense that biological elements of sexuality and gender only come to play a role through culture. I am interested in seeing how sexuality and gender are intertwined and construct each other. The chapter will start with a first impression of Malick. In the second and third section, I will look at the way he relates to girls and at his safe-sex behaviour. Malick's experiences will be put in the context of the global discourse on AIDS and notions of tradition and modernity in section four.

My interest is to understand how Malick constructs his masculinity in the interplay of the local and the global. In that respect, my approach differs from Connell's search for 'globalizing masculinities' (Connell, 1998). Connell, one of the most prominent thinkers on masculinity and men, has taken a specific stand with respect to gender and globalization, which I seek to question here. He calls the generation of male studies with a focus on the specific and the local, which has developed since the 1980s, the 'ethnographic moment' in masculinity research. He praises the intellectual fruits of this ethnographic moment, which are, very briefly, insights into the plurality of sometimes contradicting masculinities that are actively constructed in collective practices and dynamic relations of hierarchy. Despite these gains, Connell argues that one should move beyond strictly local or even comparative studies to the study of the global arena itself. Because some issues go beyond the local, he proposes to address 'globalizing masculinities': institutionalized patterns of dominant masculinity in the global gender order that become 'to some degree, standardized across localities' (1998, p. 12). I agree with Connell that the global must be considered in order to understand local masculinities. However, I do not think that 'globalizing masculinities' in itself generates an understanding of local masculinities. In fact, I will argue that the so-called 'ethnographic moment' is extremely fruitful in addressing globalization, because it makes the interaction between the local and the global in the construction of masculinities visible. As such, it allows for a deconstruction of hegemonic masculinity. In this chapter, I will focus on the local arena of Dakar in an attempt to address globalization and masculinity.

A First Impression of Malick

With his low-waist jeans, big shoes and oversized t-shirt, Malick dresses like a rapper. He lives with his father, mother, brothers and sisters in a neighbourhood outside the centre of Dakar. But he has a bad relationship with his father and is not close to his family. I met Malick for the first time during one of the focus group discussions that I conducted at a public secondary school in Dakar[2]. During the first focus group discussion (FGD) that Malick took part in, he did not say much, despite my attempts to draw him into the debate. That first time he left early. He came back a week later. At that session, we started talking about pregnancies. After a while, I asked Malick what he thought about the issues raised. He answered that he had already impregnated two girls. In the course of that FGD and in the individual interview and informal conversations that I had with Malick later, the following story unfolded.

Malick was about 14 or 15 when the first girl, Khady (17), got pregnant. He said that he had been out dancing at a '*soirée*'. Malick spent the rest of the evening hanging out with two friends and Khady at one of their homes. The two friends later left Malick and Khady alone. After having chatted for a while, Malick asked her to sleep with him. She refused. They continued talking and when he asked her again, she hesitated. But Malick thought: 'This girl, she is going to accept soon'. When he asked her again a little later, she accepted. Not only Malick but also his two friends had sex[3] with Khady that evening. Later, Malick heard that Khady was pregnant, and he was worried that he might be the father. He discussed the situation with the two other boys. Although one of them might very well be the father, they decided that all three of them would deny responsibility for the pregnancy. If they all denied their involvement, Khady could not make a convincing accusation against one of them and they would all be cleared of responsibility for the pregnancy. So, when Khady's older brother came to discuss the pregnancy, Malick denied he had anything to do with it, and so did his friends. In the end, Khady had the baby, and took care of it, without support from Malick or his friends.

The second pregnancy was with Astou, a girl (18) Malick had dated for approximately three months, although he was not really in love with her. Feeling uncomfortable about that, Malick decided to end his relationship with Astou. The day he wanted to break up with her, he 'ended up' having sex with her. Malick claims that it was the girl who 'provoked' him to have sex with her: she seduced him. Malick did not intend or expect it, so he did not have a condom and they had unprotected sex. Three weeks later, Astou told him that she was pregnant. Malick initially did not take it seriously, thinking that Astou had made it up because she was afraid to lose him. Astou's aunt, however, confirmed the pregnancy. A friend of Malick and Astou's aunt discussed the situation and decided that an abortion was the best solution, even though abortion was prohibited. Malick and Astou agreed that this might be for the best, as she was still young and at school. A 'friend of a friend' performed the abortion. Malick had to pay the 50,000 francs CFA (approximately 77 euros)[4]. Malick and Astou went to the clinic together. He remained in the waiting room during the procedure and took her home afterwards. It turned out that this abortion was carried out on the afternoon that Malick first joined the FGD. That was the reason he left early that day.

Malick's sexual history began at the age of 13, when he had his first sexual experience with a girl. He felt good and strong about it afterwards:

> I am a man now, you know. I can start dragging girls because now I am experienced

Although it is difficult to get reliable figures on sexual contacts of respondents, Malick's history suggests that he has had casual sexual relations with different girls. He indicated that during some periods he went without sex for a couple of weeks or months, while during other periods he might have had sex three or four times in one month. For example, besides Astou, he recently had sex with two other girls. One was a girl he met in a club. He called it a one-night fling, which happened because he had been drinking. The second time was with a girl that he had been seeing regularly in recent months.

So far, Malick's story matches the image of '*góor*'. '*Góor*' is the term in Wolof[5] for man, but it also points to the dominant norm of masculinity: men are expected to be '*góor*'. Sexual potency is important in this norm: a man becomes a man through penetrative sex with women. Men have to be sexually active and experienced. Impotency and homosexuality are threats to being '*góor*' and men have to show that neither of these qualifications applies to them. The Wolof word for a homosexual man is '*góorjigeen*', where '*góor*' means man and '*jigeen*' means woman. A homosexual man is labelled as a man who is a woman (Murray and Roscoe 1998, pp. 107-108). Homosexuality is therefore unmanly. The term '*doxaanante*' expresses the perceived contradictory character of homosexuality. '*Doxaan*' refers to having sex, and the suffix '*-ante*' implies reciprocity.

'*Doxaanante*' thus literally means having sex with yourself, or with somebody of the same sex. This is seen as a contradiction in terms. Men should not have sex with men, but with women – the 'other' sex.

Doubts about men's sexual capacities lead to insinuations and suspicions of impotency. Being impotent on the wedding night is a nightmare for a man. Failure of the newly-wedded husband to consummate the marriage on the wedding night can be a reason to dissolve the marriage. Although religion (both Islam and Christianity) and cultural customs value virginity and disapprove of sex before marriage, this norm is less strict for men, who are also faced with the demand for sexual potency and virility. For girls, virginity at marriage is important. Having sexual experience prior to marriage has a negative impact on their status. Boys are confronted with contradictory expectations of both virginity and being sexually experienced. Among unmarried boys in Dakar, it is commonly argued that men have sexual needs that must be satisfied; that men derive pleasure from sexual intercourse, and that men are always ready to have sex and 'seize the occasion' whenever it presents itself. The proof of virility is typically delivered by being sexually active with women, knowing how to have sex, knowing about girls and being in control of sexual encounters.

However, the notions of virginity and abstinence are not completely irrelevant. This is captured in the demand on boys to be 'serious' and not only have girls and sex on their mind. They have to think about the future, about earning money, going to school, etc. To be respected, boys have to be responsible and capable of taking care of themselves and their (future) families. Failing at school, being unemployed, and not earning your own money are often seen as a lack of responsibility. Spending the little money one has on girls, going dancing, etcetera, are also considered irresponsible. Being sexually active and knowledgeable are important in constructing one's masculinity. But at the same time, boys should not lose themselves in this. Although sexual experience is important for boys, abstinence is also an important reference point through which they can express their 'seriousness'.

Malick's behaviour clearly shows traces of a typical '*góor*', but there is more to him than that. At the end of one of our encounters, Malick asked me what I thought of him. He asked me about my own history and I told him about my boyfriends and sexual experiences. In fact, I married the only man I ever had sex with. He responded that he would have wanted to do the same thing. But, he said,

> Look at me, I am 20 years old, and I have already impregnated two girls. [....] Every day I get worse.

He feels bad about the two pregnancies:

> I tried to forget about it. [...] At that time I did not even think about it, but now I start thinking about the consequences. [...] I wanted to forget about it. I said to myself that it was a mistake of my youth, I will forget about it. But I cannot forget about it. Every time I see the kid, it comes back to me. [...] And when I see the girl, it also comes

back, you know. [...] Maybe I already have a child, and I do not even take care of it. [...] That hurts.

He does not know what to say to Khady when he runs into her. Seeing the child upsets him and he is afraid to touch it. Although he is worried about being recognized as the father, not taking care of this child that might be his is troublesome to Malick. He is also ashamed of possibly having a child out of wedlock and worries about how this might backfire on a future marriage and family. Although he wants to break up with Astou, he cannot do so because she could use the aborted pregnancy to pressure him to stay.

The picture of Malick, then, goes beyond the hegemonic '*góor*'. Malick is not proud of what has happened. He is confused and uncomfortable with the way things have worked out. He does not talk about this with anybody.

> I do not know with whom I can talk about it. That is my problem, you know. [...] Everybody will say that I am the father.

His parents do not know anything about either of the pregnancies. He prefers to talk to his friends or older brothers, but even with them he cannot talk openly about the pregnancies. Our conversations were the first time that he talked about these things with somebody. It is difficult to pin down the facts, and I am sure that there is more than what he has told me. Verification of the truth is, however, not so much my interest here. I want to explore Malick's struggles in shaping his masculinity in relation to hegemonic notions of what men are and should be. I will do that by considering his relations with girls and safe sex in the two following sections.

How to Relate to Girls?

Although Malick talks and behaves like a typical young man who chases after girls and is ready to have sex whenever the opportunity arises, he is also insecure about girls:

> I do not have my head clear with respect to girls. It is complicated. [...] They do things to you that you do not want, right. [...] When we are with them, it is very complicated; we do not know what to do.

And,

> Sometimes I think that I am sick or something like that. The fact to chase after girls like that, I tell myself that I am not normal, you know.

Malick explained that he feels he has to react to girls, that he has to do something. When a girl '*provokes*' him, he feels that she expects him to respond. It is important to take a closer look at this notion of provocation.

Provocation is a term that both boys and girls in Dakar use to describe a certain type of behaviour in girls. It is used to explain why boys cannot abstain from sex: girls are constantly provoking them. What is this provocative behaviour of girls? This could be an overt sexual remark about the potency of a boy, e.g. suggesting that he does not seem to have 'it', suggesting that he is not virile and potent. But provocation is also used to qualify behaviour that does not seem to be sexual or provocative at first sight. For example, a girl who complains about the hot weather creates an opportunity for a boy to offer her a drink. When girls do not overtly avoid contact, they create a situation in which a boy can start a conversation and make a proposition. In that sense, almost any behaviour that opens up the possibility of contact can be labelled provocative. The term has a negative connotation: a decent girl should not behave provocatively. Given the broad definition of provocation, a wide range of behaviour of girls towards boys is rendered problematic (see also van Eerdewijk, 2001b).

The effect of provocative behaviour of girls is that boys *feel* challenged: they feel they have to show their virility. Boys explain that it is difficult to resist this challenge: they have to react. Provocation puts boys in a position in which they are expected to become sexually aroused and want to have sex. Malick also experiences this. He feels pressured to have sex with a girl that provokes him, and says that he is afraid that if he does not react, she might think that he failed: 'that I am afraid, that I hesitate, things like that, you know'. She will tell her girlfriends that he hesitated, implying that he does not know 'how to do it'. This raises doubts whether he is '*góor*' enough. The notion of provocation puts men in a position to prove their masculinity.

The conceptualization of provocation creates a picture in which men are not in control of sexuality: it is the provocation of girls that makes them want to have sex and seduce girls. Provocative girls and pressure to prove one's manhood are in that way driving forces behind Malick's casual sexual relations. Establishing himself as a man through sex with women seems to be an ongoing process. Although he has slept with numerous girls so far, Malick is still insecure about this and says:

Sometimes I doubt if I really am someone who knows how to do it.

He feels insecure about his ability to seduce a girl and have sex with her, and does not know whether he can live up to the expectations that are placed on men.

This contrasts with the idea that men are in control of sexuality. Boys are supposed to initiate contacts with girls: they ask girls out. Boys also supposedly take the initiative for sex: they ask girls to sleep with them or they create situations in which 'one thing leads to another'. Girls should not take the sexual initiative. An outspoken example of this control is the encounter in which Malick (and his friends) came to have sex with Khady. Malick is the one who arranged for the three of them to have sex with her and, therefore, he feels responsible for the pregnancy.

I feel a bit ashamed, you know, because it was me who asked the girl. My friends were not there when I negotiated with the girl. I feel a bit responsible you know.

It can be argued that Malick and the two other boys could have decided for themselves whether or not to sleep with Khady. But, to what extent was Khady able to decide to have sex with them or not? Malick suggests that 'maybe' it was impossible for her to refuse. He actually talked her into it, to put it mildly, and says: 'Maybe I threatened her a little bit. I insulted her'. In fact, Malick put Khady under a lot of pressure to sleep with them. This 'confession' evidently acknowledges the power exercised in the sexual encounter between Malick, Khady and the two other boys.

The matter of control of boys over sexual encounters and girls becomes very ambiguous when one goes beyond hegemonic masculinity. Although Malick conforms to the hegemonic '*góor*' and was 'in control' of the situation with Khady, he is very confused about this and not proud. The fact that this version of what happened only came out after having met several times illustrates that the course of events is problematic to Malick. He behaves as a '*góor*', but feels bad about this and the force he employed to get sex. Hegemonic masculinity falls short in understanding Malick's situation here. His earlier remarks about being provoked and not knowing how to relate to girls raises doubts about whether boys control relations with girls and sexuality. As such, it can be acknowledged that boys are both in control and not in control of their sexuality and girls. This also comes forward in Malick's safe-sex behaviour, which is central to the next section.

Safe Sex: Abstinence and Condom Use

Malick says that he does not want history to repeat itself with another unwanted pregnancy or with a sexually transmitted infection (STI) or HIV. Basically two strategies of safe sex could have avoided the unwanted pregnancies: abstinence or condom use. Although these seem to be simple, they turn out to be complicated in Malick's life.

Every time Malick speaks about his anxieties with respect to sex and his relations with girls, he comes up with the same solution: avoiding girls. Malick says that he should spend all his time with his friends. He has to avoid being alone with a girl, and if a girl comes to see him, he should look for a friend to join him. In this way, he will not find himself in the situation where he is expected to have sex with a girl and he cannot make any more 'mistakes'. Malick proposes a solution in accordance with the dominant norm of virginity. He takes abstinence in an extreme form: no sex and limited or no contacts (sexual or other) with girls. He wants to start over again, and follow the 'right' path now. Malick proposes abstinence in an effort to show that he has more on his mind than girls and sex. He is very well aware that being too preoccupied with girls and sex is not appreciated, and that he also has to gain respect as a man by earning money and working hard at school. He has not been very serious at school and friends make jokes about him being lazy and unemployed, as he does not work during the three summer holiday months. Together with the two pregnancies, this makes it necessary to improve his life and his image. The pressures and temptations surrounding him will make it difficult for Malick to follow this strategy.

The other option is condom use. Despite the fact that the first pregnancy already dates back several years, Malick has only very recently started to use condoms. The technicalities are not the problem, but Malick just never really used them. Malick now sees condom use as one of the helpful solutions to avoid pregnancies. However, it seems that this is a rather rational line of reasoning, without much connection to his real life experiences. Many obstacles arise as soon as the issue of condom use is discussed in relation to Malick's personal experiences. He does not like condoms, because they 'spoil his appetite' when the sex play has to be interrupted for the condom. He has to go out to buy a condom, and is no longer in the mood for sex by the time he gets back. Or worse, the girl has lost interest. He does not have condoms with him all the time. This is related to a general view that considers carrying a condom as an overt indication that one is looking for sex all the time. This is an impression that Malick wants to avoid.

Further problems with condom use are that Malick feels embarrassed to use them:

> That embarrasses me, you know. I am not used to it. ... I am not used to talking about condoms with girls.

He does not feel at ease to talk about condoms with a girl. Girls do not raise the subject, so it is up to him to bring it up and he does not know how to do that. If both are afraid to mention condoms, sex takes place without protection. It is not only the talking that makes him uncomfortable, but also the act of putting the condom on. Malick indicates that he feels extremely embarrassed to actually put the condom on during sex. Another boy also said that he is afraid of the girl waiting and watching while he is fumbling about with the condom and his penis. Hence, it is worthwhile to consider in what ways condom use may be a threat to masculinity. Men are expected to know how to go about sex; they have to be experienced and in control 'in bed'. Clumsily fumbling about with a condom is not in accordance with this image. Leaving the condom aside can be a part of an unconscious or conscious strategy to keep the image of being sexually knowledgeable intact.

Malick also excuses himself from condom use by saying that he does not need them when he trusts a girl. When he knows a girl, she is considered safe and he does not need a condom. 'Knowing' is a vague term here. It applies to girls that come from the same neighbourhood for instance, but not to girls that he meets occasionally in a club or '*soirée*'. The idea is that girls that he knows carry fewer risks with them, because it is assumed that they have fewer sexual contacts. The perceived lower risk justifies not using a condom. This is different from girls that he meets when he goes dancing; he does not know whether they have multiple and casual sexual contacts. Without proof of the contrary, it is implicitly assumed that these girls are immoral and cannot be trusted. So, the argument goes, you need a condom to protect yourself against sexually transmitted infections (STIs) that such girls could carry. Nothing is being said in this argument about the risk of pregnancy.

In sum, Malick sees condoms as an effective protection on a rational and abstract level. In his real life, different problems and excuses keep him from actually using them on a regular basis. As a result, he regularly engages in unprotected sex. The strategy of abstinence is also problematic given his history. It is a socially acceptable way of protection, but goes against powerful norms to be sexually active, which Malick experiences. In the end, Malick does not deploy a resolute and determined strategy to prevent pregnancies and STI infections. This puts the issue of control in an interesting light again. In the cultural context of Dakar, men are assumed to be dominant in sexual relations and, consequently, are in a position to take the lead in safe sex. However, this control, which is assumed in hegemonic masculinity, does not seem to be present in Malick's behaviour. He does not consciously decide on a strategy of protection, and does not really opt for either condom use or abstinence. Again, dominant masculinity is insufficient for explaining the way Malick attempts to protect himself. In fact, his safe-sex behaviour is part of an ambiguous reality of ongoing negotiation of multiple masculinities.

Global Discourse on AIDS

Malick shapes his sexuality in an era in which millions of people are becoming infected with HIV through sexual contacts. It is estimated that 42 million people were living with HIV/AIDS worldwide in 2002 (UNAIDS 2002). Almost 30 million (over 70%) live in sub-Saharan Africa. In 2002, that same region saw 3.5 million new HIV infections and 2.4 million AIDS deaths. Senegal holds a special position with respect to AIDS and is labelled the 'Senegalese exception', because HIV infection rates are low at 1.8% of the adult population (UNAIDS, 1999, p. 22). Because of the early response of the government to the first HIV cases, Senegal is praised as a 'successful country' in the fight against AIDS. Examples of success factors include the establishment of a national AIDS programme, the support of religious leaders, an information campaign reaching a large part of the population, and the comparatively good availability of condoms (UNAIDS, 1999; Meda et al., 1999). Condom sales rose from 800,000 in 1988 to seven million in 1997 and condoms are used more frequently, although not on a systematic basis by young people (UNAIDS, 1999, pp. 17-18). Unfortunately, the label of a successful country does not necessarily mean that safe sex is widely practised.

The scale of the pandemic and of its impact in Africa and the world has resulted in a global effort to stop the spread of AIDS. With the continuing search for a cure[6] or vaccine, the focus of the AIDS campaigns is on care for those living with HIV/AIDS and on prevention of new HIV infections. With respect to the latter, safe-sex behaviour has become a major concern (and is still highly relevant in Senegal). Prevention campaigns are designed to inform people about HIV/AIDS and offer them strategies to protect themselves from infection. Central to this are the safe-sex ABCs: abstinence, being faithful and condom use. The AIDS discourse can be viewed as a specific construction of sexuality and sexual practices in which safe sex is hierarchically positioned in relation to unsafe sex. It defines 'good' sex as safe and healthy sex (in the sense that there is no possibility of HIV infection) and 'bad' sex in terms of unprotected and risky sexual contacts (which might result in infection with the virus). Medical perspectives dominated the original AIDS agenda, and continue to do so (Packard and Epstein, 1991; Seidel, 1993; Schoepf, 1995).

I want to address this medically framed AIDS discourse critically and show how it creates a dichotomy between tradition and modernity on a symbolic level. In order to do that, I have to discuss the way the global AIDS discourse has taken shape in time. The first studies on AIDS in Africa highlighted a different epidemiology of HIV from the West, with (1) high HIV prevalence (in contrast to other regions in the world), (2) a 1:1 ratio of male to female cases (in contrast to the 13:1 ratio in the West, meaning predominantly male infections), and (3) the absence of known risk groups such as intravenous drug users or homosexuals (Packard and Epstein, 1991; Patton, 1997; Gausset, 2001). The World Health Organization developed a geographical categorization of HIV infections in Pattern One and Pattern Two (Seidel, 1993; Patton, 1997). Pattern One describes Europe and North America, where most infections occurred through drug injection and homosexual contacts. Pattern Two highlights Africa as a place where transmission mainly took place through heterosexual sex. The effect of this geographical categorization was the 'invention of African AIDS' (Patton, 1997, p. 281; see also Arnfred, 2004), as if it were a distinct tropical disease[7]. What could explain 'African AIDS'?

The high levels of HIV infection in Africa were explained from higher levels of sexual promiscuity (Packard and Epstein, 1991). Cultural aspects of sexuality were identified that could contribute to the spread of HIV: polygamy, adultery, pre-marital sex, wife sharing, widow inheritance, circumcision and scarification rituals (with shared knives and needles), dry sex, and witchcraft beliefs (Gausset, 2001). In the state of 'emergency' of the AIDS epidemic, the practices that carried a risk of HIV infection were highlighted. Unfortunately, the complexities of their local meanings and importance were often not considered. Moreover, behaviours that were not risky or less risky, but that were just as much part of a so-called 'African sexuality', did not receive much attention. This resulted in a heavily biased view of 'African sexuality' as different from and opposed to idealized European sexuality (see Caldwell, Caldwell and Quiggin, 1989).

Despite the lack of empirical evidence for high rates of sexual partner change being the sole explanatory factor for Africa's high HIV prevalence, thinking about HIV in Africa became framed in a one-sided analysis that highlighted cultural differences. Whereas cultural aspects of sexuality and gender are certainly relevant to the spread of HIV as well as its prevention, this biased perspective meant that other potentially influential factors, such as poverty and malnutrition, which affect people's health and their vulnerability to HIV infection, were overlooked (Stillwaggon 2003). In this thinking about 'African AIDS' that centred on a view of a hyper-sexualized African culture, the demarcation between

Africa and the West was made along the lines of tradition and modernity. The blame for the spread of HIV/AIDS in sub-Saharan Africa was put on 'African cultural practices'. Getting bogged down with the politics of development and modernization (see also van Eerdewijk, 2001a), the fight against AIDS turned into a fight against 'cultural barriers' in Africa:

> AIDS prevention campaigns tell people that they should be monogamous, stop inheriting widows, stop practising dry sex, witchcraft, etc., without reflecting upon both the ethics and feasibility of such changes. In the West, one respects different cultural and sexual behaviours and one tries to make them safer without fighting against them; in Africa, one adopts the opposite attitude and one tries to eradicate what are identified as 'cultural barriers' to AIDS prevention (Gausset, 2001, p. 512).

As Stillwaggon (2003) argues, the globally circulating AIDS discourse turns out to be seriously biased by Eurocentric and racist prejudices.

It should come as no surprise that in many local discourses in Africa not tradition but modernized life styles and western practices are blamed for the spread of HIV (Dilger, 2003; Gausset, 2001). AIDS is associated with urban life styles, modern education, the breakdown of social control and moral codes, and prostitution. In this way of thinking, 'modernity' leads to promiscuity and immoral behaviour and, as such, causes AIDS. A restoration and promotion of African tradition then becomes imperative to combat AIDS. This tendency of accusing modernization is also present in Senegal. Urbanization and education have led to changes that not everybody is equally pleased with. The marriage age of girls, for example, has risen considerably and girls are now sexually mature before they enter into marriage and can engage in pre-marital sex. Getting married has become more difficult for boys because of the socio-economic problems, including unemployment, which make it difficult for men to finance the cost of getting married and the marriage ceremony, and to fulfil their obligations as (future) heads of household. Against this background, people, whether old or young, often complain about the lack of respect of young generations for what is called tradition, and especially about the sexual behaviour of unmarried girls and boys. The national AIDS campaign of Senegal has gained the support of religious leaders. In this setting, abstinence is emphasized as protection against HIV infection. As such, the campaign reinforces traditional values of virginity till marriage, and gives less priority to condom use and provision of services when it comes to young people.

Both discourses on what causes AIDS are simplifications of what is actually going on in the lives of boys like Malick. Both create a dichotomy between modernity and tradition, and attempt to fix their meanings in specific ways. Young people's sexualities become contested terrains where, in symbolic terms, the tension that is created between the two is being played out. As a result, different safe sex strategies are not neutral, but become carriers of normative representations of modernity and tradition. Whereas condoms are commonly associated with promiscuity and moral breakdown, abstinence coincides with a restoration of tradition and is therefore attractive. But premarital sex is also part of an appealing modern life style that, among others, encompasses fashion, music, radio, TV and the Internet. The global discourses impact on Malick's life in the sense that he has to position himself in relation to them. This means that his decisions about safe sex are larded with the tension that is created between tradition and modernity.

But that is not all. For people like Malick, life is not a choice between modernity on the one hand and tradition on the other. As I showed earlier, Malick's construction of his masculinity and sexuality is a constant process of negotiation of different masculinities. In Malick's struggles over his sexuality and safe-sex behaviour, the meanings of masculinity and of modernity and tradition become fluid and ambiguous. Being '*góor*' encompasses elements of both being a man by being sexually active, and of being respectable by knowing how to control one's sexuality. Malick brings these seemingly contradictory notions of masculinity together and reworks them in a way that he finds meaningful. In this dynamic process, it is difficult to establish the meanings of tradition and modernity. In the interplay between notions of modernity and tradition in Malick's life, simple dichotomies fall short. They do not provide insight into the multiple and the diverse masculinities that circulate in the context of Dakar and that characterize Malick's sexuality. This complexity of real life is not captured in the discourses on AIDS. Reality cannot easily be divided in black-and-white poles of modernity and tradition.

Reconsidering Malick, Masculinities and Safe Sex

In this chapter I analyzed how Malick constructs his masculinity and sexuality. By digging deeper into Malick's experiences I am not trying to excuse his behaviour, but seek to problematize hegemonic masculinity from the perspectives of men themselves. This chapter has shown that an understanding of men and their behaviour cannot be restricted to hegemonic masculinity. At first sight, Malick corresponds to the hegemonic '*góor*', when he engages in sex with different girls, often without using condoms. But, as an active subject, Malick shapes his gendered sexuality by negotiating the different and contradictory normative discourses on masculinity that he confronts. This chapter puts the control that men are assumed to have over sexuality and women in a different perspective. Although men have dominant positions vis-à-vis women, that does not mean that men or boys are always in control of their sexuality and their relations with women or girls. Malick experiences the power and normalizing effects of dominant discourses on masculinity. This means that hegemonic masculinity is also problematic to men themselves. Boys are both in control and not in control when it comes to girls, as is illustrated by Malick's unease and insecurity. The fact that Malick does not clearly and consciously decide his safe-sex behaviour, or lack thereof, is another example.

Malick has to relate to different discourses on HIV/AIDS. The globally circulating discourse on AIDS is one of those normative reference points. The local African discourse on AIDS is another. In both discourses, a dichotomy is created between modernity and tradition in symbolic terms. It is against this background that condom use and abstinence are not neutral strategies, but become associated with modern life styles or traditional values. Young people's sexualities become contested terrains where different and conflicting discourses meet. Malick is forced to position himself to safe sex and condom use, as well as the acceptability of sex before marriage. He does that in a context where the meaning of '*góor*' is fluid and ambiguous, encompassing both traditional and modern elements. Malick brings seemingly contradictory notions of masculinity, modernity and tradition together, and transforms their meaning. The way he shapes his sexuality and safe-sex behaviour cannot be reduced to either modernity or tradition. By contrast, Malick's struggles can only be understood in terms of multiple masculinities, in which different meanings of modernity and tradition are negotiated and reworked. Hegemonic masculinity does not capture this interplay and reworking of meanings. Malick's case, therefore, does not correspond to the standardization of masculinity that Connell speaks about. By contrast, my analysis shows how a globally circulating discourse only gets meaning in the locality of Dakar, where it is immediately reworked and embedded in local discursive practices that alter its meaning. Taking the local arena as a starting point for the study of globalization and masculinity, ambiguity and fluidity in the construction of masculinity and sexuality come forward, and dichotomies fall apart.

Notes

I would like to thank Stefan Dudink, Bard Evers, the participants of the workshop *Sexuality, gender and development: a feminist challenge to policy and research* (Institute of Social Studies, The Hague, 20-21 March 2003), and the other contributors to this volume for their critical comments on earlier versions of this chapter.

1   Both biologically and socially, women are more vulnerable to HIV infection. The chances of a woman getting HIV through sex with a seropositive man is much higher than the chances of a man having intercourse with a seropositive woman. Biological factors are the higher concentration of HIV in semen than in vaginal secretions, and the larger and more vulnerable surface of female genitals through which HIV can penetrate more easily, compared to men's genitals. In addition, menstruation can also facilitate HIV transmission to and from women. Social factors are women's lack of power to determine when, where and whether sex takes place, to negotiate protection through condom use, non-penetrative sex, or to negotiate with the partner to remain faithful (UNAIDS 2000; Schoepf 1995, pp. 30-31; Berer 1993).

2   The group consisted of six boys, whose ages varied from 19 to 22 years. All names are fictional.

3   I use expressions such as 'having sex' and 'sleeping with' for heterosexual penetrative sex. Young people in the study indicated that they use terms as '*faire l'amour*' (making love) and '*coucher*' (sleeping with) for sexual encounters in which 'the penis penetrates the vagina'. 'Not having sex', as in abstinence, means not having penetrative sex.

4   According to Malick, normally an abortion would have cost 100,000 francs CFA (approximately 155 euro), but because it was a 'friend of a friend' he 'only' paid

50,000 francs CFA (approximately 77 euro). The exchange rate is roughly 1 euro for 650 francs CFA.
5   Wolof is a dominant ethnic group in Senegal. Their language is commonly spoken in Dakar (besides French).
6   Triple combination therapies, or anti-retroviral therapies, suppress the further replication of the HIV/AIDS virus. If taken according to prescription, AIDS does not necessarily result in death and HIV infected persons live longer and are healthier. These therapies are frequently used in Europe and North America, but are inaccessible to African countries, for example, where large numbers of people need treatment.
7   Another effect of this categorization into Pattern One and Two is that heterosexuality in the West remains invisible and unchallenged: the fact that the virus affects heterosexuals in the West, and that heterosexuals need to modify their behaviour to protect themselves from HIV infection is obscured (Patton 1997; Seidel 1993).

References

Arnfred, Signe (ed.) (2004), *Re-thinking Sexualities in Africa*, Nordiska Afrikainstitutet, Uppsala.
Berer, Marge (1993), *Women and HIV/AIDS – An International Resource Book: Information, Action and Resources on Women and HIV/AIDS, Reproductive Health and Sexual Relationships*, Harper Collins, London.
Caldwell, John C., Pat Caldwell and Pat Quiggin (1989), 'The Social Context of AIDS in Sub-Saharan Africa', *Population and Development Review*, 15 (2), pp. 185-234.
Connell, R.W. (1998), 'Masculinities and Globalization', *Men and Masculinities*, 1 (1), pp. 3-23.
Dilger, Hansjörg (2003), 'Sexuality, AIDS, and the Lures of Modernity: Reflexivity and Morality among Young People in Rural Tanzania', *Medical Anthropology*, 22 (1), pp. 23-52.
van Eerdewijk, Anouka (2001a), 'How Sexual and Reproductive Rights Divide and Unite', *European Journal of Women's Studies*, 8 (4), pp. 421-439.
van Eerdewijk, Anouka (2001b), 'Beheersing en Provocatie', *Raffia, 13* (3), p. 9.
Gausset, Quentin (2001), 'AIDS and Cultural Practices in Africa: the Case of the Tonga (Zambia)', *Social Science and Medicine*, 52, pp. 509-518.
Horrocks, Roger (1997), 'Male Sexuality', in *An Introduction to the Study of Sexuality*, Macmillan, London, pp. 163-182.
Meda, Nicolas, Ibra Ndoye, Souleymane M'Boup, Alpha Wade, Salif Ndiaye, Cheikh Niang, et al. (1999), 'Low and Stable HIV Infection Rates in Senegal: Natural Course of the Epidemic or Evidence for Success of Prevention?', *AIDS*, 13 (11), pp. 1397-1405.
Murray, Stephen O. and Will Roscoe (eds.) (1998), *Boy Wives and Female Husbands: Studies of African Homosexualities*, Macmillan, London.
Packard, Randall M. and Paul Epstein (1991), 'Epidemiologists, Social Scientists, and the Structure of Medical Research on AIDS in Africa', *Social Science and Medicine*, 33, pp. 771-794.
Patton, Cindy (1997), 'From Nation to Family: Containing African AIDS', in Micaela di Leonardo and Roger N. Lancaster (eds.), *The Gender/Sexuality Reader: Culture, History, Political Economy*, Routledge, London, pp. 279-290.

Schoepf, Brooke Grundfest (1995), 'Culture, Sex Research and AIDS Prevention in Africa', in Han ten Brummelhuis and Gilbert Herdt (eds.), *Culture and Sexual Risk: Anthropological Perspectives on AIDS*, Gordon and Breach Publishers, Luxembourg, pp. 29-51.

Seidel, Gill (1993), 'The Competing Discourses of HIV/AIDS in Sub-Saharan Africa: Discourses of Rights and Empowerment vs. Discourses of Control and Exclusion', *Social Science and Medicine*, 36 (3), pp. 175-194.

Stillwaggon, Eileen (2003), 'Racial Metaphors: Interpreting Sex and AIDS in Africa', *Development and Change*, 34 (5), pp. 809-832.

UNAIDS (2002), *UNAIDS Epidemic Update: UNAIDS/WHO HIV/AIDS Regional Estimates as of End 2002*, UNAIDS, Geneva, www.unaids.org (retrieved: 16 October 2003).

UNAIDS (2000), *Men Make a Difference: Men and AIDS – a Gendered Approach*, 2000 World AIDS Campaign, UNAIDS, Geneva.

UNAIDS (1999), *Acting Early to Prevent AIDS: the Case of Senegal*, UNAIDS, Geneva.

Whitehead, Stephen M. (2002), *Men and masculinities*, Polity Press, Cambridge.

UNEXPECTED OUTCOMES: GLOBALIZATION AND THE PRODUCTION OF DIFFERENCE

Chapter 5

The Global Localization of Feminist Knowledge: Translating *Our Bodies, Ourselves*[1]

Kathy Davis

Introduction

In 1969, a group of Boston women met in a workshop on 'Women and their Bodies' at one of the first conferences organized by second-wave feminists in the US. Most of the participants were young, white, middle-class, college-educated women, who had been active in the Civil Rights movement or had helped draft resisters during the Vietnam War. For many of them, it was their first encounter with feminism and it was electrifying. They talked openly about their sexuality (a burning issue for young feminists at that time), about their experiences with pregnancy and childbirth, and they shared their frustrations with physicians. The group, which later became known as the Boston Women's Health Book Collective (BWHBC), began to meet regularly. They collected information about their bodies and health and wrote discussion papers. A year later, this collection of papers was assembled and the first version of *Our Bodies, Ourselves* was born. Originally printed on newsprint by an underground publisher and selling for 75¢, *Our Bodies, Ourselves* (*OBOS*) was a lively and accessible manual on women's bodies and health. It was full of personal experiences and contained useful information on issues ranging from masturbation (how to do it) to birth control (which methods were available and how to access them) to vaginal infections, pregnancy and nursing. It combined a scathing critique of patriarchal medicine and the medicalization of women's bodies as well as an analysis of the political economics of the health and pharmaceutical industries. But, above all, *OBOS* validated women's embodied experiences as a resource for challenging medical dogmas about women's bodies and, consequently, as a strategy for personal and collective empowerment.

The book was an overnight success. Since the first edition in 1970, *OBOS* has sold over four million copies and gone through 12 major updates (and some minor revisions). It was a catalyst for the international women's health movement as well as for various consumer and patient organizations in the US. It played a germinal role in campaigns against sterilization abuse, helped initiate hearings on the safety of silicone breast implants, and was instrumental in rehabilitating midwifery as a respectable profession in the US. The success of *OBOS* in the US can be attributed to its ability to speak to a broad spectrum of women and to provide a politics of knowledge, which was both accessible and empowering. This politics of knowledge validated women's everyday experiences with their bodies. It situates women as active knowers, rather than passive objects of the knowledge practices of others. Finally, it showed that women could gain control over their bodies, their sexuality and reproduction, and their lives by sharing knowledge with one another.

OBOS was, of course, a distinctively North American product, both in content and format. It draws upon a long populist tradition of self-help with its emphasis on self-improvement and empowerment through knowledge (Schrager, 1993). Its matter-of-fact treatment of sexuality is a radical response to the Puritan legacy of the US and a popular culture, which make sex both repressed and ubiquitous. The book's emphasis on issues involving informed consent and reproductive rights is unsurprising, given the current explosion of medical technologies and the rampant abuse of women's rights in the US health care sector (sterilization abuse, enforced Caesarean-sections), not to mention the ongoing and often violent struggle for access to legal abortions. The critique of medicine found in *OBOS* is informed by the specific problems that women face in a highly medicalized culture where health is a consumer good and the health care system puts profit above the equitable distribution of care. In a context where the government cannot be counted on to meet the basic health care needs of all its citizens, the combination of self-help and consumer activism advocated by *OBOS* made perfect sense, providing a needed corrective to the US health care system and the ubiquitous commercialization of the female body. In short, *OBOS* is – as the old saying goes – 'as American as Mom's apple pie'.

However, despite being a North American artefact, it did not remain within the borders of the US. From the beginning, it has crossed borders to become an international bestseller. As of 1998, *OBOS* has been translated into 19 languages. Five other-language versions were openly inspired by and/or acknowledge *OBOS*, and an additional 13 groups or individuals were either actively working on a translation/adaptation or had indicated that they would like to do so (*Our Bodies, Ourselves in Many Languages*, Global History and Status Report, 1998).[2]

Initially, the BWHBC did not anticipate that *OBOS* would be such an international success – or all the work that this success would entail. Norma Swenson, one of the founders, remembers only too well how surprised they all were at the book's popularity in the US. 'It took us by surprise'. But she also recalls thinking how 'utterly absurd' it was when one of the members of the collective joked that someday *OBOS* would sell a million copies and be translated into Chinese. None of the original members of the collective took the prediction seriously. However, by the mid 1970s, *OBOS* had already sold well over a million copies (nearly two million) and, by the late 1990s, it had been translated into Chinese.

The worldwide success of *OBOS* raises several questions: First, how could such a distinctively North American book become so popular in so many different contexts? What was its appeal to women in such different parts of the world? Second, how was the book translated and adapted to address the specific concerns of women in different contexts? What did the translations leave out, what was added, and, more generally, what does the process of translation say about how feminist knowledge circulates? Third, to what extent does the dissemination of *OBOS* around the world, but particularly in the so-called 'Third World', make it just another western product (not unlike Nestlé's milk or Coca Cola) that has inundated less affluent nations, undermining indigenous women's struggles to improve their circumstances? In other words, what does the history and global trajectory of *OBOS* say about the possibilities (and pitfalls) of global feminism?

Global Feminism

Although the ideal of global feminism – as epitomized by Robin Morgan's feminist opus *Sisterhood is Global* (1984) – is shared by most US feminists as well as many feminists around the world, it is an ideal that has also generated considerable critique. Feminist scholars like Cynthia Enloe, Chandra Mohanty, Jacqui Alexander, Inderpal Grewal, Caren Kaplan, Sara Ahmed and others have criticized the notion of 'global feminism' as a kind of cultural imperialism. In their view, 'global feminism' is a euphemism for what is essentially a Western – and, in most cases, a North American – version of feminism with its belief in universal sisterhood, its celebration of individuality, and its embeddedness in modernist paradigms of social action. It is imposed upon women in non-western contexts who have different problems, different struggles, and different allegiances. It does not acknowledge the unequal global relations that shape women's lives in different settings. As a model, 'global feminism', like much of Western imperialism, is little more than feminist missionary work, involving maternalistic intervention and salvation of less fortunate 'sisters' (Enloe, 1989).

The feminism-as-cultural-imperialism critique has three main arguments: First, Western feminists are accused of creating a 'common world of women' scenario, in which women are treated as 'an already constituted, coherent group with identical interests and desires, regardless of class, ethnic or racial location, or contradictions' (Mohanty, 1997, p. 258). This assumption of unity provides the possibility of a global feminist subject – a 'we' uniting different women living under highly disparate circumstances into the same feminist family. At the same time, however, it denies the historical specificity of women as sometimes subordinate or marginal, but sometimes powerful or central, depending upon their social location and local power networks. Women are not a unified powerless group, nor are they powerless in the same way. The assumption that 'we' are victims of the same kinds of oppressions and that patriarchy operates in similar ways across national borders neglects historical and material differences in women's situations, which give rise to different concerns and require different political struggles. As Kaplan (1996) noted, this move has allowed some US (and European) feminists to avoid confronting painful class or racialized differences among women in their own cultures, while obscuring the dominance of middle class women around the globe. The relative ease and perhaps preference with which middle class feminists around the world forge alliances with other women across borders – rather than with their less affluent or marginalized 'sisters' at home – attests to this.

Second, 'global feminism' has been criticized as a western model of feminism, which homogenizes indigenous struggles of 'US and Third World feminists' (Mohanty, 1997). In their attempt to stake out the world, white, middle-class, or western feminists have conveniently 'forgotten' that they are just one group among many (Alexander and Mohanty, 1997). Under the 'universal' banner of global feminism, a western model of feminism is propagated, whereby primacy is given to the individual woman and her struggles to realize her potential. Feminist interventions are centred upon women gaining entrance in the public domain. Drawing upon modernist ideals of liberal individualism and equal opportunity, women's advancement is linked to access to economic resources, vocational training and scientific knowledge. Within this modernist narrative, women from 'developing' countries appear to be underprivileged and mired in tradition. They need to be 'brought into' modernity with the help of global feminism (Ahmed, 2000). For women both within and outside the US who are struggling with the effects of racism and imperialism, such a model of feminism is often viewed with suspicion – as just another imperialist move from the west. It does not take into consideration the importance of family, community, and alliances with other anti-imperialist social movements, which many women regard as integral to their own struggle for empowerment.

Third, 'global feminism' – at least in its US variant – has been criticized for creating an untenable division between centre and periphery, whereby US feminists are the 'movers and shakers' in the centre and women of the so-called Third World are relegated to the 'periphery'. Women in non-western contexts are represented as oppressed victims of a despotic patriarchy in need of support and salvation by their more emancipated sisters in the west. This kind of dualistic thinking not only obscures the disempowering conditions under which many women in the 'centre' live, but it fails to do justice to the struggles of women in other parts of the world who grapple constantly – and with considerable creative agency – with the oppressive contingencies of their lives. It ignores longstanding traditions of feminist opposition outside the US. Indigenous women's groups contest but also adopt and transform 'Western' feminist ideas and practices to meet the demands of their local circumstances (Narayan, 1997).

In view of this critique, it is difficult to imagine how alliances between US feminists and feminists in non-western countries could be mutually empowering. However, on a more hopeful note, Grewal and Kaplan (1994) have proposed a model for what they call 'transnational feminist practices', which is based on difference rather than global sisterhood, a critique of modernity, and oppositional practices rather than identity politics. In their book, *Scattered Hegemonies*, they call for an analysis of the specific conditions ('scattered hegemonies') that structure women's lives in different locations, rather than an assumption of a common condition of oppression. As a precondition for transnational feminist alliances, western notions of modernity need to be deconstructed and, along with them, the collusion of western feminisms in their nation's histories of imperialism, genocide, slavery or colonialism. They provide examples of a 'politics of solidarity' between women that neither collaborate with Euro-centric feminism nor work for the patriarchal power groups within local communities, but rather 'create affiliations between women from different communities who are interested in examining and working against the links that support and connect very diverse patriarchal practices' (Grewal and Kaplan, 1994, p. 26).

In this chapter, I use *OBOS* as a case for assessing 'global feminism'. The feminism-as-cultural-imperialism-critique has been important in deconstructing the model of global feminism as universal sisterhood and replacing it with a model focusing on diversity and local feminisms. It has made western feminists more conscious of their tendency to engage in what Donna Haraway (1991) calls the 'god trick'. It has also paved the way for thinking about transnational feminist alliances, which are based on mutual understanding and empowerment. While I share this critique of the underlying assumptions inherent in the model of 'global feminism' as formulated by Mohanty and others, it is my contention that this critique, however theoretically and politically relevant, does not address the unpredictability and messy realities of feminist practices across national borders. It does not help us understand how concrete US-based feminist projects actually cross borders, how encounters between western and non-western women's groups take shape or how these projects might be assessed in terms of their imperialistic tendencies. To provide the feminism-as-cultural-imperialism critique with some empirical basis, I, therefore, propose taking *OBOS* as a 'test case'.[3] As a 'world traveller', it provides a unique opportunity to assess the pitfalls of global feminism or, alternatively, as I will argue, the unexpected possibilities of transnational alliances for the circulation of feminist knowledge and body/politics.

OBOS Abroad: From the US to 'the Rest'

The globalization of *OBOS*'s travels falls into three stages: from the US to publisher-based translations in Western Europe in the 1970s to 'inspired' adaptations in Asia, Africa and the Middle East, to the more recent collaborative projects sponsored by foundations, particularly in so-called 'Third World' countries and Eastern Europe. The first translations of OBOS began to appear in Western Europe throughout the 1970s in 'pirate' editions published in Japan in 1975 and Taiwan in 1976. By the early 1980s, the book had already been translated, adapted or had inspired similar books in Italy (1974), Denmark (1975), France (1977), the UK (1978), Germany (1980), Sweden (1980), Greece (1981), the Netherlands (1981) and Spain (1982). By the mid-1980s, *OBOS* had gone into its *second* stage of border crossing, 'escaping to the East and the South', as one founder put it, 'often in someone's backpack'. Translations or adaptations began to be published outside of Europe: a Hebrew version for Israel appeared in 1982 and a Russian translation in 1995. Several books on women's health were published which were inspired by *OBOS* without being direct translations: Arabic (1991), Telugu (1991) and South African (1996).

A group of Latina women (*Amigas Latinas en Accion Pro-Salud*), working under the auspices of the BWHBC, produced the first Spanish edition of *OBOS* (*Nuestros Cuerpos, Nuestras Vidas*) in the US in 1977. Although initially intended for Hispanic communities in the US, *NCNV* gradually flowed into Latin American countries where, by 1987, more than 50,000 copies had been distributed throughout the hemisphere. By the late 1990s, translations were completed or underway in Senegal, Thailand, the People's Republic of China, Indonesia, Armenia and Nepal, as well as Russia and Eastern Europe (Serbia, Poland, Bulgaria, Romania).

In conclusion, three decades after its inception in the US, *OBOS* had become a feminist export product. After taking Western Europe by storm, it crossed over into Africa, Asia, the Middle East and South America, where it continues to gain in popularity. The elements that had made OBOS so popular in the US proved to be easily translatable, as the book made its way around the world: its focus on women's bodies, its accessibility for 'ordinary' women, its validation of women's everyday embodied experiences, its authorization of women's agency as authoritative knowers, and, equally important, its commitment to women's empowerment through knowledge sharing.

Adapting *OBOS*: Continuities and Changes

From the beginning, it was clear that *OBOS* could not simply be 'translated', but would need to be 'adapted' in order to address the needs and experiences of women in different parts of the world. The BWHBC advocated that, rather than publishers, local feminist groups should take on the necessary task of adapting the book. As the various translation/adaptations of the book piled up, the collective divided them into several categories, based on the degree to which the translation resembled the original book.[4] I shall now turn to some of the ways *OBOS* changed in the process of being translated, moving from the direct translations through the adapted versions and concluding with a closer look at books that were 'inspired' by *OBOS*.

Direct Translations

Strictly speaking, very few of the foreign editions could even be considered a direct translation – that is, a verbatim rendition of the original in another language. Even the early books initiated by foreign publishing houses tended to delete or 'sanitize' parts of the original book (usually the controversial chapters on lesbian sexuality, masturbation and abortion). Direct translations were produced in some cases simply because resources were too limited to do a full-fledged adaptation. This was the fate of the Spanish version of *OBOS*, which for many years had to be content with a little 'window dressing' (e.g. including photographs of Hispanic women). Given the enormous demand for the book in Latin America, however, a translation – even a bad one – was considered better than nothing. For several projects, a direct translation was a matter of expedience; it was the only way to get funding from foundations, which were reluctant to subsidize the more intensive process of adapting the book. The translation became a 'dummy copy', which was subsequently passed on to local women's groups who proceeded to rework it, often without funding and at great personal hardship (Thailand, Indonesia, China).

Translation/Adaptations

In contrast to direct translations, the majority of the foreign editions fell under the category translation/adaptation. The original *OBOS* was reworked and contextualized in accordance with the translators' notions of what was appropriate, useful, or necessary in their particular situation. Throughout the seventies and eighties, changes in *OBOS* were fairly minimal, thus reflecting a similarity in feminist issues between the US and Western Europe. The foreign versions invariably had to take differences in abortion laws and histories of feminist struggle around reproductive health issues into account. In some countries, abortion was still illegal or controversial for religious reasons. The context not only affected how information was presented, but which issues needed to be emphasized. For example, the Japanese translators were especially concerned with unnecessary gynaecological surgery, given a recent spate of Caesarean sections in hospitals or a long tradition of pronatalist policies, which made infertility an important concern for the Romanian adaptation. The original chapter on the health care system always had to be rewritten or substantially reworked. While most translators adopted *OBOS*'s anti-medicalization approach and agreed that medical expertise needed to be debunked, differences in European welfare systems shaped the critique provided in the foreign editions. In countries with national health systems and guaranteed medical insurance, criticisms tended to be more muted and directed at improving existing facilities rather than mobilizing consumer networks.

Thus, for most of the translation/adaptations, the structure, content, and 'spirit' of the original *OBOS* was maintained. Changes entailed deleting an occasional paragraph, adding an explanatory footnote, substituting photographs and experiences of local women and providing practical information on health care services. An exception is the Spanish edition, which underwent a much more radical and comprehensive transformation in its adaptation for Latin America. The 'we women' of the original *OBOS* was problematized, while the experience of colonialism and US imperialism shared by Latina women was emphasized. The focus of the new *Nuestros Cuerpos, Nuestros Vidas* shifted from the individual woman and her ability to take care of herself to the importance of family and community for women's health and well being. The term 'self-help', so prevalent in the original *OBOS*, was banished in favour of a more community-orientated term 'mutual help'. As Ester Shapiro, the visionary coordinator of the Latin American adaptation put it: 'People need to understand that it's your relationships that keep you well… energy for collective action is part of becoming healthy'.[5] For this reason, the translators proposed a much more comprehensive vision of health – not just reproductive issues, but education, sanitation, work conditions, adequate food and shelter, social support and quality of life were treated as primary ingredients of women's health. They reasoned that, in countries where medical care can help only about 10% of people's health concerns, it made no sense to devote a whole chapter to the medical system; and opted instead for a chapter on how to make connections with community groups and feminist organizations.

'Inspired' Versions

In some cases, the decision was made not to translate or adapt *OBOS*, but rather to use it as a source of inspiration and write a new book, using the same process as the original. For example, in Denmark, a group of feminists were so enthusiastic about the original book that they could not resist writing their own. They set up a collective along the same lines as the BWHBC and proceeded to talk about their bodily experiences. They compiled position papers on various health issues to be discussed in the group. The book was published in 1975 under the title *Kvinde Kend din Krop* and went through four revisions, all under the auspices of the original Danish collective.

With the rapid expansion of the feminist movement in India throughout the 1980s, the Hyderabad Women's Health Group decided to produce a handbook on women's health in Telegu (the second most widely spoken language in India). It was to be similar to *OBOS*, but 'grounded in Indian women's experiences and concerns'. Under the title *A Hundred Thousand Doubts About Women's Health* (1991), the book became widely used among feminist groups and NGOs in India.

Several years later, another 'inspired' book appeared on another continent – *The South African Women's Health Book* (1996). The coordinator, a US expatriate living in Johannesburg, knew about *OBOS* and wanted to create a similar health book 'by and for South African women'. She helped set up the Women's Health Project with other feminist activists and health workers. The process of compiling the book resembled its North American counterpart, with chapters written by different women, read by special interest groups for accuracy or 'tone', and tested in focus groups, organized throughout South Africa. The result was a fairly weighty tome, which was criticized for being 'such a thick book' that many South African women would never be able to read it.

I shall now take a closer look at one of these 'inspired' versions of *OBOS, Hayãt al-mar'a wa'sihatuhã* (translated as 'The Life of a Woman and Her Health'), written in Arabic and published in Egypt by the Cairo Women's Health Book Collective in 1991. It is worth looking at their book in more detail, in part because they have written eloquently about what makes their book different from the North American *OBOS* (Farah, 1991; Ibrahim and Farah, 1992; see, also, Hill, 1994), but also because it provides a good example of some of the possibilities and limitations of global feminism.

The Egyptian Case

While the Cairo Women's Health Book Collective acknowledged that they had 'borrowed' much of the philosophy of *OBOS* for their book and made frequent references to their 'Boston sisters' (Hill, 1994, p. 18), they insisted that the book itself was 'couched in a cultural context alien to most Egyptian and Arab women' and reflected the 'priorities of American women' (Farah, 1991, p. 16). Thus, from the outset, they were determined to make their own book, explicitly written for a non-western audience. It would take the Egyptian and Arab cultural context into account, paying close attention to the problems facing women in the Arab world.

The authors assumed not only that Egyptian women, in particular, and Arab women, in general, have their own health problems, but also that feminist movements have their own histories of struggle and battles to fight, making both the issues and the rhetoric in which they are framed different from one context to another. Many Egyptian women see themselves as fighting not so much against patriarchy or local oppressors, but against the Egyptian government, Western cultural and economic domination, and global forces, which impose harsh economic policies and alien life styles (El Dawla *et al*, 1998, p. 103). While the Cairo Women's Health Book Collective clearly wanted to borrow from US feminism, they were also shaped by the prevailing sentiment of anti-imperialism and anti-Americanism of the contemporary political movement in Egypt (Al-Ali, 2000). Secular in orientation, they were also part of a culture where the Islamist movement enjoys considerable popularity and where most women, whether Muslim or Copt, were religious and where tradition is the locus of the most salient norms by which women are judged (El Dawla *et al*, 1998, p. 75).

In this context, the book was bound to be controversial. It required considerable juggling to make a book that would be culturally sensitive, not offend religious feelings, but still sustain a strong commitment to women's rights (Ibrahim and Farah, 1992, p. 7). The result was a delicate balancing act whereby the authors would take up potentially contradictory or contested positions, often presenting them side-by-side. The flexible strategy adopted by the Cairo group in deciding whether to include issues and how to address them is illustrated by the following three examples.

The first concerns the Cairo group's stance towards medicine. Like the original *OBOS*, the Egyptian book was critical of medical knowledge and practice. However, they described medicine explicitly as 'western'. While the authors support women's right to have access to all medical knowledge about their bodies and health (the cover of the book shows a young woman with bare arms, western attire and flowing hair, peering intently through a microscope), they are also critical of western medicine, which is often authoritarian and disrespectful to women's needs. Underprivileged women often experience demeaning treatment when they enter a 'modern' clinic in Egypt. Physicians trained in western medicine are often contemptuous of Islamic codes of modesty, which make women reluctant to be examined by male doctors or discount the importance of virginity for many unmarried women, who fear that their hymen will break during a gynaecological exam (Hill, 1994, pp. 4-5).

The second example concerned the authors' treatment of sexuality. While the explicit mention of sexuality and sexual enjoyment was a revolutionary eye-opener for the US readers of *OBOS*, sexuality was not a particularly controversial subject in Egypt, where women are expected to enjoy sexuality and where women's networks have always allowed extensive talk about the details of sex. However, sexuality outside of marriage is entirely off limits, let alone between women. Although the Cairo group took up the issue of lesbianism because it is 'regarded as a path toward liberation by many women in the west', they ultimately decided not to include it in their book, as it would have invoked certain censure from religious authorities for something that was not a 'viable life style' in Egypt (Farah, 1991, p. 17). Another 'hot item' – masturbation – was treated in a similarly ambivalent way. On the one hand, Egyptian readers were reassured that it was 'natural' for their children to masturbate. On the other hand, mothers were encouraged to tell their children to go out and play ('do something worthwhile') rather than masturbate. Rape was also controversial. Some group members felt that women brought rape upon themselves through immodest clothing, while others did not like the idea of attributing violence against women only to men (what about daughter-in-law abuse or female genital mutilation?). Ultimately, rape was included, but in a comprehensive chapter on violence against women perpetrated by both sexes.

The third example was female genital excision and, more generally, the issue of how to deal with 'cultural traditions'. The issue of female genital excision has, not surprisingly, stirred considerable debate both within and outside Egypt. As the issue on which western feminists invariably focus in connection with Muslim women, the Cairo group agonized about how to take a stand against it without alienating their readers, who had an understandable aversion to the attitude of western feminists. After much discussion, they took a stand against the practice, providing information on the psychological and social damage that it entails. However, they also explained the cultural context, which allows for the continuation of the practice among Egyptian women, particularly in rural settings.[6] As the book was being tested on different groups of Egyptian women, the authors routinely took along an imam who, in the course of the discussion, would stand up and announce that there was nothing in the *Q'uran* that required female genital excision, thereby lending the book legitimacy among religious women.

Rearticulating Feminist Body/Politics

At the outset of this chapter, I raised the question of how the globalization of *OBOS* should be viewed against the backdrop of the critique that 'global feminism' is little more than an imperialistic move by primarily white, middle-class US feminists to establish their brand of feminism as universal, while ignoring the experiences, circumstances and struggles of women in other parts of the world. Having explored how *OBOS* travelled and was adapted by different women in different locations, a picture emerges that shows that feminist knowledge circulates in surprising ways. Moreover, it is a picture that is considerably less diabolical and more optimistic than the feminism-as-cultural-imperialism critique would suggest.

Although early versions of *OBOS* were written in the spirit of 'global feminism' (universal sisterhood) that belonged to the US second-wave feminist discourse of the time, the universalism inherent in this model was also undercut by the book's claim that each woman was the ultimate authority over her own bodily experiences. The authors of *OBOS* were, to be sure, all white, middle-class feminists who, in their own words, could not pretend to 'speak for' all women. Their intention was rather to 'inspire' other women to write their own books. The translations that emerged in the three decades following the first edition of *OBOS* indicate that it was not the notion of 'global sisterhood' that travelled (although some of the translation projects, as for example, the Egyptian collective, did refer to the BWHBC as their 'US sisters'). On the contrary, what travelled was *how* the original collective wrote the book.

The image of a group of (lay) women collectively sharing knowledge about their embodied experiences seems to be what fired the imagination of women in different parts of the world and served as an invitation to do the same. While the notion of 'global sisterhood' creates a spurious universality, which denies differences among women, the process by which the original collective wrote their book could be taken up fairly easily by a diversity of women and adapted to their specific needs and circumstances. It was the method of knowledge sharing – and not a shared identity as women – that appeared to have global appeal. The practice of adapting and disseminating OBOS linked different feminist groups in a common project, compelling translators as well as the original authors of the book to acknowledge and confront the cultural and social divisions between them. OBOS generated an imagined feminist community, based on shared oppositional practices in the field of body politics, making it a case in point for a self-reflexive and mutually empowering transnational feminist body/politics (Grewal and Kaplan, 1994).

While the original *OBOS* was a decidedly North American book, firmly wedded to modernist notions of individualism and equal rights' feminism, in the process of travelling it underwent continual and often dramatic revisions. *OBOS* was not simply 'consumed' by non-western feminists as a US export product. Despite limited finances and difficult working conditions, translators reframed and adapted *OBOS* to make it culturally and politically appropriate to their local circumstances. They were critical of the content and did not hesitate to make the book less individualistic or more explicitly political (as in the adaptation for Latin America). If the cultural discrepancies were too great – as was the case with the Egyptian version – the translation collective simply made their own book. Each project, in fact, attested to the creative agency of translators in developing flexible and effective strategies for making their version of *OBOS* sensitive to the local political and cultural climate, as well as to differences and schisms within their own feminist movements. The increasing diversity in the way the book was adapted attests to the fact that feminist knowledge is not simply transferred from one context to another. It invariably requires re-working and contextualization.

What is empowering or disempowering in one context is not necessarily so in another.

   Although *OBOS* travelled from the 'West to the rest' and, in that sense, fits the trajectory described in the cultural imperialism critique, its dissemination does not fit neatly into the paradigm of US feminists at the 'centre' helping their 'sisters on the periphery'. The relations between the BWHBC and the translation projects were a complicated and ambivalent mixture of non-interventionism and interventionism, with both parties actively involved in the process. The BWHBC initially took a hands-off approach towards translations, jumping in only when necessary to do battle against exploitive publishers (France) or save contentious topics like lesbianism or abortion from state censorship. However, as *OBOS* moved farther afield, they became even more flexible about changes in the content of the book, as it became clear that ideologically charged issues presented often-insurmountable problems for local women's groups, which had to worry about censorship of the entire book if controversial passages were included.[7] As translators struggled to develop a book that would address the needs of women in their local contexts, the BWHBC was forced to become even *less* interventionist concerning the content and form of the translations. Paradoxically, however, they had to become *more* interventionist in helping women's groups from less affluent nations find resources and funding to get the book adapted and distributed. As Sally Whelan, who coordinated most of the later adaptations, put it: 'We were just glad when the book could get out at all and we did what we could to help'.[8] As the impact of *OBOS* dwindled within the US, the translation projects increasingly became the *raison d'être* of the book's continued existence. At this point in time, the translation projects might be viewed as the 'movers' and 'shakers' of *Our Bodies, Ourselves*, while the BWHBC has taken up a backseat position as facilitator.

   But – and this is my final argument – even if the BWHBC had wanted to impose their admittedly North American view of women's health on indigenous women's groups in other localities, one look at the actual process by which *OBOS* travelled should convince even the most committed critic of cultural imperialism that this would have been a 'mission impossible'. Perhaps the most salient feature of the globalization – or, more accurately – the global localization of *OBOS*[9] is the unpredictability by which the book moved, appearing unexpectedly and often inexplicably in strange places and, subsequently, taking on a life of its own. Many contemporary scholars have been critical of how globalization has been theorized because a uniformity is implied that belies the uneven, contradictory, and incomplete processes by which objects reappear in new contexts, carrying some of their original values while acquiring new meanings (see, for example, Grewal and Kaplan, 1994; Appadurai, 1996; King, 1997). Stuart Hall (1997) advocates treating globalization as a set of open-ended processes in which, somewhat paradoxically, forms of local appropriation, opposition, and resistance, are going on at the same moment as cultural homogenization and absorption.

   Nowhere is this more apparent than in the most recent developments of *OBOS* in the US. While the proposed update of *OBOS* is being pared down to a handy resource book on women's health, bearing only the faintest resemblance to the earlier classic with its focus on women's experiences and the politics of capitalist medicine, the translation/adaptations of *OBOS* are finding their way back into North America. Several Asian-American community organizations have used the Chinese language *OBOS* as a basis for discussion with Chinese women who have immigrated to the US. The French-language *OBOS* from Senegal has been adopted by a community centre in Montreal for use with Haitian women and the Bulgarian translation is being used as a resource for working with immigrant women in US cities with large Bulgarian communities. This flow of knowledge has been anything but straightforward, as community organizations attempt to balance 'culturally specific' versions of *OBOS* with the requirements of immigrant women for practical information and advice on how to negotiate the complexities of the US medical system. As one of the members of the BWHBC put it, 'the notion that *OBOS* is nothing more than an "imported ideology" ignores the fact that, in practice, nothing is "de novo": we learn from them, they learn from us'.[10]

In conclusion, during the past three decades OBOS crossed many borders and took on many different shapes and forms. The history of its translations shows that books travelled in both predictable and surprising ways. It resembles what Stuart Hall (1996) has called the continuous process of re-articulation and re-contextualization, which is what the global circulation of cultural texts is all about. Translation is not and can never be a matter of taking a project from the west and transporting it fully formed to a new cultural space, where it lives on in its original state. Invariably, some elements remain the same and certain concepts will be retained. However, the text is always rearticulated and, in the process, meanings change and a new configuration of the original text emerges. This is precisely what happened with OBOS. Or, as one collective member put it: 'You have the book and then there is the life of the book'.[11]

Notes

1   This is an abridged version of my article 'Translating Feminist Body/Politics' in *The European Journal of Women's Studies* (forthcoming). I would like to thank Anna Aalten, Willem de Haan, Judith Ezekiel, Barbara Henkes, Helma Lutz, Sawitri Saharso, Gloria Wekker, Barbara Wiemann, and Dubravka Zarkov for their helpful comments on the earlier version of this chapter. I am especially indebted to Halleh Ghorashi for her insightful criticisms of this chapter and, more generally, to the editors and many of the authors of this volume who helped me clarify my thinking. And, last but not least, I am grateful to the participants of 'Crossing Cultural Borders with *Our Bodies, Ourselves*' which was held in Utrecht on 14-16 July, 2001 for sharing their translation experiences and, more generally, for providing an inspiring glimpse of what transnational feminist practice can be.

2   Much of the information on the translation/adaptations projects is taken from *Our Bodies, Ourselves in Many Languages*, A Global History and Status Report, which was compiled by the BWHBC in July 1998, the BWHBC website (http://www.bwhbc.org) and updates from various staff members.

3   My analysis is based on oral history interviews with the BWHBC and several conversations focused specifically on translation/adaptation projects with Judy

Norsigian, Ester Shapiro, Norma Swenson, Sally Whelan, and Jennifer Yanco. I also spent the summer of 2000 in the archives of the Schlesinger Library and the BWHBC library going through minutes from meetings, correspondence with translators and publishers, internal papers, publications, and proposals for foundation grants. I have been able to talk with some of the women involved with adapting the foreign editions and have, in some instances, been able to make use of what the translators have written about the adaptation process themselves.

4   Although each foreign edition has its own translation story, I did not have access to all of them. However, for many of the adaptations, correspondence between the translators and the BWHBC was available. Translators usually kept the collective posted – at least in a cursory way – about how they adapted the book. They invariably sent copies of the finished version, which the collective was able to give to a critical reader. Translations often provide a preface with an explanation by the translators on how the book was adapted to fit their own contexts (German, Dutch, UK). The translators frequently gave interviews – in local newspapers or on visits in the US – in which they explained some of the difficulties they had encountered in doing the translation (China, Japan). And, finally, some of the translation projects wrote accounts themselves in which they reflected on the process of adapting *OBOS* (see, for example, Farah, 1991 on the Egyptian version, Shapiro, 1999 on the Latin American adaptation, and Yanco, 1996).

5   Interview Ester Shapiro, February 1999.

6   Female circumcision was officially banned in Egypt in 1959, but continues to be performed, particularly in rural settings, where it is estimated that 90% of women are circumcised, whether they are Christian or Muslim. The reasons women give for engaging in the practice range from wanting to be 'pure' to the belief that it is more 'aesthetic' to not wanting to become dependent on a man through sexual desire.

7   Remembering conversations with the Cairo Women's Health Book Collective about how there were no lesbians in Egypt, Norma Swenson notes 'Oh sure! We knew some. But they were right that they had to take the context into account'. (Interview Norma Swenson, 19 March 1999.) The collective gradually relaxed their position that every translation should contain at least all the chapters in some form.

8   Interview Sally Whelan, 25 July 2000.

9   Robertson's (1995) term 'glocalisation' has been taken up by many contemporary globalization theorists to express the interconnections between the local and the global.

10   Interview Sally Whelan, 28 May 2003.

11   Interview Norma Swenson, 19 March 1999.

References

Ahmed, Sara (2000), *Strange Encounters: Embodied Others in Post-Coloniality*, Routledge, London and New York.

Al-Ali, Nadje (2000), *Secularism, Gender and the State in the Middle East: The Egyptian Women's Movement*, Cambridge University Press, Cambridge.

Alexander, M. Jacqui and Mohanty, Chandra Talpade (1997), 'Genealogies, Legacies, Movements', in M.J. Alexander and C.T. Mohanty (eds.), *Feminist Genealogies, Colonial Legacies, Democratic Futures*, Routledge, New York, pp. xiii-xlii.

Appadurai, Arjun (1996), *Modernity at Large: Cultural Dimensions of Globalization*, University of Minnesota Press, Minneapolis.

Chen, Kuan-Hsing (1996), 'Cultural Studies and the Politics of Internationalization: An Interview with Stuart Hall', in D. Morley and K-H Chen (eds.) *Stuart Hall: Critical Dialogues in Cultural Studies*, Routledge, London, pp. 392-408.

El Dawla, Aida Seif, Hadi, Amal Abdel and Wahab, Nadia Abdel (1998), 'Women's Wit Over Men's: Trade-offs and Strategic Accommodations in Egyptian Women's Reproductive Lives', in R.P. Petchesky and K. Judd (eds.) *Negotiating Reproductive Rights*, Zed Books, London, pp. 69-107.

Enloe, Cynthia (1989), *Bananas, Beaches and Bases: Making Feminist Sense of International Politics*, University of California Press, Berkeley.

Farah, Nadia (1991), 'The Egyptian Women's Health Book Collective', *Middle East Report*, November-December, pp. 16-25.

Grewal, Inderpal and Kaplan, Caren (1994), 'Introduction: Transnational Feminist Practices and Questions of Postmodernity', in I. Grewal and C. Kaplan (eds.) *Scattered Hegemonies: Postmodernity and Transnational Feminist Practices*, University of Minnesota Press, Minneapolis, pp. 1-33.

Hall, Stuart (1997), 'The Local and the Global: Globalization and Ethnicity', in A. King (ed.) *Culture, Globalization and the World-System: Contemporary Conditions for the Representation of Identity*, University of Minnesota Press, Minneapolis, pp. 19-40.

Haraway, Donna (1991), *Simians, Cyborgs, and Women: The Reinvention of Nature*, Free Association Books, London.

Hill, Nancy (1994), 'An Egyptian Women's Health Book Inspired by *Our Bodies, Ourselves*: Is Global Sisterhood Possible After All?', Paper presented at the Eastern Sociological Society, 18 March 1994.

Ibrahim, Barbara and Farah, Nadia (1992), 'Women's Lives and Health: The Cairo Women's Health Book Collective', *Quality/Calidad/Qualité*, Vol. 4, pp. 4-11.

Kaplan, Caren (1996), *Questions of Travel: Postmodern Discourses of Displacement*, Duke University Press, Durham.

King, Anthony D. (1997), *Culture, Globalization and the World-System: Contemporary Conditions for the Representation of Identity*, University of Minnesota Press, Minneapolis.

Mohanty, Chandra Tapade (1997), 'Under Western Eyes: Feminist Scholarship and Colonial Discourses', in A. McClintock, A. Mufti, and E. Shohat (eds.) *Dangerous Liaisons: Gender, Nation, and Postcolonial Perspectives*, University of Minnesota Press, Minneapolis, pp. 255-277.

Morgan, Robin (ed) (1984), *Sisterhood is Global: The International Women's Movement Anthology*, Anchor Press/Doubleday, Garden City, N.Y.

Narayan, Uma (1997), *Dislocating Cultures: Identities, Traditions, and Third World Feminism*, Routledge, New York.

Robertson, Roland (1995), 'Glocalization: time-space and homogeneity-heterogeneity', in M. Featherstone, S. Lash, and R. Robertson (eds.) *Global Modernities*, Sage, London, pp. 25-44.

Schrager, Cynthia D. (1993), 'Questioning the Promise of Self-Help: A Reading of *Women Who Love Too Much*', *Feminist Studies*, Vol. 19 (1), pp. 177-192.

Shapiro, Ester (1999), *Crossing Cultural Borders with North American Feminism: Lessons from the Latin American Translation/Adaptation of* Our Bodies, Ourselves, Paper presented at conference 'Gender, Culture, and Translation', Budapest, October 1999.

The Boston Women's Health Book Collective (1971/1979), *Our Bodies, Ourselves,* Simon and Schuster, Inc., New York (later editions: *The New Our Bodies, Ourselves* in 1984/1992 and *Our Bodies, Ourselves for the New Century* in 1998).

The Boston Women's Health Book Collective (1998), '*Our Bodies, Ourselves* in Many Languages: Translations and/or Adaptations', *A Global History and Status Report*, internal paper, Somerville, MA.

Yanco, Jennifer J. (1996), '*Our Bodies, Ourselves* in Beijing: Breaking the Silences', *Feminist Studies*, Vol. 22 (3), pp. 511-517.

Chapter 6

Global Peace Builders and Local Conflict: The Feminization of Peace in Southern Sudan

Dorothea Hilhorst and Mathijs van Leeuwen

When I attended activities of the Sudanese Women's Voice for Peace, the members often donned their SWVP T-shirts, like a club uniform. They were bright-coloured T-shirts with the emblem of the organization imprinted on them – a dove carrying an olive branch flying over a map of Sudan. The text on the T-shirt read: 'SWVP, Strengthening traditional ways of conflict resolution'. The T-shirt definitely added to the appeal of the women's organization: worn with pride, underlining a sense of togetherness of the women. Yet, it always made me smile too. Claiming to strengthen tradition, the T-shirt addressed the members in English, while even the very notion of a T-shirt was alien to many of the bare-breasted, grassroots members of SWVP. And what did they mean by strengthening traditional ways of conflict resolution? Surely, this was not to be taken literally, for real tradition left little room for women's involvement in peace. I guess that the slogan was chosen to convey a message to outsiders: observers, friends and donors alike. So, I pictured the members of SWVP walking the dirt tracks of their villages with their children in T-shirts, meant to impress the world. Wasn't this globalization?[1]

Introduction

Since the mid-1990s, there has been an unmistakable international tendency to bring peace building into the domain of women. Worldwide, women are found at the forefront of peace initiatives, policy hopes are set on women's peace-building efforts and significant funds are allocated to strengthen women's capacities for peace. In this chapter we trace the feminization of peace to changes in present-day conflicts that are related to globalization. The conflicts of the 1990s are sometimes characterized as 'globalized' wars resulting from the disintegration of states, characterized by a lack of legitimacy of the warring parties, the importance of identity politics and heavy dependence on external support. Those so-called new wars differ from the old wars in that they are overwhelmingly intra-state in nature. Where state institutions break down or take part in inflicting violence, conventional (diplomatic) mechanisms for conflict resolution lose their relevance. International organizations have therefore shifted their focus from the negotiating table and the national level to civil society and local levels; hence, the increasing attention for the involvement of women in peace building.

The chapter first elaborates the triangular relations between globalization, gender and conflict. It then describes the emergence of a global discourse on the feminization of peace that was particularly pronounced during the Beijing women conference in 1995. The core of the chapter addresses the question of how this global discourse works in local peace-building practices. This is analyzed for the case of southern Sudan, where Mathijs van Leeuwen spent ten months in 2001 doing fieldwork, in the context of a Disaster Studies research programme on peace-building policy and practice (van Leeuwen, 2004).[2]

Globalization and Conflict

Most authors agree that conflict has undergone change in the last decades and that these changes are partly related to processes of globalization. Conflicts since the end of the Cold War overwhelmingly occur in societies where the legitimacy and representativeness of the state is low or even completely lacking, at least in the eyes of certain groups (Kaldor, 1999; 2001). Identity politics play a large role in conflicts when particular groups are excluded from power and political participation, discriminated against in the distribution of state goods and services and their cultural identity is oppressed (Frerks, 1998, pp. 6-11). Changes in the economy associated with globalization, such as the impoverishment and instability created by the transnational economies and a sharp increase in global flows of illegal or informal economic goods, also contribute to creating favourable conditions for present-day conflicts (World Bank, 2000; Collier, 2000; FitzGerald, 1999).

While the causes and underlying processes of conflict are thus changing, this chapter is mainly interested in the *everyday patterns* of conflict in practice. These can best be summarized by the phrase, the 'informalization' of conflict. Most conflict is not fought between regular armies but between factions where the boundaries between soldiers, rebels and civilians are vague or disappearing. Conflict is becoming everybody's business. International conventions and rules for warfare hardly apply and there is neither a clear beginning nor end of hostilities. In the 'battlefield', use is made of light weaponry, while 'military' tactics include rape, ethnic cleansing and starvation. With the informalization of conflict, peace is also informalized. Peacekeeping discretion is partly redirected to supranational governance bodies. In addition, there is growing attention for so-called track-two diplomacy by actors in civil society, such as media, churches, women's organizations and educational institutions. These groups may not have a direct influence on the political processes, but they are crucial in creating a critical mass to contribute to a society conducive to peaceful conflict resolution.

One relevant feature of conflict in the analysis presented in this chapter is the collapse of time and space resulting from globalization. Knowledge of conflict elsewhere is no longer reserved to diplomats and historians, but reaches everybody with lightning speed. The real time close-ups of conflict that we experience daily have a bearing on the way citizens (including members of diaspora communities) and civil society organizations can engage in debates and practices of conflicts elsewhere. On the other hand, the fact that combating parties realize that they are fighting their wars in the eyes of the world community likewise affects their strategies to legitimize their causes. Well-known examples of this are the Zapatistas in Mexico using the Internet to gather international support, and the Kurds in Iraq reporting through the Internet on the atrocities committed against them. As we will elaborate in the case of Sudan, this results in an apparent, discursive proximity between bush fighters, office holders and news consumers that are thousands of kilometres apart from each other.

Before discussing the impact of the informalization of conflict on women and peace building, let us first briefly qualify the above statements. The notion of new and informalizing conflicts is not uncontested. In the first place, it has been pointed out that the present broad attention to intra-state conflicts makes it easy to forget that, since the Second World War, over 75 percent of all registered conflicts have been of an intrastate nature (Holsti, 1996, p. 37). What appears to be primarily changing, then, is our perception and labelling of conflicts. In the second place, there is some question as to whether the developing patterns in conflicts depict a worldwide change, or are fluid and temporary. Since the Iraq war, for instance, the United Nations seems to have lost status rapidly as a governance body, while some claim that the United States has become the only hegemonic power in the world. Conflict and peace policies are being reviewed under the threat of international terrorism (Macrae and Harmer, 2003), which hints at the possibility of renewed conflict among international interests, and lead again to more nation-orientated and formal forms of conflict. Leaving aside the question of what may lie ahead in the future, the point remains that today conflict is informalized and involves a large role for civil actors.

Women and Gender in Conflict

> The terms 'vulnerable' and 'victim' are not synonymous with 'women' (Lindsey, 2001, p. 212).

The international interest in the problems experienced by women in situations of armed conflict snowballed when it came out that many women were raped in Bosnia in 1992. International organizations started to pay systematic attention to the plight of women in war. In October 2000, the UN Security Council passed resolution 1325 on Women, Peace and Security, stipulating that a study should be carried out on the impact of armed conflict on women and girls, the role of women in peace building and the gender dimensions of the peace processes and conflict resolution.

Women are severely affected by war. Conflict reduces women's '*lebensraum*', confronts them with (sexual) violence and deprives them of their husbands, sons and resources. In many cases, they are left with the responsibility to take care of their children without having the means to do so. Many women – lawyers, doctors, artists, farmers, traders – see their social roles reduced to rearing children for the 'fatherland'. In the process of militarization, women are often seen as the bearers of culture, which raises expectations about their behaviour and makes them particularly vulnerable targets (Byrne et al., 1995; 1996).

The idea that women are particularly vulnerable in conflict is toned down on two accounts. Firstly, some international reports (e.g. Lindsey, 2001) draw attention to gender and conflict rather than women and conflict and point to the vulnerability of men in war. Conflict takes the lives of more men than women, produces overwhelmingly male prisoners, subjects unknown numbers of men to sexual violence and imposes restricted and very demanding notions of manhood on men expected to fight. Secondly, women are not only victims but fulfil different roles in conflict (Moser and Clark, 2001). Women may provide shelter and assistance to fighting parties. Conflict may also empower women. In the absence of their husbands, they may take on new economic roles or assume leadership in their communities, or in Non Government Organizations (NGOs) and political groups. Furthermore, with the informalization of conflict, the number of women combatants is also increasing, which may be seen as another token of empowerment.[3] Analogous to what the editors argued in the introduction to this book about popular notions of globalization as something 'outside' of women, denying women's agency in the process, it can be said that conflict is often analyzed as something outside of women. Hence women are either seen as victims or (as will be elaborated below) as opposing conflict. A more nuanced reading of the roles of women in conflict would reveal how women are also agents in creating the conditions and manifestations of conflict.

Women as Peace Builders

> LYSISTRATA: 'Of course we should, by the goddesses twain! We need only sit indoors with painted cheeks, and meet our mates lightly clad in transparent gowns of Amorgos silk, and perfectly depilated; they will get their tools up and be wild to lie with us. That will be the time to refuse, and they will hasten to make peace, I am convinced of that!' (410 BC Lysistrata by Aristophanes)

In the play 'Lysistrata' by Aristophanes (ca. 447-385 BC), the women of Athens get tired of losing their sons on the battlefield. They conspire to occupy the treasury and deny their husbands sexual intercourse until they make peace with the Spartans. Lysistrata maintains her appeal in today's globalized world. She became a symbol against the impeding war of the Bush administration in Iraq in 2003. The Lysistrata project was launched early in February of that year and, thanks to the Internet and e-mail, was soon taken over by women and men all over the world. On 3 March 2003, barely a month after its first announcement, Lysistrata was simultaneously played by volunteer actors for packed audiences in 1,029 readings in all 50 US states and a total of 59 countries.[4]

The ancient Greek idea that women are more interested in peace than men was highlighted in the last decade. An international discourse has come about to emphasize the crucial role of women in peace building. A key event in the development of this discourse was the Fourth UN World Women's Conference in Beijing in 1995. Partly inspired by the large presence during the conference of the 'Women in Black' international peace network,[5] the conference declaration identified women and armed conflict as a critical concern. Strategic objectives were included to increase the participation of women in conflict resolution at decision-making levels and to promote women's contribution to fostering a culture of peace.[6] Beijing gave rise to many follow-up activities in the United Nations, donor and recipient countries and among international NGOs to enhance women's role in peace building.

It is interesting to note that, in the midst of this event, a counter discourse was also present, but gained much less attention. Women connected to the Philippine National Democratic Front distributed pamphlets to warn participants against the 'gender trap' that lured women into peace-related activities instead of mobilizing them for class-based, anti-imperialist activism (Hilhorst, 2003, p. 70). They organized a march attended by hundreds of women to protest against the presence of Hillary Clinton during the NGO conference and to demand the right of women to engage in armed conflict in order to attain social justice.

The success of the international discourse on women and peace building can partly be explained by geo-political trends. Policies and statements attributing peace-building qualities to women never ignore the fact that the women's capacity may reach all levels of political decision-making, but is in practice particularly associated with grass roots initiatives (Rupesinghe, 1996). In fact, the prominent role attributed to women rarely leads to a proper representation of women in official peace diplomacy. Women and women's organizations act as informal negotiators, lobby groups, campaigners and demonstrators. The interest in women as peace builders could thus partly be inspired by international political motives that consider local peace-building activities as less costly, less diplomatically risky and less insecure than engaging in international military interventions or international diplomatic efforts for peace (Duffield, 2001). This raises the question as to whether the interest in women for peace bears evidence of an elevated respect for women's leadership qualities or, rather, whether it concerns the degradation of peace building to the low-profile, informal domains that are mainly inhabited by women.

What is the rationalization of the discourse on women and peace? There are several explanations of why women are more inclined than men to undertake peace activities. Some authors believe that women are innately more peaceful than men. Empirical research does not sustain this claim. Women's direct contribution to violent conflicts is generally less than that of men, but is not absent. Women in some instances have turned out to be ferocious fighters, and have often had an indirect supportive role to conflict. With the 'informalization' of conflicts, as discussed above, this appears to be increasingly the case. Over the last decades more women have participated in armed forces. They have played leadership roles in revolutionary movements in Nicaragua, El Salvador, Angola, Eritrea and a host of other struggles. The conflicts in Sri Lanka and Rwanda have also provided many examples of women actively contributing to fighting and killing. Nonetheless, the idea that women are more peaceful by nature than men lingers on in some of the peace literature. Shelley Anderson (1999, p. 230), for instance, states:

> Women's strengths for reconciliation are many. They include good listening and communication skills, the willingness and flexibility to compromise, extensive experience in practical problem solving, and caring for real people above abstract principles.

Others believe that women are more inclined to peace because they are mothers. Olive Schreiner illustrated this by saying, in 1911:

> There is perhaps no woman whether she has borne children, or is a potential child bearer who could look down on a battlefield covered with the slain, but the thought would rise in her 'So many mothers' sons! So many bodies brought into the world to lie there' (P. Villanueva, 1995, quoted in Kant, 1998, p. 12).

Although this is true for many mothers, motherhood can also have the opposite effect because coming to the real or imagined defence of their children can also bring women to commit or condone violent acts. Besides, we cannot assume that women act as they do *because* they are mothers. Women, as social actors, may also strategically use their motherhood to justify their actions for building peace as well as being engaged in conflict (Ferris, 1993). In many cases, women can only make themselves heard by speaking as mothers, as is prominently illustrated by the Mothers of the Plaza de Mayo (Davids and van Driel, 2001).

Still other authors assume that women's supposed peacefulness is related to particular roles in society. In those cases where women carry the main responsibility for livelihood, they feel more constrained in their everyday practices by conflict situations. Women who cannot feed their children or who see their trade activities interrupted are clearly more affected by the negative effects of war. Another example is formed by women who, through exogamous marriage practices, live their adult lives in alien social groups (e.g. Somalia). In these cases, women may have much to lose by conflict and may tire of war more easily than men (Kant, 1998).

When we emphasize the discursive nature of the international attention for women and peace building, we do not mean to suggest that this discourse is not grounded in reality. It is undoubtedly so that in many local situations women take the initiative and are at the forefront of peace-building efforts. All the above-cited explanations have some validity in certain situations. Women's active engagement in peace building may be explained in particular cases by one or a combination of them. However, we are concerned with the generalizing nature of the discourse around women and peace. There is a high diversity of gender roles and ideologies. Besides, women have a multiplicity of identities and the identification with ethnicity or whatever social group may be stronger than gender. The discourse also homogenizes women. It tends to be forgotten that there is so much social differentiation among women that it could very well lead to conflict or competition among them.

Globalized Conflict in Southern Sudan

Since 1955, southern Sudan has suffered heavily from civil conflict. Internationally, most attention goes to the conflict between the Government of Sudan (GOS) in Khartoum and armed opposition movements in the south. This so-called 'North-South conflict' has several dimensions, including post-colonial governance heritage, cultural and religious domination and competition over oil and other resources. Besides, there are multiple conflicts within the South, East and West of the country. In the South, in 1983, the Sudan People's Liberation Movement/Army (SPLM/A) started to bring down the central government, but has been plagued by factionalism resulting in diverse militia groups and fighting at regional level. At the local level, the insurgence and related factionalism has inflamed or further intensified local conflicts, fuelled by the widespread availability of light weapons resulting from GOS strategies to arm splinter factions. Those include inter-ethnic and inter-factional conflicts and conflicts about resources such as land and cattle, conflicts between communities and between displaced and local populations (Pax Christi, 1999).

The last ten years has witnessed a series of international diplomatic interventions to address the North-South conflict, which remained unsuccessful (see Verney, 1999). Early in 2002, however, the two major factions in the South joined forces. In July 2002, the Sudanese government and the SPLM/A signed a framework agreement to end the civil war. Under the agreement, southern Sudan will be able to hold a referendum on possible secession after a six-year, power-sharing, transitional period. At the time of writing, March 2004, negotiations were still ongoing.

Conflict in Sudan is international and even global, in several respects. In 2002, approximately 490,000 Sudanese were refugees or asylum seekers (UNHCR, 2003). Neighbouring countries support different parties in the civil war and international companies are very interested in Sudan's oil revenues. Revenues from oil operations by firms from various countries, including Canada, Sweden, China and Austria, reportedly have enabled the government to increase its offensive capabilities (Christian Aid, 2001). International involvement in the cross-border trade of light weapons further contributes to the conflicts. On the other hand, the involvement of western countries has played a crucial role in the recent peace process. The United States in particular has put pressure on both sides, wanting to make sure that Sudan is not a refuge for foreign terrorists, while African oil is regarded as a strategic national interest.[7]

Conflict in Sudan is also 'globalized' because different stakeholders consciously address the international arena to defend their interests and gain international legitimacy. Sudanese refugees living in Nairobi, Europe and the USA have become very important in such activities. As a result of the efforts of

Sudanese intellectuals abroad, the SPLM/A has been effective in improving its international image. In its early years, the armed wing of the SPLM/A was notorious for its human rights record (Amnesty International, 1995), and its political structures that left little room for the emergence of local organizations (Prendergast, 1997). Recently, however, SPLM/A has gained respect from western governments, resulting in promises for assistance to the movement for the reconstruction of southern Sudan. One of the major strategies in winning 'the hearts and minds' of foreign governments was the establishment in 1994 of a civil structure separate from the military movement (SPLM, 2000; Lesch, 1998). Leaving open the possibility that the movement is really prepared to hand over power to these structures, there is no doubt that at least part of the effort was made to oblige the international community. In addition, the SPLM/A has adopted strategies to effectuate women's political participation. A secretariat for women, gender and child welfare was established in 1998, with the aim of mobilizing women for development and the exchange of viewpoints. In 2003, SPLM/A was involved in women's conferences in the different southern regions. The women's secretariat, however, has been severely under-resourced and remains a top-down structure. At higher levels of policymaking, the involvement of women is limited. For instance, only three women participated in the peace negotiations facilitated by the Intergovernmental Authority on Development in Nairobi, Kenya.

Local Peace-Building in Southern Sudan and the Role of Women

> The equality discourse of the movement always concerns the men from the North and the South, not the men and the women (Co-ordinator of a network of indigenous NGOs, interview 12 October 2001).

Since the humanitarian operation in southern Sudan is one of the longest in history, the idea has taken root among UN organizations and International Non-Government Organizations (INGOs) that relief efforts should be made relevant to development and peace building. Many organizations have adopted peace building among their objectives. To some extent, all of them involve Sudanese indigenous organizations. Over the last ten years, an estimated 65 southern Sudanese NGOs have been formed.[8] Most have their main offices in Kenya or Uganda, established and run by Sudanese in exile. They mainly provide relief, in particular food distribution and health programmes, and many have secondary objectives regarding peace building. Some work primarily on peace. Because NGOs have very restricted access to national or international peace-building efforts, their activities are mainly geared to the local level.

Sudanese and international NGO people often attribute to women an important potential in local peace-building practices in southern Sudan (Simonse, 1999; AU/IBAR, 2003). It is said that women from different sides share similar experiences, which enables them to transcend ethnic borders. There are many stories from different regions in southern Sudan about women speaking out in peace meetings. Skilfully playing with cultural repertoires (e.g. taking men on their laps and asking them to listen to their mothers; questioning the need of bearing sons that will be killed in the fighting) they urge their husbands to reconcile. Women rarely initiate reconciliation meetings and in many instances are not even represented in peace councils. Nonetheless, women do intervene in conflict, for instance, by informing the authorities or traditional community leaders about imminent fights or interfering with plans to raid cattle. The impact of women on local conflict fluctuates regionally and situationally. In the Nuba Mountains, for instance, women are taken more seriously than in Eastern Equatoria, because the soldiers in Nuba are from among the community, and because of a different status of women. Of course, it should also be acknowledged that women could have a role in promoting conflict. In workshops facilitated by the Inter-African Bureau for Animal Resources of the African Union (AU/IBAR) in Eastern Equatoria, for example, women related how they incite youngsters to raid cattle, and praise and chant at the cattle raiders upon their successful return (see also Simonse, 1999).

The limited role of women in peace building is interlaced with the room allotted to women for participating in public affairs. In many cases (cultural) impediments and prejudices to women's political participation still prevail. Women are ignored or simply 'forgotten'. One of the elements that accounts for the slow penetration of women in the political structures is the fact that political positions are often reserved for ex-fighters of the SPLM/A (*cf.* Enloe, 1990). Despite the constraints to women's political participation, Sudanese women's organizations started to emerge in the 1990s. From the start, this was strongly facilitated by international organizations, where a discourse on gender and peace had become increasingly popular. The Netherlands' embassies in Nairobi and Khartoum initiated Engendering the Peace to increase the participation of women in the peace process. The Women Waging Peace project of the University of Boston is another initiative to bring together Sudanese women's groups in pursuit of peace.

The Sudanese Women's Voice for Peace

For some years, the Sudanese Women's Voice for Peace (SWVP) was one of the most prominent women organizations in southern Sudan. SWVP resulted from a meeting of wives of political leaders, organized by an East African NGO, the People for Peace in Africa. People for Peace had approached the women, hoping that they would influence their husbands to break the impasse in the peace negotiations and strike an accord. At the end of the workshop, however, the women decided that they did not want to engage in politics. Instead, they formed an organization promoting the interests of the women of all ethnic and religious backgrounds. In 1994, this became the Sudanese Women's Voice for Peace.

The initial membership of SWVP consisted of wives of political leaders and women active in civil society organizations and peace-building initiatives. Their ethnic origin was diverse. They were relatively highly educated and lived in exile in Nairobi. The women wanted to attain a southern Sudan-wide women's movement for peace, emphasizing the central role of women in the resolution of conflict. According to the founders, women as mothers are united in their desire to end conflict. Besides, women are considered to have more interest in peace because they suffer more than men from the war. The SWVP also believed that women are natural peacemakers by character and traditional heritage.

In its first year, SWVP organized several events on the plight of women and children in the war. They were able to get modest support from different organizations, including church bishops and the United Nations Development Fund for Women (UNIFEM) office in Nairobi. They trained their members and made a visit to southern Sudan, where they had a workshop and introduced the SWVP to the military command in the area. Within one year after having had just one activity in southern Sudan, the organization was launched internationally. A delegation of SWVP was invited to attend the Beijing Conference in 1995, where they were exposed to international discourses around women and peace. Their presence in Beijing furthered the visibility of SWVP and attracted increasing international support in the form of training, funding, and invitations to international events. Immediately after the initiation of SWVP, the organization thus became discursively and organizationally intertwined with the international development community.

In the five years following Beijing, SWVP wanted to move from a city-based membership organization to a countrywide women's movement. Several international organizations offered training in conflict resolution and civic education to the Nairobi members. These in turn trained women in southern Sudan, until they formed a network of ten organizations. Part of the local training was facilitated by international experts flying in for the occasion. SWVP also started a socio-economic programme called Seeds for Peace. Four 'Peace Demonstration Centres' (PDC) were going to be set up in southern Sudan for increasing awareness, training, and income generating activities. A Dutch peace organization, with which SWVP had related for several years, helped to develop and write the proposal and secured its funding through the Netherlands Ministry of Foreign Affairs.

Unfortunately, Seeds for Peace turned out to be so problematic that it severely damaged SWVP and was stopped halfway through the intended project duration. The failure was partly related to logistic difficulties involved in working in a country in conflict. Mainly, however, it came about because of internal problems in SWVP, problems that were partly brought about by the Seeds for Peace programme itself. SWVP had never had large projects to administer, and suddenly had to transform from a voluntary membership organization to an NGO. This created friction between salaried women and volunteers, raised unrealistic expectations among target communities in southern Sudan and fed rumours about misuse of funds. The Seeds for Peace programme triggered a number of slumbering personal problems among the women and painfully revealed that a heritage of war and autocracy had not equipped the women with problem-solving capacities in their organization. More and more women left the organization and SWVP lost its multi-ethnic character. While SWVP and the Seeds for Peace were crumbling, the relation with the Dutch peace organization became increasingly strained. The Dutch requested, facilitated and eventually demanded increased accountability and more visible activities in southern Sudan, but to no avail. At the end of 2002, they decided to withdraw support to SWVP and stop the programme.

Distance and Identification

The SWVP is not an exceptional women's organization in Sudan. Others faced similar conflicts over leadership, problems of financial management, and difficulties in implementing activities in southern Sudan. Yet, funding agencies eagerly continued to fund these organizations. From their distant vantage point, they only perceived the organizations' *discourses*. Discourse refers to frames of understanding the world around us. Much more than simply providing rationale on women and peace building, for instance, discourse also embodies codes for practice. In the case of development, for example, discourse encompasses the way organizations should function (democratically, with accountability and project-orientation), along with the primacy of the interests of grassroots people. In their rationales as well as organizational set-up, the local NGO discourses are made to fit international discourses on gender and peace building and provide a good basis for identification.

An inverse relation between distance and identification therefore comes about: the larger the distance, the stronger the identification. A Sudanese representative of an INGO was painfully confronted with this tendency. At one time, this person's INGO received a request for funding an income-generating project by a women's peace organization. Not convinced of the quality of the proposal and the capacity of the organization, he rejected the proposal. The women's peace organization then complained to the agency's back-donor in the USA, and the back-donor called upon the local representative to review the decision and support the project.

What did donors fail or refuse to see from a distance? They failed to see how little tradition, problem-solving strength and organizational capacity civil society has been able to build up in southern Sudan, where room for civil society had always been restricted under the successive rules of the British, the Government of Sudan and, until very recently, the SPLM/A. They did not realize the additional strain that civil society actors undergo in times of conflict, when personal resources are destroyed and every salaried person carries the burden of maintaining numerous unemployed relatives. Nor did they realize the traumatic effects that years of conflict inflict on people, not just on their target groups but also on the NGO officers themselves.

Equally important, in their eagerness to pursue peace in southern Sudan, they indiscriminately funded local organizations without thinking how their support could be sustained (*cf.* Van Rooy, 1998). They appeared not to see the devastating effects of their haphazard search for fundable organizations and programmes.[9] Donor practices tended to drown or divide promising initiatives, while refusing to commit to long-term capacity building. With the funding available for peace, many local NGOs started to present themselves as peace organizations. Besides, the interest of donors in peace building had created a context in Nairobi where people had no incentive to solve problems. Instead, they would simply leave and establish an organization of their own to realize personal ambitions for leadership. A culture was created in which local organizations became more concerned with boosting their images, than with the substance of their work.

There is yet another dimension to the twisted relation between distance and identification underlying the global discourse around women and peace. The means of communication in a globalized world appear to make it possible to turn the apparent commonality stemming from a shared discourse into practice. In the age of the Internet, e-mail, global conferences and cheap air traffic, it is easy to be deluded by a sense of proximity in what Appadurai calls 'virtual neighbourhoods' (Appadurai, 1995). The Dutch peace organization, convinced that SWVP had the same goals in mind as they, closed the distance between a European-based funder and a Sudanese organization. Enabled by communications technology, the Dutch organization stepped largely into the implementing space of SWVP. It helped to dream up the Seeds for Peace programme, and did most of the writing of the project proposal, which was inspired by experience of peace organizations in Colombia. It undertook several initiatives to get the project afloat and often sent representatives to talk directly with the SWVP women. The apparent proximity, however, was soon overtaken by local realities on the two sides of the interface. The Dutch agency increasingly felt pressured by its back-donor, frustrated that SWVP did not live up to its promises to reach out to southern Sudan and powerless in its incapacity to make SWVP deliver the project as envisaged. SWVP, on the other hand, increasingly felt abandoned by the Dutch agency, which showed little appreciation for their international and Nairobi-based lobby work, appeared to claim ownership of the project by forwarding accountability demands and finally by bluntly displaying its power to withdraw the funds unilaterally. On both sides, experience with the Seeds for Peace programme led to feelings of betrayal, frustration and disillusion.

Global Discourse in Local Practice

The question remains, what happened to the local SWVP women's groups in southern Sudan? In terms of project implementation, the local SWVP groups were not very successful. The few that succeeded did so on account of support from entities other than SWVP, such as local representations of churches or UN-agencies. These groups were able to make significant progress and construct centres where women came together and organized activities.

More interesting, however, than documenting what failed or did not happen is to analyze how women locally evolved their activities, altering the discourse on women and peace building in the process. This was done in the case of Narus, a village located just over Sudan's border with Kenya in SPLM/A-held territory. The community started as a displaced camp, but is now a permanent settlement. Its population of around 8,000 people consists of a majority of Dinka, a large number of Toposa (originating from the region), and some other ethnic groups. Though far from the front-line, Narus has been hit several times by bombardments from the Northern Sudanese army. There are also different kinds of local conflicts. There is tension resulting from the past, when SPLA occupied the area and forcibly recruited soldiers from among the local population. This tension had an ethnic dimension because the SPLA mainly consisted of Dinka. Another source of local conflict was cattle raiding and related violence. The insecurity and high levels of domestic violence in Narus partly resulted from the wide availability of homemade alcohol.

The local women's group of SWVP started out as a multi-ethnic project organization. In the course of time, when the group was not able to realize a Peace Demonstration Centre, it turned increasingly into the embodiment of a single-ethnic network of mutual support. At the start, the Narus women were highly motivated to work for peace, except that they did not see an opportunity to do so. The North-South conflict and the bombardments of their area were clearly beyond their realm of influence. Since the majority of members were not from cattle-owning families, they saw little scope in addressing the conflicts resulting from cattle raiding that were quite common in their area. Addressing alcohol-related violence found no constituency in the group because many of the PDC women brewed alcohol to earn an income. Besides, although peace was important for the women, it did not have the overwhelming priority outsiders attribute to it. They were primarily occupied with the demands of making a living and driven by the desire to realize good community relations and strengthen the solidarity networks.

To critical outsiders, the credibility of the women's group was undermined by some contradictions. Their talk was about inter-ethnic peace but their activities were mainly single-ethnic and focused on livelihood. For the women, the different interests were not pressing realities, but became expressions of peace. They developed a definition of peace that started from below, from the unity of the home. They focused on 'peace among ourselves', in their families and social networks. In addition, they viewed development as a prerequisite for peace: 'You cannot have peace in your mind without peace in your stomach'. In this definition, participation in income-generating projects becomes peace building. In fact, much of the activities of the women in Narus were continuations of coping practices they had devised in their social networks. That these networks were usually single-ethnic was so self-evident in the local conditions that they were perhaps not even conscious of it – and certainly did not question it.

Yet, some things had changed. Even though the everyday activities continued, the women now conceived of these activities as contributing to peace: creating peace in the stomach and peace in the home would eventually contribute to peace in society. Where possible, they continued to advocate for peace in the wider context of Sudan. As SWVP, they were regularly invited to activities where they could bring out their message for peace. As a result, while the official projects of the women were largely failing, a discourse on peace nonetheless became a reality in the locality and vicinity of Narus. Through the SWVP, the concept of peace entered the vocabulary of people in the community, dignifying the coping activities of women and contributing to a slowly growing constituency of peace. This effect radiated far beyond the immediate activities. The fact that the women belonged to a movement for peace was widely known and appealed to many people in and outside of Narus. The SWVP in Narus became a social space where the concept of peace gained local meaning and a process towards peace was imaginable.

Conclusion

This chapter started by examining the claim that women are more interested in peace than men and by explaining why this notion is so powerful in present geo-political conditions. The discourses on women and peace building were then 'put to the test' for the case of southern Sudan. This does not lead to univocal conclusions, but rather to a myriad of observations on the working of global discourses.

First, we can see that the global discourse on development – and especially on women and peace building – affects the way in which local actors perform conflict. Interviewees in the SPLM/A, for instance, gave the impression that the movement's advocacy for including women and their capacities for peace was part of an effort to legitimize their movement in the eyes of the international community. In practice, space for women is not effectively created. On the other hand, the installation of women's desks, no matter how perfunctory, nonetheless provides some women with room to manoeuvre, to start discussing and expanding their roles in the movement and in Sudanese society. What starts out as the strategic embrace of a discourse may thus very well gain social reality in the end.

The case of the Sudanese Women's Voice for Peace in Nairobi provides a different picture. The international attention to women and peace building enlarges women's manoeuvring room, while the feminization of peace contributes to societal respect for women. But there are severe setbacks too. The case shows how misplaced the sense of identification and proximity with 'other' women can be and how easily it becomes in a globalized world to project one's images onto those 'others' and to mistake them for real. The case also reveals how damaging these mistakes are. Whereas both the Sudanese women and their supporters appeared to share common goals and intervention models, underlying cultural patterns and interests on both sides of the interface turned out to be stronger. Unintentionally, patterns and paces of change are imposed on local women, while the conditions for a meaningful political participation are lacking.

The case of the local SWVP women's group is yet again different. There, we see how a project fails, while the underlying discourse nonetheless gains meaning in the locality. At the start of the chapter we raised some questions about the use of T-shirts with printed English text in southern Sudan, suggesting they were mainly used to impress outsiders. However, in practice, the adoption of a discourse on women and peace does appear to make a difference. Even though the everyday coping practices of women stay the same, the symbolic meaning of these activities turns them into contributions to a more peaceful society. If this is true, then it does make perfect sense, after all, to wear the T-shirts in the isolated villages of southern Sudan. At the same time, the case brings out how discourse is being altered in local practice. Both the meaning of peace and the way it can be affected are renegotiated in the locality. The discourse on the feminization of peace works, but not in ways intended or predicted, and gains local meaning in the process.

Together, we believe these diverse observations corroborate the major tenet of this book. Globalization has a diverse impact on women and is altered by women's agency in their everyday practices. Our chapter has substantiated this principle for women and peace building. It particularly brings out the working of discourse in processes of globalization. On the one hand, global discourses are 'things' that can be imposed or strategically adopted in power-laden interactions. There is, however, a duality to discourse (Hilhorst, 2003). While discourses may be employed strategically, they tend to become real in ways that cannot be orchestrated but that are the cumulative result of everybody's agency. In the process, discourse is given local meanings. This is how the global becomes local.

Notes

1   Field notes of Mathijs van Leeuwen.
2   Additional interviews in 2002 and 2003 were conducted as part of evaluation missions.
3   The question remains, of course, whether the broadening of women's roles is sustainable (Byrne et al. 1995/1996).
4   For more information, see http://www.lysistrataproject.com.
5   Women in Black is an international peace network that started in Israel in 1988 and consists of groups of women coming together in vigils for peace. http://www.womeninblack.net.
6   Beijing Declaration and Platform for Action, 1995.
7   BBC news 7 January 2004.
8   Stocktaking of the Sudan Ecumenical Forum, 2001.
9   For a similar argumentation regarding post-communist Hungary civil society, see Miszlivetz and Ertsey, 1998.

References

Amnesty International (1995) *The Tears of Orphans*, London, Amnesty International.
Anderson, S. (1999) 'Women's Many Roles in Reconciliation' in: *People Building Peace: 35 Inspiring Stories from Around the World*, Utrecht, European Centre for Conflict Prevention, pp. 230-236.
Appadurai, A. (1995) 'The Production of Locality' in: R. Fardon (ed.) *Counterworks: Managing the Diversity of Knowledge*, London, New York, Routledge, pp. 204-223.
AU/IBAR (2003) *Pastoral Women as Peacemakers*, Community Based Health and Participatory Epidemiology (CAPE) Unit, Nairobi, African Union/Inter-African Bureau for Animal Resources.
Byrne, B., R. Marcus and T. Powers-Stevens (1995/1996) *Gender, Conflict and Development: Volume II: Case Studies Cambodia, Rwanda, Kosovo, Algeria, Somalia, Guatemala and Eritrea*, Brighton, Institute of Development Studies.
Christian Aid (2001) *The Scorched Earth: Oil and War in Sudan*, Christian Aid media report, London, Christian Aid.
Collier, P. (2000) *Economic Causes of Civil Conflict and their Implications for Policy*, Working Paper, Development Research Group, World Bank.
Davids, T. and F. van Driel (2001) 'Globalization and Gender: Beyond Dichotomies' in: F. J. Schuurman (ed.) *Globalization and Development Studies: Challenges for the 21st Century*, Amsterdam, Thela Thesis, London, Sage, pp.153-175.

Duffield, M. (2001) *Global Governance and the New Wars: The Merging of Development and Security*, London, Zed Books.

Enloe, C. (1990) *Bananas, Beaches and Bases, Making Feminist Sense of International Politics*, Berkeley, University of California Press.

Ferris, E. (1993) *Women, War and Peace*, Research Report, Uppsala, Life and Peace Institute.

FitzGerald, V. (1999) 'Global Linkages, Vulnerable Economies, and the Outbreak of Conflict', *Development*, 42(3): 57-64.

Frerks, G.E. (1998) *Omgaan met Rampen: Inaugurele Rede*, Wageningen: Landbouwuniversiteit.

Hilhorst, D. (2003) *The Real World of NGOs: Discourses, Diversity and Development*, London, New York, Zed Books.

Holsti, K.J. (1996) *The State, War and the State of War*, Cambridge, Cambridge University Press.

Kaldor, M. (1999/2001) *New and Old Wars: Organized Violence in a Global Era*, with an afterword, January 2001, Cambridge, Polity Press.

Kant, E. (1998) *Engendering Peace, Women, Armed Conflict and Reconciliation*, Women and Development Division, The Hague, Ministry of Foreign Affairs.

Leeuwen, M. Van (2004) *Local Initiatives for Peace in Southern Sudan and the Support Given to Those by Outsiders*, Utrecht, Pax Christi.

Lesch, A.M. (1998) *The Sudan: Contested National Identities*, Bloomington and Indianapolis, Indiana University Press, Oxford, James Currey.

Lindsey, C. (2001) *Women Facing War: ICRC Study on the Impact of Armed Conflict on Women*, Geneva, International Committee of the Red Cross.

Macrae, J. and A. Harmer (2003) *Humanitarian Action and the 'Global War on Terror: A Review of Trends and Issues'*, Humanitarian Policy Group Report, London, Overseas Development Institute.

Miszlivetz, F. and K. Ertsey (1998) 'Hungary Civil Society in the Post-Socialist World' in Alison Van Rooy (ed.) *Civil Society and the Aid Industry: The Politics and Promise*, London, Earthscan Publications Ltd., pp. 71-103.

Moser, C. and F. Clark (Ed., 2001) *Victims, Perpetrators or actors? Gender, Armed Conflict and Political Violence*, London, New York, Zed Books.

Pax Christi (1999) *Strengthening Civil Society Inside Southern Sudan: A Transformation to Peace*, Utrecht, Pax Christi.

Prendergast, J. (1997) *Crisis Response: Humanitarian Band-Aids in Sudan and Somalia*, London, Chicago, Illinois, Pluto Press.

Rupesinghe, K. (1996) *From Civil War to Civil Peace: Multi-Track Solutions to Armed Conflict*, Unpublished manuscript, London, International Alert.

Simonse, S. (1999-draft) *Opportunities and Constraints for Women Peace Groups in Southern Sudan*, Consultancy report commissioned by Pax Christi Netherlands, Utrecht, Pax Christi.

SPLM (2000) *Peace Through Development: Perspectives and Prospects in the Sudan*, Sudan People's Liberation Movement.

UNHCR (2003) *2002 Annual Statistical Report: Sudan*, Geneva, UNHCR.

Van Rooy, A. (1998) 'The Art of Strengthening Civil Society' in A. Van Rooy (ed.), *Civil Society and the Aid Industry: The Politics and Promise*, London, Earthscan Publications Ltd., pp. 197-220.

Verney, P. (1999) *Raising the Stakes; Oil and Conflict in Sudan*, West Yorkshire, Sudan Update.

World Bank (2000) *Poverty in an Age of Globalization*, Washington, D.C., The World Bank.

Chapter 7

Gendered Travels:
Single Mothers' Experiences at the
Global/Local Interface

Annelou Ypeij

Introduction

Sara (29), a divorced mother of three sons, was born in Morocco. Her migration to the Netherlands was not of her own choosing. It was a consequence of her forced marriage, which was arranged by her father. Her husband turned out to be a violent man. He raped her several times, twice resulting in pregnancies from which two of her sons were born. Despite her grief and shame, Sara told her life story with high spirits and energy. She certainly misses Morocco, but she is very definite in her decision to stay in Amsterdam.

Philomena (33) is from Surinam, a single woman and a mother of two. The relationship with the father of her children ended when she migrated to the Netherlands. She left her two small children behind with her sister in Paramaribo. After saving for years, she was able to pay for the children's plane tickets. At the time we met, she lived with her children in Amsterdam and she was proud to be working as a civic city guard.

Shirley (25) migrated from the Netherlands Antilles to Amsterdam with her mother when she was 13 years old. At the time of the interviews, she was a single mother of two children. She has a relationship with the father of her second child, but intends to break up with him by moving to a small town, northeast of Amsterdam. Counting on the support of her mother who already lives there, she hopes to be able to return to school.

Though these three women have different cultural backgrounds, life histories and migration trajectories, they share the experience of single motherhood and their migration to the Netherlands. As single mothers, they attract the attention of researchers and policymakers because they are supposedly in financial difficulties. As is argued through the feminization of poverty discourse, female heads of households supposedly belong to the poorest of the poor (Chant 1997). As migrants, the three women also provoke concern because the integration of migrants into a new society is often considered to be problematic. However, statistical data on the Netherlands show that women who migrate from Surinam are successful, considering their levels of education, income and participation in the job market. Regarding the latter, they even outperform indigenous Dutch women. Many Surinam women, especially Creole women, are single mothers (28 per cent of the total number of Suriname women in the Netherlands). In accordance with the severe criticism that the feminization of poverty discourse received, their single motherhood doesn't automatically result in low levels of job participation or high risks of poverty (for this criticism see Moore, 1994; Chant, 1997; Davids and van Driel, 2001). The participation of Antillean women in the Dutch job market, in general, is relatively high. However, being a single mother – as 38 per cent of the Antillean women in the Netherlands are – considerably reduces this participation. Moroccan mothers, whether married or not, have the lowest levels of education and job-market participation (Hooghiemstra and Merens, 1999, pp. 58, 69).

These data are intriguing because they suggest that many differences exist among migrant single mothers in the Netherlands. Nevertheless, it is my view that reducing the lives of Sara, Philomena and Shirley to levels of poverty, education and job participation in their new country will not do much to help understand the differences among them. Such a reductionistic approach negates their agency as architects of their own lives and doesn't do justice to the complex processes that direct their life trajectories (*cf.* Davids and van Driel, 2001). As migrants and as single mothers, the women's experiences can be placed in the context of two social trends that occur at a global scale, which are indications of the gendered character of globalization processes. The first trend is that worldwide, during the last decades, the number of single-mother households has risen considerably (Chant, 1997; Moore, 1994). The second trend concerns increasing flows of international migration, especially female migration. Somehow, the experiences of Sara, Philomena and Shirley are related to those gendered processes of globalization. This chapter attempts to place the experiences of the women within globalization processes by approaching migration as a process and by using a gender analysis.

Boyd and Grieco suggest that, to understand the experiences of female migrants, migration theory has to be sensitive to gender hierarchies. They criticize the neoclassical and push-pull demographic models of the 1970s and 1980s, which emphasized migration as a decision of rational individuals – which means male individuals. Even when, under the influence of gender studies, the household began to be integrated in their analyses, it was considered to be a harmonious entity. Decisions to migrate were, again, perceived as being taken in a calculating way with the aim of improving the well-being of all members of the household. Migrant women were mainly perceived as wives who willingly accompanied the migrant male (Boyd and Grieco, 2002). However, as the life histories of Sara, Philomena and Shirley show, migrant women are not always married. Furthermore, if they migrate as married women, their households – instead of being harmonious entities – may be venues of conflict and violence, as is shown by the case of Sara. Gender relations, hierarchies within families, the marital status of women and their potential motherhood affect the migration process. As a consequence, migration processes produce gendered outcomes that result in differences between migrant women and men and among migrant women themselves. In other words, migrants travel as gendered persons to new locations. Gender hierarchies, discourses and practices travel with them and are reinterpreted and redefined in the new locations.

The question is then how do migrant single mothers deal with gender hierarchies and discourses. What are the possibilities and limitations that they experience and how are gender hierarchies and discourses that have travelled from abroad redefined in the new location? Boyd and Grieco distinguish three stages where gender directs the process of migration: the pre-migration stage, the stage of transition across state boundaries and the post-migration stage in the new country. These stages relate the economic opportunities and gender hierarchies in the country of origin to the immigration policies and the experiences of the migrant in the new country. Moreover, the stages provide room for an analysis of the social relationships between the migrants and their families and friends who stayed behind.

As I will argue, transnational networks are important in understanding the experiences of the migrants. The organization of this chapter follows the distinction between the pre-migration stage, the transition stage and the post-migration stage. A comparison will be made between Surinamese, Antillean and Moroccan women. This is based on research in Amsterdam on poverty in the Dutch welfare state. Including Sara, Philomena and Shirley, we interviewed 36 women who are migrants and single mothers[1]. All women have an income around the social minimum level. Within the group of women interviewed, Sara represents an exceptional case. While the majority of the interviewees originate from Surinam or the Antilles, she is the only Moroccan woman. In my view, using her experiences as a starting point for a comparison between Surinamese, Antillean and Moroccan migrant women provides many additional insights into the gendered character of migration. The advantages of such an analysis outweigh the methodological problem of extrapolating an argument from a single case.

Pre-migration Stage

In this section I will make a comparison between Morocco, the birth country of Sara, and Surinam and the Antilles, where Philomena and Shirley were born. I will limit myself to the dominant gender discourses and practices that the women have to take into account and that may have limiting or enabling effects on their opportunities to migrate.

Morocco

In Morocco, notions concerning honour and shame are important for understanding the patriarchal relationships between women and men. Although the sexual division of labour ascribes to women care and household tasks, they are allowed to earn incomes, especially when this is agreed on in the marriage contract. Males are supposed to be breadwinners and to maintain the family. Male domination and authority is confirmed by Moroccan family law, legitimized by the husband's responsibility for the honour of the whole family. Wives may threaten the family's honour by indecent behaviour and by not showing respect or obedience to the authority of their husbands. To protect the family's honour, men try to control and limit the mobility of their wives and daughters. Practices of arranged marriages are commonplace, as is the practice of marrying off girls at an early age. Divorce is allowed and, as a matter of fact, Moroccan divorce rates are among the highest in the world, probably partly due to practices of repudiation of wives by their husbands. The social position of divorced women and single mothers is weak. They normally fall back on their families for economic security and are remarried off as soon as possible (Bartels, 1993; Mernissi, 1987; Eldering and Borm, 1996). The dominant position of men attributes to the fact that women who migrate often do so as dependent family members under the wings of their fathers and husbands. However, as the De Haas study shows, migration of men, especially international migration, may challenge gender hierarchies. It has a positive effect on girls' education. Besides, the generally well-educated and partly 'westernized' daughters of Moroccan families that live abroad may be important role models for female kin that have stayed behind. The fact that the number of Moroccan women who independently migrate to other countries has risen recently should be placed in this light (2003, pp. 196, 363).

Surinam and the Netherlands Antilles

The Creole family system in Suriname and the Antilles is often analyzed as a product of the colonial past and depicted as matrifocal in the literature (Terborg, 2002). Within this family system women are pivotal in both economic and emotional respects, while the roles of men as fathers and husbands tend to be more marginal. Motherhood comprises both effective care and responsibility for earning the household income. In this value system, sexual faithfulness to one partner and having children with one man are not always considered to be very important and single motherhood is commonplace. Marriage may be the ideal but is often associated with a civil status for the economically more successful. The bond between a mother and her children is the foundation of domestic units. While these units may exist independently as single-mother households, they may also include other relatives and thus give rise to extended households. Mutual support among female relatives characterizes this family system.

    In the Antilles, mothers frequently live and work within extended family networks. Such family networks provide women with more security than an individual male partner would. Although mothers ultimately bear individual responsibility for their children, they tend to share parenting and care with others (Venema, 1992; Dijke et al., 1992; Wekker, 1994). In the last decade, however, the economic crisis and poverty in Surinam and the Antilles have lead to a disintegration of female networks and an increase in women's dependency on men. Despite the matrifocal family system, gender hierarchies in the Creole community are also rooted in a patriarchal ideology. The latter is noticeable in the image of male authority and as heads of households. Men are inclined to restrict women's movements out of fear for their sexual infidelity. Women, however, only accept male authority when their partners' financial input in the household meets their expectations (Terborg, 2002). As the migration histories of the women we have interviewed show, because of their relative independence and autonomy, Surinamese and Antillean women can take the decision to migrate free from male interference. They are able to migrate individually, as single mothers or otherwise.

Most of the women interviewed migrated to escape from the poverty they experienced in their countries of origin. Only one woman from Hungary migrated as a political refugee. Two others, namely Sara and a Polish woman, migrated with the aim of being reunited with their husbands. For the majority of the other women, the hope of improving their living conditions – through receiving education and finding jobs or medical care – was the main reason to migrate. The eight women, who were single mothers before their migration, stated that being a single mother made their migration even more urgent because in Surinam and the Antilles, the countries they originated from, they lacked the economic means to raise their children on their own. Some women migrated immediately after they were separated from their husbands. Besides economic reasons, women may have additional reasons for leaving their countries of birth. I can identify only five cases among the women we interviewed where marriage and the nuclear family played a role in the migration of the women. None of the other women interviewed migrated together with a husband, as a marital strategy or as a child with both parents. They migrated as children with their single mothers, as an individual, as single mothers with their children or, as in one case, together with a sister. The image in the literature of married women who migrate with their husbands is not apparent in the migration histories of the women we interviewed.

Transition Across State Boundaries: Immigration Policies

Legal migration from one country to another is made possible by the immigration policies of the host country, in this case the Netherlands. During the second half of the twentieth century, various policies and programmes characterized international migration to the Netherlands. In the 1960s a flow of male labour migrants started from Mediterranean countries such as Morocco. Those labour migrants were recruited by large industrial companies and by bilateral governmental agreements with the aim of filling vacancies in Dutch industries. Initially, the migration was perceived as temporary, in the government's point of view as well as in that of many migrants. With the economic crisis of the early 1980s and increasing unemployment in the industrial sector, labour migration came to an end. Many migrants experienced financial difficulties, which made return migration problematic. The government developed the *family-reunion and family-formation immigration programme* that enabled the permanent migration of the wives and children of the male labour migrants. Also, potential wives and husbands were allowed to migrate and to form a new family with an already migrated person (Graaff, 2002, pp. 6-7).

Surinam, a former Dutch colony, became independent in 1975. In the years before complete independence, during the so-called transition period (1975-1979), the Dutch government gave migrants from Surinam an opportunity to choose between Surinamese or Dutch nationalities. Because of feelings of uncertainty about an independent Surinam, large numbers of Surinamese chose the Dutch Nationality and moved to the Netherlands to settle permanently during the second half of the 1970s. As of 1980, free migration from Surinam was no longer permitted. Currently, Surinamese migration is only possible under the above-mentioned family-reunion/formation programme or under the so-called *political asylum programme* that allows the entrance of political refugees. Concerning the Netherlands Antilles, another former Dutch colony, the decolonization process has not (yet) resulted in independence of the island group. Though its status is one of self-governance, the island group is still part of the Dutch Kingdom. This means that Antilleans have Dutch nationality. They can migrate and take up residency in the Netherlands freely. Migration from the Antilles tends to fluctuate with the economic situation on the islands. With the closing of the Shell refinery on Curacao in 1985 and, more particularly, during the last decade, large numbers of poor, unemployed Antilleans have tried their luck in the Netherlands (Hulst, 1997; Niekerk, 2000; Oostindie and Klinkers, 2001).

Comparing migration under the family-reunion/formation programme with that from the former colonies reveals an important difference. The family-reunion/formation programme is based on the notion of the nuclear household with the breadwinning male and the dependent wife and children. People are allowed to migrate as dependent wives, children, and potential marital partners. The policy of free migration from the former colonies is based on the historical ties between the 'mother country' and former colonies. This migration policy lacks the gender bias of the family-reunion/formation programme. In the past, it has allowed all Surinamese, regardless of marital status or gender, to migrate to the Netherlands. Nowadays, it is still possible for Antilleans to move freely to the Netherlands, as individuals or as members of larger families. Since the Antilles are still part of the Dutch Kingdom, Antilleans' migration does not have the permanent character of that of the Surinamese. Antilleans can always return to the Antilles, while Surinamese need a visa to visit their country of origin and return migration is complicated by complex bureaucratic procedures[2].

The majority of the women we interviewed come from the former Dutch colonies and their migration histories followed the above pattern. Most Surinamese respondents came to the Netherlands before the 1980s, and most Antillean women during the 1990s. Two women, including Sara, migrated under the family-reunion/formation programme. This meant that their residence permits depended on those of their husbands. Women who migrate as dependent wives and who divorce their husbands within three years after their migration lose their residence permits and have to return to their countries of origin. Women who divorce their husbands between five and ten years after their arrival in the Netherlands are entitled to residence permits under specific conditions, such as having children under six years old, speaking fluent Dutch, having a job with an income above the poverty level or giving up one's own nationality. Only after a stay in the

Netherlands of more than ten years are migrant women entitled to residence permits without any conditions (Hooghiemstra and Niphuis-Nell, 1995, pp. 52-55; Clara Wichmann Instituut, 2000).

Divorced women from North Africa and other Islamic countries who have migrated under the family-reunion/formation programme may be in a particularly disadvantaged position. For example, the Islamic-based family law of Morocco still doesn't acknowledge a divorce that is pronounced under Dutch law, though a thorough reform of the family was implemented as of February 2004. It is nearly impossible for women who are not divorced under Moroccan law to visit their families in Morocco. They may be accused of not fulfilling their marital obligations or run the risk that their ex-husband and his family will take away the children because they are considered to belong to the husband's family (Jonkers, 2003, p. 104; Eldering and Borm, 1996, p. 62). Moroccan women such as Sara, who are married to abusive husbands, may be forced to postpone their divorces. Although, as divorced women, they may have to leave the Netherlands, returning to Morocco is not an option[3].

At this point of the analysis, the conclusion is justified that, in the case of female migration from Morocco to the Netherlands, women's subordination and gender hierarchies – characteristic of Moroccan patriarchy – are being reconstructed through the Dutch family-reunion/formation programme. Also, in the case of Surinamese and Antillean women, the migration policy towards residents from the former colonies reconfirms existing gender relations. However, in the case of Antillean women, who can migrate freely regardless of gender or marital state, the migration policy reconfirms their autonomy and not their dependence within the matrifocal family system, as was the case in the past with Surinamese migrant women.

Transition Across States Boundaries: The Emergence of Transnational Networks

What is so specific for our new era of globalization is not migration in itself – people have been migrating ever since the early stages of mankind – but the speed with which international migration is taking place and the fact that, through international air travel, telecommunication and global banking systems, distances are being compressed. This enables migrants to maintain intensive contacts with their families and friends that have stayed behind. Those contacts have created transnational networks through which people move back and forth, send money to each other, find their marriage partners and take care of new or returned migrants. People tend to migrate to those countries to which their transnational networks extend (Staring 2001). Present research confirms these insights. For the two women who migrated under the family-reunion/formation programme, the transnational networks functioned as a marriage market. At the time that Sara was married off, she was living with her father and his second wife in Brussels, Belgium. Her father used his transnational network to find her a husband. A friend of his who lived in Amsterdam was prepared to marry his daughter. On the occasion of the engagement, during the holidays, Sara travelled to her family in Morocco, where she met her husband for the first time.

For the Surinamese and Antillean women, the existence of transnational networks was an important incentive for migrating to the Netherlands. As I have stated before, mutual support among female relatives characterizes the matrifocal family system. Family members may facilitate the voyage of new migrants, both by offering support on leaving Surinam and the Antilles and on settling down in the Netherlands. As the case of Philomena shows, she left her children in the care of her sister in Paramaribo and built a life in the Netherlands before she sent for her children six years later. Migration may also be motivated by the wish to live close to migrated family members. A Surinamese woman of 41 years old, who migrated at the age of sixteen, answered our question as to why she migrated to the Netherlands as follows:

> Well, for a better future. Because you live in Surinam and your sister lives in the Netherlands. You hear about the Netherlands in Surinam: You have better chances there. You are born in Surinam and you don't belong to the highest classes. My mother was a single mother. Then you are poorly off. And you have an older sister who says: I will send for you, so you can go to school here and study better. So she sends for you and in that way you arrive in the Netherlands.

The migrated family members gave information about the Netherlands and their life styles. They may stimulate and actually support other family members to migrate, too. Many women related that, after their arrival in the Netherlands, they started living in the houses of their female kin. The previously migrated family members served as a safety net and a springboard for the recently arrived. New migrants receive shelter, emotional and practical support that makes it easier to start a new life in the Netherlands. Having family in the Netherlands makes the decision to migrate easier.

Migrants' Experiences in the Host Countries: Gender Dynamics

The Netherlands may be characterized as a rapidly changing society where gender relations undergo a constant process of reformulating and redefining. In the 1960s, marriages between women and men, including the traditional division of labour between them, were regarded as normal and socially desirable. Married women were responsible for household chores and childcare, while their husbands had jobs outside the home to support the family. Since then, women have entered the Dutch labour force in massive numbers. Marriage as a socially desirable and lifetime form of coexistence between women and men has become the subject of heated debates. Nowadays, one third of marriages end in divorce (Hooghiemstra, 1997, p. 35). Alternative forms of coexistence, such as 'living-apart-together' relationships, unmarried cohabitation and single-mother families are on the rise. Although the sexual division of labour has changed significantly, the trend has not entirely eroded traditional notions. In fact, studies reveal that even though the daily activities of women and men are becoming more similar, women remain responsible for most of the childcare, while men perform the lion's share of paid employment. Women may take paid jobs but tend to consider this a matter of choice. The idea that nobody can take care of the children as well as the mother is still very vivid (Hooghiemstra, 2000, pp. 106, 121; Hooghiemstra and Keuzenkamp, 2000, p. 125).

Social policy tends to reflect gender discourses and transformations – and the Netherlands is no exception. In the literature, the Dutch welfare system has been defined as a strong, male breadwinner state, though the system is currently being reformed at a rapid pace (Plantenga, 1999). Social provisions were initially designed based on the notion of the male breadwinner and the caring wife. If a husband's income was lost through his death or the couple's divorce, the state replaced the income of the male breadwinner. Between the 1960s and 1980s, single mothers' income was rather steadily secured by a general policy that facilitated full time care. This strong state focus on women as caretakers and men as breadwinners has also contributed to the definition of care as a private matter of the family and of women, which subsequently results in a scarcity of public care provisions. With the New Assistance Act of 1996, the position of single mothers changed. The state no longer automatically replaces the incomes of male breadwinners and the status of full-time motherhood is no longer undisputed. Nowadays, single mothers are increasingly considered to be workers and, to be eligible for benefits, they are required to be available for entering the job market (Bussemaker et al., 1997, pp. 48-49; Plantenga, 1999, pp. 14-15).

Women who migrate to the Netherlands arrive in a society where gender discourses express ambiguity and contradictory messages. Women's importance for the labour force is stressed, along with their traditional roles as full-time caretakers, mothers and wives. In the case of single mothers, although they are entitled to welfare benefits, the conditions are becoming more and more strict. Increasingly, unemployment or social security benefits are only intended to cover a short period without work. For migrant single mothers such as Sara, Philomena and Shirley, who came to the Netherlands with their own interpretations of gender relations, the ambiguities and contradictions that they encounter in the Netherlands may enable them to seize opportunities, resulting in a variety of reinterpretations and redefinitions.

Within the matrifocal family-system of the Caribbean, motherhood is defined as emotional as well as material care. 'Your first husband is your diploma' is a popular saying used by the interviewees (*cf.* Terborg, 2002, p. 278; Distelbrink, 2000, p. 44). It expresses the need for women to rely on themselves and earn their own living, instead of counting on their husbands' support. Philomena, for example, migrated from Paramaribo to Rotterdam, the Netherlands' second largest city. She lived there for several years and tried to find a job without success, while living off her social-security benefits. Then she heard of a subsidized job programme in Amsterdam. Since she was very determined to find a job, she decided to move to Amsterdam and to try her luck there. During the interview, she expressed her happiness that she was able to get a job as a civic city guard. It is not without reason that Creole-Surinamese single mothers participate in the Dutch labour market in large numbers (Mérove and Merens, 2004, p. 91; Niekerk, 2000, p. 233). As a result of their self-definition of caretakers and income providers, they take advantage of the opportunities offered by the Dutch labour market.

Interviews with other Creole-Suriname and Antillean respondents demonstrate that – within the Dutch context – they have reinterpreted and redefined notions of motherhood and parenthood. Given the deplorable economic conditions in Suriname and the Antilles, women are often unable to subsist without financial assistance from a male partner, despite their pursuit of economic and emotional independence. Financial contributions from male partners need to be reciprocated by what Creole women refer to as 'bedroom duties', i.e. a woman's sexual obligations toward her partner in exchange for the goods and services received from him (Wekker, 1994, p. 127). Because men often dominate women, women genuinely fear that they will lose control over their lives by accepting such financial contributions. In the Netherlands, as mentioned before, single mothers with small children are entitled to welfare benefits, which protects women from becoming financially dependent on men. Shirley, who is on welfare, explained that she had lived with one of the fathers of her two children. She kicked him out when he became involved with another woman. For a long time he didn't give her any support, because he was upset that he had been dumped. He has recently started giving her money, hoping to resume sexual relations with her. Shirley, however, was not interested. Her welfare benefits enabled her to break the vicious cycle of financial contributions from men in return for sexual favours. It also improved Shirley's negotiating leverage with respect to the father. She said that she might resume sexual relations with the father in the future, but that first she wanted him to become more involved in raising her child. As a mother, she was using her sexual favours to renegotiate the matrifocal values with respect to fatherhood. Her benefits enabled her to increase her autonomy towards her child's father.

The benefits to which single mothers are entitled in the Netherlands enable them to be full-time mothers. Some women experience their social-security benefit as an opportunity to be full-time mothers. This tendency, however, has little material basis as a general redefinition of motherhood among Surinamese and Antillean women, since the Dutch state is increasingly questioning single mothers' entitlements to social-security benefits. Besides, full-time care may not always be the result of free choice. Since public nursery facilities are scarce in the Netherlands, single mothers – especially those without a support network – may find it hard to combine care and paid work. Other women are full-time mothers because they cannot work for health reasons. One woman interviewed was a kidney patient, another one had breast cancer and two women had seriously ill children who needed full-time care. The migration of these women gave them access to health care and financial security through their social-security benefits.

Literature concerning the Moroccan gendered notions of honour and shame make clear that, through migration, cultural notions may receive different emphases in the context of Dutch society. Moroccan migrants, men as well as women, consider the behaviour of indigenous Dutch women as indecent and shameful. Bartels argues that the threat of dishonourable femininity within Dutch society places emphasis on the sexual morality of Moroccan women. This leads to a further limiting of mobility and autonomy of women. Women whose husbands have migrated before them may have experienced some liberties while still living in Morocco. After their arrival in the Netherlands they are very dependent on their husbands. They do not speak the language and they are unfamiliar with the structures of Dutch society. On a daily basis, they have to adapt to their husbands whom they do not know very well. Women may become very isolated, especially in the early stages after their migration to the Netherlands (Bartels, 1993, p. 197-199). Marital problems and husbands who mistreat their wives are often reported among Moroccan couples. Sara, who is divorced because of her abusive husband, cannot relate to this period of her life without choking up. However, she has no intention of returning to Morocco, not only because her Dutch divorce isn't valid there, but also because she enjoys the freedom of Dutch society, her financial autonomy through her social-security benefit and the opportunity to develop as a person (*cf.* Eldering and Borm, 1996, p. 62). At the time of the interviews, she had intensive contacts with welfare workers who prepared her for the job market with a Dutch language course and other training. The Dutch juridical system enabled her to divorce her husband; the Dutch welfare system enabled her to become financially independent and to get an education.

Moroccan women, who came to the Netherlands as daughters, show a different pattern. More often than their mothers, they acquire an education and find jobs. Gender relations may be especially challenged when they marry men from Morocco, which many young Moroccan women do (Hooghiemstra, 2003). In cases where men migrate as potential husbands to marry women who already live or were born in the Netherlands, the Dutch family-reunion/formation programme may support this challenging of gender relations. Under this programme, the woman needs to have an independent income from work before the potential husband is allowed to migrate. As research shows, during their marriage, these women keep working. Their new husbands need to learn the language and to integrate in the Dutch labour market. They are dependent on their wives for their residents' permits (Jonkers, 2003). The migration policy confirms the daughters' wishes for autonomy. In the process, Moroccan patriarchal relations are being undermined. The dependent status of the husband may be an explanation for the rising divorce rates among young Moroccan couples in the Netherlands.

Migrants' Experiences in the Host Countries: Transnational Networks

The interviews with the majority of the single mothers provide evidence of the exchange of emotional, material and practical support among family members, irrespective of whether they have migrated. As stated above, within the matrifocal family system mutual support among female kin and friends is very commonplace. The interviewees mentioned cousins, sisters, mothers and aunts as their main sources of support (Ypeij and Steenbeek, 2001). The women are often as close to aunts on their mothers' side as they are to their own mothers, and the children of these aunts are like sisters to them. Among Surinamese and Antillean female family members, the emotional involvement and trust in each other runs very deep. An Antillean woman and mother of two children stated:

> We help each other, my family and I. The four of us form a unit: my aunt, my sisters, my cousin and myself. When I go to class in the evening, my cousin baby-sits for me. If one of us has problems, we get together. That's how we live. My sisters and my mother are the most important of all, but my mom lives in Curacao. She sends things for the kids, especially trousers.

Her last remark shows that social support is being exchanged between migrants and family members who have stayed behind. Contacts between the country of origin and the Netherlands are maintained intensively in various cases. Gifts and money are sent back and forth. However, since the intensification of the economic crisis in Surinam as well as in the Antilles, money flows have increasingly moved in one direction – towards the Caribbean. The exchange of social support between female kin is related to notions of motherhood and the matrifocal family system. Many Antillean and Surinamese mothers raise their children without involvement of the fathers, but this does not mean that they are on their own (Dijke et al., 1992; Wekker, 1994). Referring to them as single mothers is ethnocentric. As mothers, they rely on people other than the fathers, especially their female kin. When a woman becomes a mother, the exchange network is mobilized. The efforts the women make to help their female kin to migrate to the Netherlands should be placed in this context. If their family kin live close by, they are able to receive the social support they need as single mothers and they are able to combine paid work with care more easily (Distelbrink, 2000, p. 46). Also, the formation of extended households, a common practice within the matrifocal family system, should be seen in this light. As the interviews show, after their migration to Amsterdam, the majority of the interviewed Surinamese and Antillean mothers lived in extended households with other female kin for a certain period of time. The interviews with Surinamese and Antillean women make clear that the support networks may offer women opportunities to migrate and start new lives as single mothers in the Netherlands. Simultaneously, through the exchange of support, the notions of motherhood as emotional and material care, in relation to the support of female kin, are being reconstructed.

Not all interviewees are so well connected that they have access to support networks after their migration. Within the literature, especially the situation of Antillean single mothers has been described as one of social isolation and loneliness (Dijke et al., 1992; Zwaard, 1999). An explanatory factor might be that migrant networks tend to be ethnically homogeneous. Because the migration from the Antilles only took on massive proportions during the last decade, Antillean single mothers might need more time to establish satisfactory networks. Another factor is that Antillean single mothers may find difficulties combining care with a paid job. In their countries of origin, many women were able to work because their female family helped them with their care tasks (Dijke et al., 1992). In the Netherlands, they may lack the support of female kin and friends, public nursery facilities are scarce and they are forced to live on the dole (Mérove and Merens, 2004, p. 125). Their relative poverty may complicate maintaining contacts with kin that live further away. Also, return migration to the Antilles is occurring at a relatively large scale. This may result in fragmented, only partially functioning, networks on both sides of the ocean. Our own interviews do not particularly show that Antillean mothers are isolated, which may be related to the small number of interviewees. However, social isolation does occur among the interviewees. In some cases it may be compensated by support from family members abroad.

Also, Sara's interview contains many references to the fact that her life was characterized by long periods of social isolation and loneliness. When she arrived in Amsterdam with her husband at the age of sixteen, they moved into her parents-in-law's house. Despite her husband's infidelity, long periods of absence, aggressiveness and unwillingness to give her money, her mother-in-law persuaded her time and again to stay with him. Only when Sara moved with her husband to another house, where she became friends with a Dutch couple next door, did she realize that she could change her situation. With their support, Sara managed to get police protection against her violent husband, to divorce him under Dutch law, to apply for welfare and to move to another house, this time in her own name. She stated:

> My whole life was in the dark. I was always closed in the house, always in the dark. I was always scared. But I did two things, I got the divorce and I moved into the new house. Now I am not scared anymore. I am free. Nobody is the boss about me. I feel strong. I am going to give my children a future. I am a mother and a father for my children. I am a man in a woman, because I want to live alone with my children.

Sara paid a high price for being free and having a new future. She had to break with her parents-in-law and her father. She was stigmatized by the Moroccan community, which might have offered her friendship and support during the difficult time of her divorce. Moroccan women started gossiping about her and called her a 'bad woman'. Sara turned her back on the Moroccan community and did her utmost to make new contacts with people from other ethnic backgrounds (*cf.* Eldering and Born, 1996, pp. 91, 107). At the time of the interviews, she had a Pakistani friend who had proposed marriage to her. Sara's forced isolation from her community and family made her very sad. But, simultaneously, it opened up avenues to a new life, to a new future and to friendships outside her community. As an independent mother with many responsibilities living on social-security benefit, she might not be willing to give up her autonomy for a marriage based on traditional gender roles and the subordination of the wife.

Final Remarks

To understand the lives of migrant women, it is important to analyze their migration as a process and to realize that gender directs all stages of that process. As this comparative study has shown, Surinamese and Antillean women have been able to migrate as autonomous persons. In their countries of origin, the matrifocal value system attributed to the fact that they could take the decision to migrate as individuals, a position that was reconfirmed through the immigration policy of the Dutch government. In the Netherlands, Surinamese women in particular have been able to rebuild their support networks of female kin. Due to these networks, they have been able to reconstruct the matrifocal notion of motherhood as a combination of material responsibility and care. But the Dutch context also allowed for reinterpretations of gender notions, such as the redefinition of motherhood as full-time care or fatherhood as social responsibility.

As the case of Sara shows, it is much harder for Moroccan women to migrate to the Netherlands as individuals. In the case of female migrants, the patriarchal interpretation of gender notions is reconfirmed through the family-formation/reunion policy of the Dutch government. Once in the Netherlands, Moroccan women may have difficulties with their residence permits and divorce under Dutch and Moroccan law can be complicated. If they are able to overcome these limitations, they might be eligible to receive social-security benefits. However, stigmatization by other Moroccan people could lead to social isolation. Fortunately, Sara had the strength to become 'a man in a woman' and to build a new life that included a multi-ethnic network. Also, the transnational networks of Antillean women may be too fragmented to offer support and emotional satisfaction. Many Antillean single mothers experience social isolation, loneliness, welfare dependency and poverty. These cases make clear that we should not be too romantic about migrants' transnational networks. Also, the Netherlands is a rapidly changing society. Migration policies are characterized by ever increasing restrictions. Nowadays, Surinamese can only migrate under the family-reunion/formation policy; in other words, as dependent men and women, as daughters and wives. Welfare transformations threaten the position of single mothers, regardless of their ethnicity. Single mothers' access to social security has been severely reduced. The Dutch government no longer intends to replace the role of the male breadwinner and increasingly forces single mothers to work. Nevertheless, public nursery provisions remain scarce. Finally, not least important, the economic recession has reduced job opportunities.

As migrants and single mothers, the women interviewed provoke the concern of policymakers and researchers who conceive their situation as problematic. However, the present analysis shows that the women are capable of building new lives. Contrary to the feminization of poverty discourse, they are not victims of their situations. I would certainly not deny the fact that they may encounter many problems and severe limitations, including financial ones, but they are very active in dealing with them, in finding solutions and making decisions, particularly by redefining gender notions and discourses. The ambiguity and contradictions within the gender discourses that migrant women encountered in the Netherlands may offer room for new interpretations and deconstruction of existing meanings. As daughters, migration policy may enable women to marry men from their countries of origin and to challenge traditional gender relations. Because of their entitlement to welfare, married women have opportunities to leave their husbands and become single mothers. As single mothers, they can choose between a combination of work and care and being full-time mothers. As a result of their migration, their gender interpretations are being shuffled, redefined, and reinterpreted. Gender discourses are being mixed into a new brew.

This opens up new room to manoeuvre. It enables single mothers to seize opportunities unknown in their country of origins. At the global/local interface, the combination of migration and single motherhood may turn women's agency into an engine of gender change and transformation.

Notes

1   The women were interviewed between 1997 and 1999. We spoke with 22 mothers from Surinam, eight mothers from the Antilles and six women who came from Hungary, Poland, Morocco, the Caribbean, and Ghana. I would like to thank the Ministry of Social Affairs and Employment, the Ministry of Health, Welfare and Sport and NWO/MaGW for their subsidies and financial support, which made this research possible.

2   See Palet Newsletter December 2002 published on the web (http://www.paletweb.nl/nieuwsbrief/dec2002/4.htm).

3   The Dutch government is considering granting residence permits to battered wives on humanitarian grounds (NRC, 18-10-2003, 'Mishandelde partner krijgt verblijfstitel' page 3). Women who are divorced under Dutch law have to start separate divorce proceedings under Moroccan law, which takes six months (NRC, 10-02-2004, 'Vrouw kan niet meer worden gedumpt' page 5).

References

Bartels, Edien (1993), *Eén Dochter is Beter dan Duizend Zonen: Arabische Vrouwen, Symbolen en Machtsverhoudingen Tussen de Seksen*, Utrecht, Jan van Arkel.

Boyd, Monica and Elizabeth Grieco (2002), *Women and Migration: Incorporating Gender into International Migration Theory*, Washington, D. C., Migration Policy Institute.

Bussemaker, J., A. van Drenth, T. Knijn and J. Platenga, 1997, 'Lone Mothers in the Netherlands' in J. Lewis (ed.) *Lone Mothers in European Welfare Regimes: Shifting Policy Logics*, London: Jessica Kingsley Publishers, pp. 96-120.

Chant, Sylvia, 1997, *Women-headed Households: Diversity and Dynamics in the Developing World*, London, Macmillan.

Clara Wichmann Institute (2000), *Commentaar van het Clara Wichmann Instituut inzake Notie over de vreemdelingrechtelijke rechtspositie van vrouwen in het vreemdelingenbeleid*, 8 May, www.clara-wichmann.nl.

Davids, Tine, and Francien van Driel (2001), 'Globalization and Gender: Beyond Dichotomies', in F. Schuurman (ed.), *Globalization and Development Studies: Challenges for the 21ˢᵗ Century*, London, Sage, pp. 153-177.

Dijke, A. van, H. van Hulst and L. Terpstra (1990), *Mama soltera: de positie van alleenstaande Curaçaose en Arubaanse moeders in Nederland*, The Hague, Warray.

Distelbrink, Marjolijn (2000), *Opvoeden zonder man: Opvoeding en ontwikkeling in Creools-Surinaamse een- en tweeoudergezinnen in Nederland*, Assen, Van Gorcum.

Eldering, Lotty and Julie-Anne Borm (1996), *Alleenstaande Marokkaanse moeders*, Utrecht, Jan van Arkel.

Graaff, Thomas de (2002), *Migration, Ethnic Minorities and Networks Externalities*, Amsterdam, Thesis Publishers.

Haas, Hein de (2003), *Migration and Development in Southern Morocco: The Disparate Socio-Economic Impacts of Out-Migration on the Todgha Oasis Valley*, PhD. thesis, Nijmegen, Catholic University of Nijmegen.

Hooghiemstra, Erna (1997), 'Demografische ontwikkelingen', in M. Niphuis-Nell (ed.) *Sociale Atlas van de vrouw. Deel 4. Veranderingen in de primaire leefsfeer*, Rijswijk, SCP, The Hague, Vuga, pp. 17-52.

Hooghiemstra, Erna (2000), 'Denken over verdelen', in S. Keuzenkamp and E. Hooghiemstra (eds.), *De kunst van het combineren: Taakverdeling onder partners*, The Hague, SCP, pp. 101-24.

Hooghiemstra, Erna (2003), *Trouwen over de grens: Achtergronden van partnerkeuze van Turken en Marokkanen in Nederland*, The Hague, SCP.

Hooghiemstra, Erna and S. Keuzenkamp (2000), 'Verdienerstypen en de kunst van het combineren', in S. Keuzenkamp and E. Hooghiemstra (eds.), *De kunst van het combineren: Taakverdeling onder partners*, The Hague, SCP, pp. 124-44.

Hooghiemstra, B.T.J. and J.G.F. Merens (1999), *'Variatie in participatie: Achtergronden van arbeidsdeelname van allochtone en autochtone vrouwen'*, The Hague, SCP.

Hooghiemstra, Erna and M. Niphuis-Nell (1995), *Sociale atlas van de vrouw: deel 3: allochtone vrouwen*, The Hague, SCP.

Hulst, Hans van (1997), *Morgen bloeit het diabaas: De Antilliaanse volksklasse in de Nederlandse samenleving*, Amsterdam, Amsterdam University Press.

Jonkers, Marina (2003), *Een miskende revolutie: Het moederschap van Marokkaanse vrouwen*, Amsterdam, Aksant.

Mernessi, Fatima (1987) *Beyond the Veil: Male-Female Dynamics in Modern Muslim Society. Revised Edition*, Bloomington and Indianapolis, Indiana University Press.

Mérove, Gijbert and Ans Merens (Ed.), (2004*), Emancipatie in estafette: De positie van vrouwen uit etnische minderheden*, The Hague, SCP, Rotterdam: ISEO.

Moore, Henriette (1994), *Is there a crisis in the family?* Geneva, World Summit for Social Development, Occasional paper 3.

Niekerk, M. (2000), *De Krekel en de Mier: Fabels en Feiten over Maatschappelijke Stijging van Creoolse en Hindoestaanse Surinamers in Nederland*, Amsterdam, Spinhuis.

Oostindie, Gert and Inge Klinkers (2001), *Het Koninkrijk in de Caraïben: Een korte geschiedenis van het Nederlandse dekolonisatiebeleid, 1940-2000*, Amsterdam, Amsterdam University Press.

Plantenga, J. (1999), *Alleenstaande moeders en de systematiek van de verzorgingsstaat: Een vergelijkend onderzoek naar de sociaal economische positie van alleenstaande moeders in Nederland, Denemarken, Duitsland, het Verenigd Koninkrijk en Italië*, Utrecht, AWSB.

Staring, Richard (2001), *Reizen onder regie: Het migratieproces van illegale Turken in Nederland*, Amsterdam, Het Spinhuis.

Terborg, Julia (2002), *Liefde en conflict: Seksualiteit en gender in de Afro-Surinaamse familie*, PhD. thesis, Amsterdam, University of Amsterdam.

Venema, Tijo (1992), *Famiri Nanga Kulturu: Creoolse sociale verhoudingen en Winti in Amsterdam*, Amsterdam, Het Spinhuis.

Wekker, Gloria (1994), *Ik ben een gouden munt: Constructies van subjectiviteit en seksualiteit van Creoolse vrouwen in Paramaribo*, Amsterdam, Vita.

Ypeij, Annelou and Gerdien Steenbeek (2001), 'Poor Single Mothers and Cultural Meanings of Social Support', *Focaal – European Journal of Anthropology*, 38, pp. 71-82.

Zwaard, Joke (1999), *Met hulp van vriendinnen: Moeders uit lage inkomensgroepen over rondkomen en vooruitkomen*, Utrecht, SWP.

Chapter 8

Reproductive Rights Violations: A Comparison of Export-Oriented Industries in Mexico and Morocco

Fenneke Reysoo[1]

Introduction

The debate on gender and globalization has come a long way and Davids and van Driel have taken up a challenging endeavour by inviting us to analyze how globalizing processes are mediated by local contexts, actors and meaning systems. Although globalization has been conceptualized as pervasive and all-encompassing, we – the contributors to this book – took a common stance against globalization as an autonomous, external and homogeneous force. In order to understand the mediation of global processes at local level, ethnographic research takes us to concrete arenas where social actors develop strategies to earn their livings. Or, as Kalb (2000, p. 20) put it, 'empirical analyses tend to convey the idea that the process and outcomes of globalization depend on social power relationships, local development paths, territorially engraved social institutions and the nature of possible action within social networks, and cannot simply be deducted from any general framework (…)'. For a number of scholars within the CERES (Netherlands) research school, this has led to a programmatic approach in which scholars are sensitive to accounting for complexity, contingency, diversity and contradiction (also see Kalb, Pansters and Siebers, 2004).

The intellectual puzzle presented in this chapter originates from two interesting observations in my fieldwork settings[2]. In the maquila sector of Mexico, women have to undergo pregnancy screenings upon recruitment and are more or less forced to quit their jobs once pregnant, whereas in another labour frontier country, Morocco, female workers are not subjected to pregnancy tests and hardly any information is available as to pregnancy-related dismissals. I was puzzled by this state of affairs and I wondered if the occurrence (Mexico) and the absence (Morocco) of pregnancy discrimination could be explained by a difference in gender representations. In an era of globalized economic restructuring, the Mexican and Moroccan governments have elaborated comparable strategic development policies to attract direct foreign investments but, as we noticed, firm management recurs in different recruitment practices. How can we understand the production of these differences at the local level? My aim is to reflect on the articulation of management's practices regarding (potentially) pregnant workers and local gender representations and identities.

Before delving into the multifaceted outcomes of recruitment practices at the local level, I first present a quick overview of the creation of export-oriented manufactories in both Mexico and Morocco. I then elaborate on the characteristics of the female workforce in these industrial factories. More precisely, why do these firms preferably recruit and employ young female workers? The gendered context of this workforce is questioned in terms of socio-economic changes and transformations of gender identities and relations. My focus on pregnancy-screening practices touches upon the ambivalence of the productive and reproductive capacities of women. Firm management tends to combine the exigencies of a globalized monetary logic and the constraints related to local cultures. Comparing the Mexican and Moroccan local contexts provides insight into the production of differences.

Export-Oriented Industries in Mexico and Morocco

The creation of Free Trade Zones for export-oriented industrial factories, among others, is part of the globalization of the world market economy and the liberalization of global trade. Under pressure of various policies of the International Financial Institutions (IMF and World Bank) and with the creation of the North American Free Trade Alliance (NAFTA) and the Barcelona Agreements, both countries under review have become integrated in a process of constructing free-trade areas through economic and financial partnerships. Demographic growth exceeded economic growth and both governments had to formulate policies aimed at the creation of jobs for the increasing number of unemployed or underemployed. It led to a profound restructuring of their domestic economies. Import-substituting industries had to close down and export-oriented industries took over.

International companies oriented towards the world market were seeking ways of reducing the overall costs of production and looking for consumer markets closer to home. They weighed infrastructural, marketing and political conditions against legal contexts and the availability of cheap labour, especially labour-intensive companies such as assembly lines or textile manufacturers. Manufacturers were attracted by all kinds of incentives, such as tax-free privileges, provision of infrastructure, easy profit repatriation, 'total or partial exemption from laws and decrees of the country concerned' (Ong, 1991, p. 283) and the abundant availability of cheap labour, not only in terms of low wages, but also little or no employee protection, few or no employers' contributions to social charges, etc. In this international game, the national economies of Mexico and Morocco, as many others, are dependent on companies' decisions to stay or to change the locations of their production factories. In our age of time-space compression, lower wages in Bangladesh, for example, have delocalized textile industries from Morocco as a consequence; and Central American countries are drawing companies out of the Mexican maquila sector[3].

Over the last three decades Mexican and Moroccan governments have constantly tried to attract and to keep these industries within their national borders in order to create wealth (GNP) and employment. In the 1960s, for example, Mexico created the maquila sector in the northern frontier area. The majority of the industrial factories were assembly lines (cars, computers) or textile manufactories. U.S. legislation (Offshore Assembly Provision) made it possible to export semi-manufactured products to be assembled abroad and to pay only taxes on the value added offshore. On the Mexican side, the law allowed the exemption of taxes on semi-manufacture on condition that they be exported after assembly. U.S. companies took advantage of cheap labour and – as a derivative – prevented Mexicans from migrating to the US. Many Mexicans from other parts of the country migrated to the Northern provinces and cities (Tijuana, Ciudad Juárez, Nuevo Laredo, Matamoros etc.), among them many young women, sisters who joined their brothers, friends who accompanied friends (Zagema, 2003, pp. 29, 41, 43, 50).

Morocco is another labour frontier country. Whereas Mexico lies at the southern side of the US, Morocco faces the European Union. Its government has focused on boosting textile and clothing industries and has made foreign investments attractive by creating Free Trade Zones in the outskirts of cities like Tangier, Rabat-Salé and Casablanca (Anon., 2002). Moroccan textile and clothing industries benefited from relocation of French and British clothing industries in the 1980s. During the period 1984-1990, employment growth in the export sector was 24.5 per cent annually, compared to 2.8 per cent annual growth in the domestic sector. However, real wages in the export sector declined by 2.6 per cent per annum, while they increased 1.6 per cent per annum in the domestic sector (which reflects the weakness of unionization in the export sector). Lower paid and temporary employment increased two-and-a-half times as fast as total employment. It resulted in a massive incorporation of women into the workforce (World Bank, 1993: op cit. in Joekes, 1995, p. 46). According to Belghazi (1995), in the carpet industry 42 per cent are female workers, in the knitwear industry, 71 per cent, and in the garment industry, 79 per cent (op cit. in Bourquia, 2002, p. 67).

Although not so often explicitly mentioned in the literature dealing with macro-economics, 'paternalistic' forms of labour control, low levels of labour militancy, the quiescence and obedience of female workers all add to the decisions of implanting an industrial factory in one location or another. The gender dimension of these decision-making processes was documented by several authors (Joekes, 1995; Ong, 1991; Pearson, 1998; Sassen, 1999). Local gender relations and specific recruitment practices in Mexico and Morocco have contributed to the massive integration of female workers in the newly created, labour-intensive industries (Belghazi and Baden, 2002; Bourquia, 2002; Fernández-Kelly, 1983; Salzinger, 1997).

To summarize, it appears that at least three parties seem to derive benefits from the creation of export-oriented industries in Mexico and Morocco. In the first place, the foreign company operators, who produce tradable items by keeping their operating costs as low as possible, seem to benefit. In the second place, the national governments benefit by attracting foreign investments and devices, creating jobs and increasing GNP. In the third place, an increasing number of (unskilled) workers in search of regular and formal incomes have found employment, including many women.

On 'Paradigmatic' Female Workers

In many articles and books one can read that 'the most interesting point about these world-market factories is that the vast majority (over 80 per cent) of the workers who are employed in them are young women between the ages of 13 and 25 years' (Moore, 1988, pp. 100-101; also Miller and Vivian, 2002; Salzinger, 2003; Wright, 2003; Zagema, 2003). Salzinger even argues that 'young, Third World women have emerged as transnational capital's paradigmatic workers' (Salzinger, 1997, p. 549; see also Ong, 1991, p. 281). Thus, the dominant idea, which has turned into global orthodoxy, is preferably to recruit young, unmarried women. This global orthodoxy is underscored by the findings of some researchers, such as Salzinger (2003, p. 65) who informs us that the hiring quota in the industrial factory she observed in Mexico constitutes 80% women among production workers, who are on average 17 years old.

Young women are employed *because* they are young, unmarried and women, so there is a clear link between age (read vitality), matrimonial status (read availability), gender (read nimble fingers) and production efficiency (read obedience and non militancy). These young, unmarried women are good for production not only because they do not mix multiple social roles (productive, reproductive or communal), but also because they are expected not to stay on the job once they get married (*cf.* Bourquia (2002) on Morocco; Wright (2003) on Mexico). By stressing that working in the manufacturing factories is a great opportunity for young, unmarried women to save some money before entering marriage, paid work for women is constructed as temporary. As a corollary, there is a strong sub-text of gender representation, of men as breadwinners. This historical construction of women as workers with inferior degrees of value has underscored long-held industrial traditions for paying them less and not recognizing their skills (Wright, 2003, p. 26).

Although a closer look at the sociological characteristics of female workers on the production floor in export-oriented industries in Mexico and Morocco shows that many more women are concerned, such as single mothers or divorcees, women whose husbands do not earn subsistence incomes, etc., for the purpose of my argument I want to elaborate on the so-called transnational capital's paradigmatic workers mentioned above. Besides being a productive device, young, unmarried, diligent, non-militant female workers also represent a gender. Most interestingly, this gender is expressed differently in various local contexts and therefore influences the room to manoeuvre by firm management – see below – when it comes to recruitment and dismissal practices of the female workers.

In Mexico, the creation of the maquila sector induced a particular socio-economic and cultural dynamic. It attracted many people, both young men and women, from other, often rural, areas of Mexico. In the newly industrialized cities, these migrants created collective housing arrangements, such as 'casas de la mujer', public eating places ('comida corrida') and places of entertainment and consumption (Zagema, 2003, p. 41ff). On Saturday nights, after a week of hard working, far away from family and kin, the newly immigrated workers became part of consumptive and leisurely lifestyles mirrored by the nearby US. Without (geographical or cultural) roots in their new residential resorts, they had to create new forms of social life. Dating and engaging in 'noviazgo' (betrothal) relationships had become part of this life stage of a new social category of autonomous adolescents and young adults. The other side of this newly gained autonomy is that new meanings were given to sexuality. A study by Fernandez-Kelly (1983, p. 129) informs us how young women use their charms and sex as bait to find employment. In the factories, voluntary and involuntary sexual requests or harassments are reported as part of the 'maquila culture' (Ong, 1991, p. 294, note 6). An American manager was struck by the sexual energy (sic) in the workplace and reported that in the previous months 10% of his workers had become pregnant (Weisman, 1987, p. 31). Besides the fact that women working in the factories may be seen as a subversion of the representation of the typical Mexican woman as mother and 'ama de casa' (homemaker), these observations of moral laxity have led to surveillance practices. There are complex controls exercised between brothers and sisters, (absent) fathers and daughters, fiancés and girlfriends. The ambivalence of the young, working women in the maquila sector is that they transgress gender boundaries in order to generate material autonomy. These changes put an enormous strain on existing gender-power relations.

The recurrent idea is that many maquiladoras seek to hire young women workers because they work harder than men do and are especially equipped, emotionally and anatomically, to do such work. The engendered myth is that women are more diligent and hard working, women's hands are more adept at executing the repetitive motions necessary for rote assembly work, they have a sound work ethic, are less informed about their rights, less insistent in demanding them and unlikely to unionize (Beneria and Roldan, 1987, p. 48). Furthermore, it is believed that young women do not aspire to long-lasting careers and promotion opportunities, since they want to become mothers and raise families. This is illustrated by what a human resource manager at a maquila in Mexico told Wright (2003, p. 33). She (the manager) did not think the women workers would be there for a long time. 'Most will come and go. They will start a family,' she argued.

In Morocco, the majority of the young, unmarried workers in the production factories live with their families. Bourquia (2002, p. 68) observed that 'the majority of female workers are single and come from poor social classes'. In a context of growing poverty, a daughter's income is very much appreciated as a complement to the insufficient income of her father. Sometimes a sister's income is used to finance her brother's schooling. From a man's perspective, it is less shameful to accept that his daughter is going outside to earn a (complementary) household income than to let his own wife join the labour force. The metaphors of 'dutiful daughters' and 'sacrificing sisters' are valid as part of gender representations. Furthermore, among the working and lower middle classes, there is a strong ideology of woman as housewife and mother[4]. A recurrent theme in research reports is that women ideally want to be taken care of by getting married (*cf.* Adam, 1972; Bourquia, 2002; Collectif 95 Maghreb Egalité, 1999). Many authors conceptualize that it as an interlude to marriage, since marriage and motherhood are the key aspects of an adult women's gender identity.

In terms of social autonomy, contrary to the maquila sector in Mexico, the labour-absorbing factories in Morocco are commonly located in the outskirts of the bigger cities. Female workers return home after working hours. Nevertheless, some emancipatory velleities are noticeable. They earn their own money and gain some material autonomy, which may gain them more respect in their families. To a certain extent, it is part of an upward mobility plan, 'enabling them to earn wages and freeing them from their family duties, as well as allowing them to escape direct authority and parental control, at least during factory hours' (Bourquia, 2002, p. 71). Earning their own incomes allows them to adopt consumer lifestyles (also see Joekes, 1985). Interestingly, Bourquia (2002, p. 71) elaborates on absenteeism among young female workers. She relates this absence to bad working conditions and low level of commitment to work ethics, but she also informs us that the girls pretend that they are going to work, while in fact they take the road to the shops in the city centre. Thus, they are actively escaping control of fathers, brothers and patrons and choosing to have a good time with their peers.

Behind the idea of young, unmarried and temporary workers, a number of socio-economic conditions relate to the daily realities in the countries concerned. Indeed, the industries provide opportunities for unskilled workers to earn incomes. The alternatives for unskilled, young women for earning a living are limited to a few options, such as domestic work, prostitution or the informal urban economy. The international companies at least provide a regular income and, in fortunate cases, also a contract and social security. So there are many plausible reasons to understand why young, unmarried women enter jobs in export-oriented industries. Poverty and the need for their own money are incentives to leave home and to become 'integrated' in productive and consumptive activities.

Another ambivalence of working women in the industrial factories is that their situations could be explained both in terms of being victims of impoverishment and being agents of making their own life decisions. They are more than just 'a natural fuel' to be exploited by 'global capital' (Wichterich, 1998). But how do these young, unmarried women combine this newly-acquired autonomy and integration in the world economy with their reproductive capacities? More importantly, how does firm management deal with the (potential) risks of having to pay legally-recognized maternity benefits to pregnant workers?

Mexican and Moroccan Companies Dealing with (Potentially) Pregnant Workers

In violation of Mexican labor law, maquiladora operators oblige women to undergo pregnancy testing as a condition of work. Women thought to be pregnant are not hired (Ralph, 1998, p. 1).

My starting point was that, in many articles on the maquila sector, I ran across passages concerning pregnancy discrimination of female workers. At the same time, articles on gender and female labour force participation in Morocco never hinted at practices concerning pregnancy tests or dismissals because of pregnancy. Since I do not believe that the transnational corporations operating in Morocco are more ethical than those in Mexico in terms of respecting labour codes and legal dispositions concerning sex and pregnancy discrimination, I opted to analyze this 'production of differences' in terms of gender representations.

Two critical, well-documented reports by Human Right Watch in 1996 and 1998 (LaShawn, 1996 and 1998) reported that, in the course of the hiring process, women in Mexico are submitted to mandatory pregnancy exams and are asked intrusive questions. These practices have been observed in the cities of Tijuana, Reynosa, Matamoros, Río Bravo and Ciudad Juárez (ibid). 'Pregnancy testing is conducted in several ways, most commonly through urine samples – often obtained in the course of legal pre-hire medical exams given to the job applicants' (LaShawn, 1998, p. 1). 'Maquiladora personnel also request information from women applicants about their menstruation cycles, sexual activity and use of contraceptives' (ibid, p. 1). These are preconditions for getting the jobs.

'Once hired, women who become pregnant face the prospect of being forced to resign because of their pregnancy' (ibid, p. 2). As a consequence, women workers are regularly asked to show used sanitary napkins to keep their jobs. Furthermore, probationary contracts of thirty to ninety days were given as a mechanism to refuse to offer permanent positions to pregnant women workers (ibid, p. 2). 'Rafaela Rojas Cruz, twenty-three years old, started working at a [...] maquiladora in Matamoros in July 1997. She had been working under a three-month probationary contract when her supervisor realized she was pregnant [...] then the supervisor informed her that at the end of the probationary contract she would not be given another contract' (ibid, p. 2). It is important to know that, to be eligible for the IMSS (Mexican Social Security Institute) maternity leave wage subsidy, workers must contribute for thirty weeks out of twelve months, prior to taking maternity leave (Human Rights Watch, Anon., paragraph 7).

Wright (2003, p. 35) informs us that 'Indeed, as in many maquilas, a policy both for refusing to hire pregnant women and for encouraging those who become pregnant to leave their jobs was tacitly enforced, although such practices violate federal legislation prohibiting discrimination on the basis of pregnancy'. The policies seem to be so widespread that even female hiring personnel practice the discriminatory criteria. 'We all know we're not supposed to hire pregnant girls', says Mary the supervisor, 'It's that way in all the maquilas' (Wright, 2003, p. 35). Women workers interviewed by the Human Rights Watch team worried about getting pregnant, because they might lose their jobs in the maquiladoras. Women concealed their pregnancies in an effort to avoid being fired and avoided seeking prenatal care so that they would not have to miss any time off from work. Once pregnant, women are overtly or indirectly forced to quit their jobs: they are forced to work unpaid overtime, to do more physically difficult work, and refused seated or lighter work assignments. Employers also threatened to refuse to allow women to return to work after maternity leave (LaShawn, 1998, p. 1). All this happens, since 'maquiladora employers say that they don't hire pregnant women because they want to avoid the cost of maternity benefits' (Human Rights Watch, Anon., paragraph 2)[5]. They use their own medical personnel or those of nearby private clinics to test women. No factual evidence, however, exists to assess the real cost effect of maternity benefits against the overall costs of doing business and the enormous contribution female workers make to maquiladora industry (Human Rights Watch, s.a., paragraph 7).

These intrusive mechanisms of control led to collective actions in the late 1990s by female workers, supported by international and national networks, such as the Women's Rights Project of the Human Rights Watch, the Maquiladora Health and Safety Support Network, the Mexican National Association of Democratic Lawyers (ANAD) (Brown, 1999), and the local NGOs Yeuani and Factor X (Cornejo, 2001). These countervailing power movements resist violation of women's rights and question these mechanisms of controlling women's bodies.

In Morocco, on the contrary, a striking silence surrounds the reproductive capacities of young female manufacturing workers. A quick tour of questioning in my Moroccan researchers' network resulted in the following statements: it is a deliberate strategy of textile industries only to employ unmarried girls, because they will not be bothered by pregnancy related issues; Morocco is a Muslim country; therefore, we do not practice pregnancy screening among young, unmarried female workers; girls will hide their pregnancies and quit the workplace because of shame.

What are the characteristics of the work environment in these factories in Morocco? As we saw, the arrival of export-oriented manufacturing factories has created an unprecedented opportunity for paid work for many young women in urban areas. However, the majority of authors agree on the fact that young female workers in textile industries do not aspire to life careers in production work. 'Although women are obliged to work for economic reasons, their aspirations appear to lie elsewhere: the ideal is a position of economic and social security provided by a breadwinning husband' (Bourquia, 2002, p. 67). The other side of this representation is the fact that employers do not appreciate married workers, because they have to combine productive and reproductive tasks, religious holidays and family obligations, which causes tardiness and repeated absenteeism (Bourquia, 2002, p. 93). They genuinely prefer to employ a young, temporary workforce.

In this context, management of export-oriented factories combines a number of representations of the feminine gender to organize production. Not only do they construct their recruitment policies on the gendered aspects of obedient, diligent and docile women and their dependency on a male provider by paying them low salaries, they also count on the temporary nature of their professional careers. A recurrent complaint by female workers – and to a certain extent by trade unions – concerns the laxity of industrial companies to invest in processes of 'fidélisation', such as paying bonuses, creating good working conditions, allowing career planning and providing vocational training (Bourquia, 2002, pp. 87-91). Paradoxically, while this representation of temporary careers allows them to realize (labour) cost effectiveness, managers complain about the high turnover rates. They perceive their female workforce as unstable, lacking commitment and observe that they give no priority to job performance and are rarely available for overtime work (Joekes, 1995, p. 13). The doubtful moral capacities of the female workers are thus constructed as being the justification for the absence of better secondary provisions in the workplace.

In such a context, reasons for young urban women to engage in waged labour are more complex that one would think at first sight. On top of generating a complementary income to an insufficient household income and saving some pocket money, other reasons explain women's interests in creating a safety net for themselves. Divorce rates are high and the dreams of creating a happy family are eroding, if we look at the demographic evidence concerning women who have never been married. Between 1994 and 1998, the number of unmarried women between the ages of 34 and 39 years increased by 65 per cent (1994: 15 per cent, 1998: 25 per cent) (Indicateurs sociaux, 2001). The stereotype of the dependent spouse is losing its empirical basis. Guennoun (1999, p. 2), who interviewed manufacturing workers in Casablanca, revealed that many young women do not have the illusion that the charming prince will come and take care of them for the rest of their lives. They know very well that these stories will end up with a child to care for and an absent father. A member of Attac-Maroc recognizes that women are looking for economic autonomy and an independent status related to their wish to get away from their 'home prisons', 'l'enfermement domestique' (Chengly, 2000, p. 7). Therefore, casual working relations and flexible organization should be addressed by the trade unions in order to avoid arbitrary dismissals. The author, however, does not speak of or hint at pregnancy discrimination.

Discussion

Controlling the space of the worker's body is related to a wider corporate perception of women's 'nature' (Ong, 1991, p. 291).

Asking female job applicants if they are pregnant or planning to become pregnant, or mistreating, abusing or firing pregnant workers violates the Mexican Constitution (articles 4, 123), the Federal Labour Code (articles 3, 56, 133, 164, 166, 170) and the ILO Convention 111[6]. Although pregnancy discrimination is illegal in Mexico, the practice seems to be widespread in the maquila sector. The intrusive questions, the demands for urine tests and showing sanitary napkins upon demand, is a far reaching mechanism of control of women's individual and sexual lives. The context here is one in which young women are not only constructed as diligent workers, but also as sexually active.

The workforce in the Mexican maquila sector indeed comprises young dynamic women, the majority of whom have come from far away rural places to take part in waged labour. Escaping the control of (absent) fathers and brothers, they lead lives of their own while benefiting from entertainment offered by discos and other establishments. Dating and going out with boyfriends is a common pastime. Free unions are a culturally recognized form of living together and the institution of 'noviazgo' (betrothal) is common practice among young people in Mexico. These liberties are characterized by the social figure of a freewheeling, sexually active female actor. This figure is also seen as a transgressive one and a cause of moral decadence and the loosening of the social system. This gender representation of a sexually active female actor influences the shape and practices of recruitment policies by manufacturers, concerning the containment of production costs. In other words, pregnancy screening during recruitment and intrusive questions concerning the sexual behaviour of female workers is the reflection of how female gender is represented in this part of Mexico. From our point of view, we see a contradiction, since the productive capacities of these young, female workers are recognized, but their civil and reproductive rights are not guaranteed. Hence the struggle of various organizations against these gender discriminating practices directed at the 'abusive' monetary logic of the (mainly US) companies and the failure of the Mexican government to protect women against the violations of some of their basic human rights.

In Morocco, the religiously legitimized prohibition of premarital sex apparently is reason enough for employers to elude setting up pregnancy screening instruments for job applicants. It would be culturally offensive to ask unmarried women to present urine samples to prove that they are not pregnant (i.e. sexually active). Even talking about contraceptive use would be interpreted as hinting at sexual activities, which for an unmarried woman is a contradiction in terms at the normative level. However, reality is changing more rapidly than the normative frame. A recently released report on unmarried mothers (Délégation régionale du Grand Casablanca, 2003) shows that, of their sample (N=5040), 66 per cent of the unmarried mothers were employed at the start of their pregnancies. This report is official proof of the sexual activity of young, unmarried working girls. However, neither foreign nor national companies can formally employ recruitment policies designed to control women's bodies or sexual activities. In the first place, the control of women's sexuality is the responsibility of the men of the family and not an anonymous stranger or company manager. In the second place, the Islamic canons do not allow sexuality out of wedlock. Islam thus becomes a justification for the absence of pregnancy testing of unmarried female workers during recruitment. The internalization of the norm means that unmarried workers who happen to be pregnant will not even think of seeking jobs and/or will quit their jobs.

Nor do these companies employ dismissal procedures, since it is believed that unmarried pregnant women will leave their jobs out of shame. A recently released report by the Spanish NGO Setem shows that 'pregnant women lose their positions' (Setem, 2002)[7]. It is not specified if it concerns married or unmarried women. If this were the tip of the iceberg, more (inter) national networking would be needed with Moroccan women's rights groups to initiate the struggle against pregnancy discrimination. The absence of overt pregnancy screening of the manufacturers' paradigmatic female workers in Morocco is based on a representation of the feminine gender of young women as being sexually inactive.

Conclusions

The intellectual puzzle I intended to solve in this chapter leads to the conclusion that globalization, seen from two local contexts, is a situated and multifaceted process and leads me to argue that we could conjugate globalization in the plural. The advantage of using a local perspective opens up spaces and insights in the unpredicted outcomes of so-called global and homogenizing processes. The process of implanting transnational manufacturers in Free Trade Zones, with the aim of being competitive on a world market, follows a global monetary logic of cost effectiveness. To do so, the recruitment of preferably young, unmarried, obedient and diligent female workers has created the image of a 'paradigmatic' worker. Although many more categories of (unskilled) women are looking for paid employment and stable incomes, I have chosen to concentrate my analysis on how the managers of transnational companies deal with these 'paradigmatic' workers, especially when it comes to pregnancy screening during recruitment and overt or indirect dismissals of pregnant production workers.

We have seen that both in Mexico and Morocco. These women share the sociological characteristics of being young, uneducated and unmarried. They also have in common the fact that they work in order to complement their fathers' insufficient household incomes or to realize a project of personal upward mobility. These (unprecedented) employment opportunities for women are contributing to profound social transformations. In view of traditional gender stereotypes of men as breadwinners and women as homemakers and mothers, the newly created life stage of waged labourer goes hand in hand with new social identities. These young women, who have some money of their own to spend, enjoy life, give in to consumerism and postpone marriage. These processes, however, have different forms and outcomes, depending on local power relations and gender representations.

In Mexico, the maquila sector is absorbing migrant workers from all over the country and beyond. The young women who arrive to earn an income have to make a living on their own, or with friends, far from their native families. Traditional patriarchal mechanisms of control cannot be applied as usual, which gives them more room to manoeuvre with regard to spending their money and enjoying leisure. Firm management in this context employs mandatory pregnancy tests during recruitment, because the probability of young women getting pregnant is real and pregnant women have a negative effect on production costs. The gender representations held by these company operators is built on a social actor with multiple identities, both productive and reproductive.

In Morocco, the female workers in the factories happen to live with their families and are not supposed to be sexually active. Islamic law prohibits premarital sex. The transnational companies are said to prefer hiring unmarried women because they are sexually inactive. By local cultural constraints, they equate unmarried female workers with non-occurrence of pregnancy-related problems and production costs. The work is represented as an interlude to marriage, and this idea of temporariness prevents these companies from investing in processes of 'fidélisation'. Secondary working conditions and enforcement of labour laws are weak. Paradoxically, the company operators are complaining about high turnover rates.

While young, unmarried female workers are represented as diligent workers and sexually active women in Mexico, in Morocco they are represented as disposables and sexually inactive women. In Mexico, it is a preoccupation with cost effectiveness that is performed through the control of women's wombs, whereas in Morocco it is the representation of sexually innocent women waiting to get married that prevents them from asking questions about their sexual activities. Both local situations induce different types of management styles. Both local situations also produce their own specific forms of resistance against potentially abusive work conditions. In Mexico, women's health and human rights' advocates have denounced violations of civil and reproductive rights; in Morocco, women act in isolation, shamefully withdrawing from the scene in cases of premarital pregnancies. The analysis of the articulation of management's practices regarding (potentially) pregnant workers and local gender representations and identities sheds light on the complexity and diversity of the global-local nexus.

Notes

1   With special thanks to Rachid Filali, Nora Habafy, Fatima Agnaou, Malika Ladjali, Soumaya Naamane-Guessous, Carlos Sevilla, Maria Cristina Fuentes Zurita, Pien Bos and the co-authors of this book, especially Kathy Davis for their substantive support.

2   Ethnographic fieldwork was conducted in Morocco over the period 1982-1998 and in Mexico in 1999-2000.

3   A maquiladora is a Mexican Corporation which operates under a maquila programme approved for it by the Mexican Secretariat of Commerce and Industrial Development (SECOFI). It entitles the company to special customs treatment, allowing duty free temporary import of machinery, equipment, parts and materials, and administrative equipment such as computers and communication devices, subject only to posting a bond guaranteeing that such goods will not remain in Mexico permanently. Ordinarily, all of a maquiladora's products are exported (Mexico Business Directory, 2004).

4   Women from upper middle and upper classes generally are more educated and can afford to employ domestic workers to do the cooking and cleaning tasks at home.

5   Article 170 (paragraphs II., IV., and V.) of the federal labour code guarantees pregnant workers, among other things, six weeks maternity leave before birth, and six weeks after birth, with full pay. While on maternity leave, women workers have the right to keep their job, as well as the rights they acquired under their labour contract. Maternity benefits do not cost employers very much. All workers and their families receive medical and maternity care, disability compensation and pension, as part of the benefits they receive from the Social Security Institute (IMSS).

6   Many Mexican laws are violated by practising pregnancy testing, among them:

- Article 4 of the Constitution, which guarantees that men and women are equal before the law, and that each person has a right to decide on the number and spacing of her children.
- Articles 3 and 56 of the federal labour code, which prohibit distinctions among workers based on sex.
- Article 133 (I.) of the federal labour code, which prohibits employers from refusing to hire workers because of their sex.
- Article 164 of the federal labour code, which states that women have the same rights and obligations as men.
- Article 123 (A) (V and XV) of the Constitution and Articles 170(1) and 166 of the federal labour code, which guarantee that pregnant women have the right to work in safe conditions, and prohibits employers from forcing pregnant women to work in jobs that are dangerous to their health in relation to their foetus.

Pregnancy discrimination also violates International Human Rights and Labour Law. Experts who interpret these laws agree that pregnancy discrimination is a form of sex discrimination. For example, the International Labour Office (ILO) Committee of Experts has interpreted the scope of Convention 111 on Discrimination in Respect of Employment to prohibit pregnancy discrimination as a form of sex discrimination. The Mexican government has signed and agreed to abide by these international instruments:

ILO Convention 111 on Discrimination in Respect of Employment and Occupation prohibits pregnancy-based employment discrimination. The North American Agreement on Labour Co-operation under NAFTA obligates Mexico to promote the elimination of sex discrimination in the labour force. The International Covenant on Civil and Political Rights prohibits discrimination based on sex. The Convention on the Elimination of All Forms of Discrimination against Women expressly outlaws pregnancy-based employment discrimination. The American Convention on Human Rights prohibits discrimination based on sex.

7   A Moroccan employer has to provide twelve weeks unpaid maternity leave. Only when female workers are matriculated to the Caisse nationale de sécurité sociale (CNSS) may they receive some indemnities. As long as the working relationship is informal, workers can easily be dismissed.

References

Adam, André (1972), *Casablanca*, Paris: CNRS.
Anon. (2001) *Indicateurs sociaux 2001*, Rabat: Royaume du Maroc, Département de la prévision économique et du plan.

Anon. (2002, 30 August) 'Morocco's Government Launches New Textile Plan' (3 paragraphs), *Emerging Textiles.com* (online newsletter), retrieved on 3rd of March 2004 from www.emergingtextiles.com/?q=art&s=020830-coun&r=free&n=1.

Belghazi, Saad (1995), *Emploi Féminin Urbain et Avantage Compétitif du Maroc*, Geneva, UNRISD, mimeo.

Belghazi, Saad and Baden, Sally (2002), 'Wage Discrimination by Gender in Morocco's Urban Labour Force: Evidence and Implications for Industrial Labour Policy' in Miller, Caroline and Vivian, Jessica (ed.) *Women's Employment in the Textile Manufacturing Sectors of Bangladesh and Morocco*, Geneva, UNRISD, pp. 35-60.

Beneria, Lourdes and Roldan, Martha (1987), *The Crossroads of Class and Gender. Industrial Homework, Subcontracting, and Household Dynamics in Mexico City*, Chicago, University of Chicago Press.

Bourquia, Rahma (2002), 'Gender and Employment in Moroccan Textile Industries', in Miller, Caroline and Vivian, Jessica (ed.) *Women's Employment in the Textile Manufacturing Sectors of Bangladesh and Morocco*, Geneva, UNRISD, pp. 61-101 translated from Bourquia, Rahma (1999), *Genre et Emploi dans l'Industrie Textile Marocaine*, Geneva: UNRISD, Occasional Paper 11.

Chengly, Lotfi (2000), *Chômage, Précarité et Zone de Libre Échange*, Rabat: Attac Maroc.

Collectif 95 Maghreb Egalité (1999), *Les Maghrébines Entre Violences Symboliques et Violences Physiques: Algérie, Maroc, Tunisie*, Rapport annuel 1998/1999 – Rapport Algérie. Ce rapport a été élaboré sous la coordination de: Cherifati Doria [Algérie], Horchani Malika [Tunésie], Rhiwi Leila [Maroc] avec l'appui de la Fondation Friedrich Ebert.

Délégation régionale du Grand Casablanca, UNICEF and UNFPA, (2003) *Enquête Statistique sur les Filles-Domestiques Âgées de Moins de 18 Ans dans la Wilaya de Casablanca*, Royaume du Maroc, Ministère de la Prévision Economique et de Plan.

Fernández-Kelly, María Patricia (1983), *For We are Sold, I and my People: Women and Industry in Mexico's Frontier*, Albany: State University of New York.

Guennoun, Souad (1999), *Ouvrières: Nouvelle Génération*, Casablanca: unpublished paper.

Human Rights News (1996) 'Mexico's Maquiladoras: Abuses against Women Workers', *Human Rights News*, retrieved on 28th of April 2003 from http://hrw.org/press/1996/08/mexicomaq96.htm.

Joekes, Susan (1985), 'Working for Lipstick? Male and Female Labour in the Clothing Industry in Morocco' in Afshar, H. (ed.), *Women, Work and Ideology in the Third World*, London: Tavistock Publications, pp. 183-213.

Joekes, Susan (1995), *Trade-Related Employment for Women in Industry and Services in Developing Countries*, Geneva: UNRISD, Occasional Paper 5.

Kalb, Don (2000), 'Localizing Flows: Power, Paths, Institutions, and Networks' in Kalb, Don (ed.), *The Ends of Globalization: Bringing Society Back In*, Lanham/London: Rowman and Littlefield, pp. 1-32.

Kalb, Don, Wil Pansters and Hans Siebers (2004), *Globalization and Development. Themes and Concepts in Current Research*, Dordrecht/Boston/London: Kluwer Academic Publishers.

La Jornada (2001), *Des Maquiladoras de Tijuana Licencient Chaque Année 900 Femmes Enceintes*, www.transnationales.org.

LaShawn, R. Jefferson (1996), *No Guarantees: Sex Discrimination in Mexico's Maquiladora Sector*, Human Rights Watch Report, Vol. 8, no. 6B.

LaShawn, R. Jefferson (1998), *A Job or Your Rights? Continued Sex Discrimination in Mexico's Maquiladora Sector*, Human Rights Watch Report.

Moore, Henrietta (1988), *Feminism and Anthropology*, Polity Press, New York.

Ong, Aihwa (1991), 'The Gender and Labor Politics of Postmodernity', *Annual Review of Anthropology*, Vol. 20, pp. 279-309

Pearson, Ruth (1986), 'Female Workers in the First and Third Worlds: The Greening of Women's Labour' in Purcell, K. (ed.), *The Changing Experience of Employment: Restructuring and Recession*, Reprinted in Pahl R. (ed.), *On Work*, Oxford: Blackwell (1988).

Pearson, Ruth (1998), '"Nimble Fingers" Revisited: Reflections on Women and Third World Industrialisation in the Late Twentieth Century', in Jackson, Cecile and Pearson, Ruth (eds.), *Feminist Visions of Development: Gender, Analysis and Policy*, London and New York: Routledge, pp. 171-188.

Salzinger, Leslie (1997), 'From High Heels to Swathed Bodies: Gendered Meanings under Production in Mexico's Export-Processing Industry', *Feminist Studies*, Vol. 23(3), pp. 549-574

Salzinger, Leslie (2003), 'Re-forming the "Traditional Mexican Woman": Making Subjects in a Border Factory', in Vila, Pablo (ed.), *Ethnography at the Border*, Minneapolis: University of Minnesota Press, pp. 46-72.

Setem (2002), *The Responsibility of Spanish Garment Retailers for the Social and Working Conditions in Small Production Centres in Northern Morocco*, Madrid: Clean Clothes Campaign.

Weisman, A. (1987) 'The Other Side of Nogales', *City Magazine*, The Arizona Republic, Ucson, February, pp. 34-41.

Wichterich, Christa (1998) *Die Globalisierte Frau: Berichte aus der Zukunft der Ungleichheit*, Reinbek: RoRoRo Aktuell.

Wright, Melissa W. (1997), 'Crossing the Factory Frontier: Gender, Place, and Power in the Mexican Maquiladora', *Antipode*, Vol. 29(3), pp. 278-302.

Wright, Melissa W. (2003), 'The Politics of Relocation: Gender, Nationality, and Value in a Mexican Maquiladora', in Vila, Pablo (ed.), *Ethnography at the Border*, Minneapolis: University of Minnesota Press, pp. 23-45.

Zagema, Bertram (2003), *Casino Mexico: Winnaars en Verliezers van de Globalisering*, Rotterdam: Lemniscaat.

GLOCALIZED GENDER IDENTITIES: TRADITION AND MODERNITY DECONSTRUCTED

Chapter 9

Dowry in India: Respected Tradition and Modern Monstrosity

Marion den Uyl

Introduction

The custom of paying dowry, a gift that goes with the bride at the time of her marriage, is seen as increasingly dangerous for women in India. A recent report warns that the 'ancient practice of dowry perpetuates violence against women in India' (Reddy, 2002). One of the reasons that dowry is labelled a dangerous custom lies in the fact that it is difficult to afford the rising amounts of dowry, which makes daughters even less welcome in a culture that has had a strong preference for male children for centuries. Moreover, dowry is seen as the main force behind the increased incidence of neglect of girls, female feticide, female infanticide and the killing of married women, so-called bride burning, in order to marry a new wife who will bring a new dowry (Miller, 1997; Menski, 2000; Seghal, 2003).

When I visited India for the first time, more than twenty years ago, I found that the dowry system formed one of the major problems for women in India, because it was a source of unhappiness in married life, of young girls' fears, suicides and violence against women (den Uyl, 1995). However, I expected that this custom, linked to ancient practices, would disappear in the course of time with the ongoing modernization of Indian culture and economy. Although the Indian economy did grow, especially after the liberalization of the economy in the 1990s, this did not bring the disappearance of the despised ancient practice. Instead of dying out, the custom spread and blossomed.

A recent survey of the All India Democratic Women's Association (AIDWA) shows an 'epidemic-like spread and intensification of the practice of dowry' (AIDWA, 2003, p. 1). Research among ten thousand people in eighteen states reveals a rapid increase: 'Dowry spreads its tentacles across India' (Seghal, 2003). Rajni Palriwala, one of the leading researchers of AIDWA, links modern dowry to gender inequalities as well as to economic and political transformations. She states that:

> In a concentrated form dowry encapsulates contemporary and intensified inequalities and oppressions – caste, class and gender. It encapsulates the materialist and

consumerist desires of today, the new religion of liberalisation (Palriwala in AIDWA, 2003, p. 1).

Dowry develops itself hand in hand with the increase of capital, the opening of markets, and – in the eyes of many Indians – modern feelings of greed and individualism. Several authors have noted that the increasing foreign influence in India is experienced as threatening, especially by the Indian middle classes. This fear is expressed in stress on Hindu traditions, which results in revitalization of cultural and religious practices and values (Corbridge and Harris, 2000; Kapadia, 2002).

According to the World Bank, the Indian economy is doing well, especially since the ruling Hindu party liberalized the economy in the early 1990s. It is one of the fastest growing economies in the world, with an average growth rate of 5 percent in the 1990s (Collier and Dollar, 2001). However, economic development in itself does not say much about social and cultural developments. The interplay of economic and social forces is complex. The anthropologist Ulf Hannerz (1996) is one of the authors who has noted that economic, political and cultural processes of global flow have accelerated in recent years (Hannerz, 1996). These flows from the centre interact with local traditions in the periphery. The force of local habits, often unconscious ways of coping with day-to-day living, form a strong focus of resistance to change, a source of development of new local habits and a source of hybridization or creolization of culture. Hannerz states that 'the cultural processes of creolization are not simply a matter of constant pressure from the centre towards the periphery, but a much more creative interplay' (1996, p. 265). Although there exists an unequal power relation between the centre and the periphery, this does not mean that the centre simply compels its standard – he uses the metaphor of a linguistic standard and dialects – on the periphery. Creolization also increasingly allows the periphery 'to talk back', when Third World Music becomes world music, for example (Hannerz, 1996, p. 265). The outcome of processes of creolization is open: new forms may develop, but it is also possible that the initial process of creolization is taken over by the dominant culture, and the standard becomes the rule in the periphery.

In this chapter I will look at what lies beneath the tentacles of dowry that have spread through India, and consider how it can be explained that the era of globalization witnesses the blossoming and spread of an old and seemingly old-fashioned tradition. One question that arises when we look at dowry is whether modern dowry actually is the same kind of ritual payment that used to be given at marriages in past centuries, or has dowry changed in form and meaning? Can we – in the context of processes of globalization – interpret the growth and spread of dowry as a form of creolization and can we find a 'periphery talking back', or do we find a process of cultural domination, where the standard becomes the rule?

Respected Tradition and Modern Monstrosity

The custom of dowry is rooted in the religious traditions of patrilineal and patrilocal Hindu culture (Altekar, 1962; Goody and Tambiah, 1973; Srinivas, 1996). In traditional Hindu culture the highest form of marriage was, according to the sacred texts of Manu laid down in the 6th century, the Brahmin form of marriage. This Brahmin marriage, associated with the highest caste of priests, centred round the *kanydan*, the gift of the virgin daughter. It was considered the father's *dharma*, religious plight, to give his daughter to another man without asking compensation; otherwise he would, according to Manu, sell her and treat her like cattle.

The gift of a daughter was accompanied by other gifts, such as jewellery and costly clothing; the origin of dowry might be found in these gifts that went along with the bride (Altekar, 1962; Srinivas, 1996). The well-known sociologist, Srinivas, remarks that there were actually two important kinds of gifts that accompanied the *kanydan*, the virginal gift. On the one hand there was the *dakshina*, the gifts to the groom, and on the other hand there was the *stridhan*, or *stridhana*, the gifts to the bride, which should be considered her property (Srinivas, 1996, p. 162). Both kinds of gifts, *stridhan* and *dakshina*, might have formed the basis on which the practice of dowry developed.

According to several authors, the custom of *stridhan* has to be seen as a consequence of the Hindu system of inheritance. It is argued that the institution of *stridhan* stems from the fact that women in patrilineal patrilocal societies do not share in their father's property and live in the houses of their husbands. Dowry has to be perceived as a kind of pre-mortal inheritance (Goody and Tambiah, 1973; Gaulin and Boster, 1990).

During the 19th century, or maybe even earlier, the value of gifts that accompanied the bride started to increase. The Indian social historian, Altekar, explains this increase by pointing to changes in the labour market and the level of education in the 19th century (the first edition of his work on Indian women appeared in 1938):

> It is only during the last 50 or 60 years that the amount of dowry has begun to assume scandalous proportions. A good education, a lucrative appointment, or a good footing in a learned profession improved enormously the social and economic position of a youth, and made him immensely attractive as a son-in law. He naturally acquired a high price in the marriage market (Altekar, 1962, p. 71).

Altekar refers to changes in marriage payments – increasing sums, scandalous proportions – that he relates to changes in the educational system, the labour market and the wider economy. Here I would like to comment on the ambiguous nature of the concept of dowry. Because he writes in English, Altekar (1962) uses the term dowry instead of Indian terms such as *stridan* or *dakshina*, or one of the numerous local words that indicate either *stridhan* or *dakshina*. The English term, dowry, originally referred to the bridal wealth of the daughters of European nobility. The educated Indian upper castes and classes adapted this term to use it in official circles, in law books and in scientific texts, but generally not in daily practice. Because of the ambiguity of the concept of dowry, with respect to the origin of dowry, we cannot say whether Altekar (1962) meant that *stridhan* and/or *dakshina* grew to scandalous proportions, or that *stridhan* and *dakshina* disappeared and were taken over by a *new* custom, dowry.

To get a better understanding of this question, Srinivas' essay (1996) on dowry is illuminating. Srinivas proposes making a sharp distinction between traditional Indian marriage practices and recent developments. He speaks of *modern dowry* when he refers to practices of his time (the first edition of his essay on dowry appeared in 1962). This *modern dowry* differs from the traditional practice because it is given on demand. Instead of being a voluntary gift embedded in religious tradition, the groom's party asks for huge sums of cash, jewellery, clothing, and furniture. To equate this to *dakshina* is, in the words of Srinivas, '…only an attempt to legitimate a modern monstrosity by linking it with an ancient and respected custom' (1996, p. 163). Modern dowry differs also from traditional *stridhan*, which was intended to be under the bride's control. It is difficult to say whether the bride will have any control over the cash, clothing, furniture demanded by the groom's party, or even over the jewellery given to her (1996, p. 162).

Srinivas makes here a distinction between a respected custom and a modern monstrosity. He uses the concept of *modern dowry*, which makes it possible to distinguish the present practice from older practices. Unfortunately, probably through the lack of a better English equivalent, most of the time he uses the term dowry to refer to traditional as well as to present practices, which is also done by other authors. As a consequence, dowry generally refers to *both* traditional as well as present-day practices.

In a more recent study the term dowry is used to encompass three different kinds of marriage payments. Madan (1985) found that among different castes in Delhi the custom of paying dowry has been fashionable for several decades. He found that present-day dowry embraced different elements. The most common element of dowry included firstly the gifts to the bride, such as jewellery, which should ideally be treated as her *stridhan*. Secondly, there were gifts to the bridegroom, the *dakshina*, such as a golden watch and a suit, along with modern luxury items such as a scooter, a television set or a flat. Thirdly, some gifts were donated to the bridegroom's kin (1985, p. 10). It seems that, in this case, both *stridhan* and *dakshina* were absorbed in the new custom of dowry. It is also clear that modern luxury items such as scooters or cars, available on the new consumer market, were recently added to the dowry.

Although Srinivas distinguishes modern dowry from what he sees as a respected ancient custom, he also perceives continuity; gradually the modern monstrosity grew out of the traditional practice:

> Young men who had salaried jobs, or careers in the professions were sought after as
> bridegrooms. They were 'scarce commodities', and their scarcity was exacerbated by
> the rule of jati endogamy and the need to marry a girl before she came of age. The
> parents of the lucky youths demanded cash and such goods as cycles, woollen suits,

etc. as part of the wedding agreement. The monster of modern dowry has grown from such humble beginnings (1996, p. 161).

The rise of dowries is related to the growth of the bureaucracy under British rule and the emergence of a capitalist economy. Madan (1985), several decades later, in the 1980s, places the changes in dowry payments in the context of a changing economy. He concludes that dowry developed from a 'social institution of gift of a non-monetised economy' into a 'commercial institution of dowry in a free market and commercial economy' (Madan, 1985, p. 35).

Historian Veena Oldenburg (2002) holds a different view on the origins of the commercialization of dowry. She states that this process originated in the Indian countryside when the British rulers started land and tax reforms in the 19th century. Before the British reforms, there were no fixed dates to pay rent, nor was there any need to pay rent when harvests failed. Landlords and tenants were mutually dependant, caught in a web of duties and rights. The land reforms forced the peasants to have cash, to pay rents on fixed dates and to pay when harvests failed. Because they needed cash, the tenants started to ask dowries in the form of – more and more – money; as a result, the nature of dowry changed and dowries started to rise. Oldenburg stresses that in former times dowry had been valuable to women. She recalls that, in her youth in the Punjab, dowry – she refers here to dowry as a woman's property – had been worthwhile for women. Their jewellery gave them some independence when their husbands died or left; it was a safety net. According to Oldenburg (2002), this safety net twisted into a deadly noose.

Although the views of Oldenburg, Srinivas and Altekar on the origins of the process of commercialization of dowry may differ, they agree on the fact that British imperialism and economic transformations are to blame for the original changes in traditional Hindu marriage payments. They also agree on the fact that a custom with a positive value for women changed into a harmful practice.

In a more recent study about Indians and the dowry problem, the sociologist Krishnamurthy (1981) devotes attention to the harmful effects of dowry. There is the danger that the groom's family might try to raise the price during the marriage negotiations and that families could suffer financial ruination for the sake of their daughters. He thinks that it is wrong for marriage arrangements to be dominated by money and demands. Marital ties should not get interwoven with commercial interests such as profit, greed and consumerism, because the marital ties must provide a safe, caring climate for raising children and looking after future generations. He states that dowry is anti-social, even perverse, and it has a negative influence on the Indian national character because it stimulates selfishness and greed (1981, pp. 9-10). The Indian government forbade dowry in 1961, but since that time dowries have continued to rise. Neither local nor national governments have been able to implement the law.

If we now consider the question of whether modern dowry has to be considered the result of a process of cultural creolization, arguments have been put forth that provide an affirmative answer to this question. We can consider India as part of the periphery of the British emporium. The traditional Indian marriage customs changed under the influence of the early processes of globalization;

imperial rule imposed changes in education, bureaucracy, the labour market and land tenure. These transformations led to changes in traditional marriage practices, especially because marriage became a means of obtaining cash. The new marriage payments even received a new, foreign name: dowry.

If we take Hannerz' concept of the standard and the dialects, we do not find a growing dominance of the standard, because the creolized form of Indian marriage practice still continues. Western style 'standard' marriages (not arranged by parents, without dowry, without Hindu religious rituals) never got off the ground in India.

Cannibalizing All Other Local Customs

Dowry, which was especially a custom of North Indian high caste Hindus, began to spread during the course of the 20th century, or maybe even earlier. South India adapted the practice from North India and lower castes took over the customs of the higher castes. This process of spreading accelerated in the second half of the twentieth century, after India became independent and developed a national identity.

Traditionally, there existed important differences between North and South Indian marriage practices. In North India marriages were hypergamous, between families of unequal status, but of the same caste. To marry off one's daughter to a family with a higher social status could improve the social status of one's own family. Dowry could be used to attract a desired groom and to raise the status of the family (Van der Veen, 1972; Srinivas, 1996). The exchanges between the families were not equal: the bride's family gave, the groom's family received. The sociologist, Upadhya, describes the northern Indian marriage system as one that was characterized by 'hypergamy, non-reciprocity between wife-givers and wife-takers, and the unidirectional flow of gifts' (1990, p. 32).

In contrast to North Indian marriage, South Indian marriage involved the union of two *jati* (sub-caste) groups of equal social status. In South India, bride price, which was paid to the family of the bride, was the rule until the middle of the 20th century (Srinivas, 1996, p. 160). Marriage payments were on an exchange basis; the family of the groom paid a bride price; the family of the bride covered the costs of the wedding. Some castes favoured marriages of distant cousins, whereby the children of a brother and a sister married each other. The marriage system of South India could be characterized by 'reciprocity, equality, and the exchange of women within small groups' (Upadhya, 1990, p. 33).

When the different castes in South India adapted dowry, especially in the second half of the twentieth century, the change from paying a bride price to paying dowry involved much more than a change in the direction of marriage payments. This adaptation involved an orientation towards dominant Hindu cultural values; hierarchy replaced reciprocity and equality.

Dowry not only spread from North to South India, and from high castes to low castes, but also from Hindus to other religious groups, such as Christians,

Muslims, and Buddhists (Srinivas, 1996; Menski, 2000). These different religious groups, which had known a variety of different marriage and inheritance customs, adapted dowry when it was already in a process of transformation. They adapted dowry in a commercialized form, expressed in luxury items, based on the demands of the groom's party. It was this modern dowry, the 'monstrosity', rather than the 'respected ancient custom', that spread through India's different regions, castes and religious groups, although it might still have been called by – respected – local terms used for *stridhan* and *dakshina*.

In the AIDWA study, the spread of dowry is summarized as a process of cannibalism, in which one cultural practice overrules all other local traditions. Moreover, this process has been harmful for women:

> The plurality of marital practises among the various castes, religions, regions and classes has now shifted in favour of one homogenous upper-caste Hindu model which is further ensuring the devaluation of women. Dowry has cannibalised all other rituals and gift-taking relationships, thereby precipitating and intensifying gender inequalities in our society (Palriwali in Sehgal, 2003, p. 3).

When we take Hannerz' ideas about centre, periphery, creolization and the cultural dominance of the standard, we discover a process of cultural domination inside India. Taking Hindu India as the centre and low castes, non-Hindu religious groups and southern regions as the periphery, we can see that the standard (dowry) became dominant in the periphery, where it replaced traditional marriage rituals and customs.

The spread of modern, commercialized dowry has contributed to growing gender inequalities. Rising dowries are a major cause of growing gender inequalities because it is becoming increasingly expensive to raise daughters. A son will bring a bride into the house, along with a dowry. He will perform the necessary religious rites for his parents. He has always been the preferred child. A daughter, unlike a son, will leave the house and, when she marries, her parents will have to pay. A well-known Indian proverb says that bringing up a daughter is like watering one's neighbour's land. Rising dowries worsen the fear of parents that they will not be able to marry off their daughters, which is socially unacceptable. An unmarried daughter shames the honour of a house.

The increasing burden of daughters comes to the forefront when we look at the sheer number of men and women in India. The sex ratio between males and females has been declining since 1901. There were 972 females to every thousand males in 1901, but only 927 in 1991 (Census of India, 2001). The census figures from 2001 reveal that the child population (ages 0-6) shows an increasing gap between the number of girls and boys. While in 1991 there were 945 female children to every thousand male children, in 2001 there were only 927 (Census of India, 2001). The number of boys below the age of seven exceeds the number of girls below that age by six million. The greater natural incidence of male births may account for around three million of the observed difference, but explanations for the remaining three million must be sought in neglect of female children, female infanticide and abortion of female foetuses.

The numerical imbalance between the sexes is found to be most prominent in relatively prosperous states like Punjab, Gujarat and Hariyana, and in larger cities like Delhi and Mumbai. In Punjab there were only 793 and in Delhi only 865 girls for every thousand boys below the age of seven (Census of India, 2001). What is alarming about these figures is that they suggest that the growing imbalance in the sex ratio, which is an expression of dislike of girls, is a problem more prominent in cities, in relatively prosperous areas, among literates, higher castes and classes. It is a problem of modernity rather than of tradition, of 'progress' rather than of 'underdevelopment'.

Sanskritization: 'Becoming Civilized'

In the southern state Kerala the marriage customs of the dominant Hindu culture, which can be seen as the 'standard', replaced the traditional marriage customs of many different castes and religious groups. For centuries bride price was the common payment at marriages of the lower castes, former slaves and untouchables. They started paying dowries in the 1940s, 1950s and 1960s (Alexander, 1968; den Uyl, 1995).

The change from bride price to dowry can be placed in the context of adaptation to higher caste values and customs, which is an important means for increasing status and gaining respectability. Srinivas has called this 'tendency of the lower castes to imitate the higher' (1956, p. 30) a process of *sanskritization*, a term that he preferred above *brahmanization*, which is also used to refer to these processes of hierarchical cultural adaptation.

Kerala is famous for its matrilineal tradition, which gave women land rights, freedom of movement and a relatively large amount of sexual autonomy. It is also famous for its high degree of literacy and active labour union movement. However, the leftist political orientation, social reforms and matrilineal tradition did not prevent a large-scale adaptation of dowry among all castes and all religious groups.

In one village, I was able to follow changes over time among the *dalits*, the former untouchable slave castes. The *dalits* explained the adoption of dowry (and the disappearance of bride price) based on the fact that they 'had become cultured', 'had become civilized', 'that it had to be done' (den Uyl, 1995, pp. 129-135). By civilized, they were referring to changes such as literacy and improvements in their living conditions due to the struggle of the communist party and the labour unions. They clearly remembered the fact that formerly they were associated with dirt and impurity and were not allowed to enter temples, public roads, to wear shoes or cover their upper bodies. As slaves, at the bottom of the social hierarchy, they were forced to go through life half-naked and dirty (George, 1990). To the *dalits* emancipation meant acceptance as Hindus, to be part of the caste system instead of being outcasts. The struggle of the *dalits* is known as the Temple Entry Movement. Their struggle resulted in a victory in 1936, which allowed them to enter the Hindu holy places.

Among the *dalits*, multiple sexual relationships, polyandry, and polygyny are associated with 'old days', 'wildness', and 'being untamed'. Monogamy is associated with 'becoming civilized' (den Uyl, 1995, pp. 129-135). Formerly polygamous and bridal-price-paying *dalits* told the Kerala anthropologist Alexander that sexual fidelity in women, a central quality in the rise of monogamy, had become the most desired quality of a bride, while before it had been important that she was a good worker (Alexander, 1968, p. 155).

When I had an opportunity in 2000 to spend a few weeks in the village where I had done research twenty years earlier, I found that the outlook of the village had changed. There were new houses, made of brick, and there was more furniture than before. Some people even had television sets. Twenty years earlier the majority of *dalit* women worked in the rice fields. In 2000, the majority of the women were housewives. Rice cultivation no longer provided work and, besides, manual labour was something educated *dalit* women did not like to do. Three generations of former agricultural labourers show the profound transformations in society and culture. In the generation of grandmothers, nearly every woman went to the fields. Marriages among the former slave castes were very unstable, divorce was common, widows' remarriage was accepted and dowry was unknown. In the generation of mothers, fewer and fewer women went out to work, although the majority worked during the harvest season. The marriage system changed, dowry was introduced and the remarriage of widows was frowned upon. The daughters stayed at home, as housewives, were literate and did not want to work in the fields.

In 2000, dowry was the regular form of marriage payment, as it had been twenty years earlier. Differences between the *dalits* and higher castes are to be found in higher amounts of dowry and in demands for luxury items such as scooters, cars or television sets. The *dalits* only ask for money and gold, not more than the income of one or two years' work. In a few cases, land will also be given. Although the dowries are not high compared to those paid by the middle classes, they confront the *dalits* with serious problems. One way to avoid paying dowry lies in arranging marriages between distant cousins, which are traditional South Indian marriage arrangements. Also, in the case of love marriages – not uncommon in the loose marriage traditions of the slave castes – no dowry is paid. Those marriages are socially undesirable but eventually accepted, especially after a child is born.

In Kerala, excessive dowry demands are to be found among the middle classes, who more often work in the Gulf states, are higher educated and possess more land and other property. Among the higher castes in Kerala, marriages are occasions for public displays of wealth. The dowry items, such as cars or scooters, are exposed in huge marriage halls and hundreds of guests are invited, who will be treated to a luxurious meal. New trends in dowry items are a ticket to the United States or to the Gulf, or an elaborate dinner with many guests in a luxury hotel. The AIDWA study found that the flooding of the consumer market with more and newer goods and the display of wealth at the marriages of the rich and powerful influences all classes in society. In the spread of dowry, television serials and films play negative roles, as they depict 'ostentatious marriages, fancy trousseaus and docile woman' (AIDWA, 2003, p. 3).

Kerala is famous for its high degree of literacy, but literacy does not seem able to stem the increase of dowry or gender inequality. One journalist complained that Kerala education narrows the minds of girls instead of broadening them (Menon, 2000). They learn to adjust to the chaste and obedient role of Sita, the docile heroine of the Ramajana. K. Saradamoni, a well-known Kerala sociologist, recalls that in her youth educated women travelled, listened to Western music, danced, read novels, discussed socialism and literature and had different sexual relations. This has changed. The younger generation of university-educated women is subjected to a more rigid regime. Their marriages are arranged, dowries are high and they have to behave properly. The decline of the traditional matrilineal culture of Kerala and its replacement by a patrilineal Hindu culture has contributed to these new attitudes of young women. Saradamoni (1991) observes that marriage is central in the minds of young girls and that they see marriage as their only future.

Looking at the developments in dowry payments among the *dalits* in Kerala, with the ideas of Hannerz in mind, we can depict a process of cultural domination: their original customs are replaced by the dominant Hindu custom of dowry. However, the present marriage customs of the *dalits* are not exact copies of those of high caste Hindus. They pay smaller amounts of dowry, they do not ask for luxury items and there is less public exposure of wealth. Furthermore, they have retained several traditional marriage arrangements such as marriages among distant cousins and marriages for love. Taking a closer look at the development among the *dalits* from Kerala, we find several aspects of creolization.

Honour and Hierarchy

The shift from bride price to dowry, apart from the aforementioned process of sanskritization, can also be explained on other grounds. Bride price and dowry are often presented as opposing systems of circulation of goods and women (Goody and Tambiah, 1973; Gaulin and Boster, 1990). Bride price is considered to compensate a family for the loss of a daughter, whom they have raised and who will bear children for another lineage. When bride, goods and money go in the same direction, there is a 'negative bride price' (Rajaraman, 1983, p. 275). Gaulin and Boster (1990) propose that bride price can be seen as a compensation in systems where males compete for women, while in systems wherein women compete for males, dowry will be found. In their eyes dowry is a system of female competition.

Rajaraman (1983) ascribes the transition from bride price to dowry to the fact that during the 20th century women's contributions to productive labour declined in India, which resulted in declining contributions by women to family incomes. In her view, these declining contributions are the major force behind the disappearance of bride price and the rise of dowry. In her analysis, both dowry and bride price are defined as economic categories. They express the value of (gendered) human productive capital.

The aforementioned explanations of the transition from bride price to dowry consider marriage payments as economic transactions that take place in a more or less open market. However, it is doubtful whether the nature of bride price as well as that of dowry could be considered as strictly economic. It also seems doubtful that one could speak of an open marriage market. The marriage market in India is closed in the sense that the only persons available as marriage partners are persons of the same *jati*, or sub caste. Randeria and Visaria (1984) argue that bride price and dowry should be seen as sociological rather than economic transmissions. Bride price in India was fixed, its character was to a large extent symbolical and it was part of a general pattern of exchange of presents at the time of marriage. Dowry should be interpreted as a payment related to honour and status.

In the Kerala village where I did research, changes in labour productivity and female contributions to the household could hardly explain the adaptation of dowry. Dowry was adopted in a time when *dalit* women still worked in the fields. When they stopped going to the fields, the dowries did not rise, but remained relatively constant. It seems more likely that both the withdrawal of women from work outside the home and changes in marriage customs are products of the process of sanskritization, the long-term effort of the lower castes to rise in social status. This means that, although economic factors, such as labour value, monetization and a changing labour market may have played a role in the change of bride price to dowry, they could never fully explain the transition. An important role has to be attributed to cultural and psychological factors related to the caste system, such as respectability, status and sanskritization.

Srinivas (1996) states that Indian marriages are occasions for conspicuous spending, where families give expression to their status, involving the articulation of kin and caste (1996, p. 176). Both families, that of the bride and that of the groom, are sensitive to considerations of status, honour and shame. In his research in Delhi, Madan (1985) found that *izzat*, or honour, actually was the most important reason for paying dowry. Other reasons such as setting up a new household, custom or the avoidance of social taints were mentioned less often. More than 60 per cent of the respondents of different castes said that dowry was important because it was a means of getting *izzat* (1985, p. 48). *Izzat* is an important element in Indian social relations and personality. It is connected with a well-developed sensitivity to the feelings of others and alertness to status hierarchy (Kakar, 1978). Status hierarchy is such a central element in Indian society and personality that the French anthropologist Louis Dumont (1972) even speaks of the 'Homo Hierarchicus'.

The importance of one's image and that of one's family in the eyes of others play important roles with respect to honour and shame. One of the girls in the research village explained why she felt it was important for her father to pay dowry. She explained the feelings of honour and shame:

> I would be ashamed to go without dowry. Suppose I were to marry without any money or gold and I were to go to my husband's house then the neighbours would say: Ayoo! She has brought nothing! What sort of family does she have! And then

my husband and his family would feel ashamed! (Sixteen-year-old *dalit* girl, in den
Uyl, 1995, p. 210).

Present-day dowry is as much related to *izzat* as it is to economic gain. To analyze
dowry as a mere economic or even monetary phenomenon misses the essentially
ambiguous nature of dowry. The spread of dowry is tied to the hierarchal nature of
Indian society and personality, and to the ongoing process of *brahmanization* or
sanskritization.

Pure Hinduism: 'Talking Back' ?

Modern dowry is embedded in a social and political climate of growing Hindu
fundamentalism. The sociologist Sucheta Mazumdar (1992) has pointed out that
conceptions of purity played an important part in the nationalist movement and the
creation of Hindu India. Nationalist identity was linked to Hinduism and Hinduism
was linked to conceptions of purity, especially expressed in female purity. The
process of nation building involved an 'invented tradition' of Hindu unity, while in
reality there was a patchwork of local versions and variations of religious rituals
and conceptions throughout India. Nationalist struggle implicated the
condemnation of the West. In the process of nationalist struggle and the creation of
national identity, women became 'the repository of the Hindu Spirit, a symbol not
to be polluted by the West' (1992, p. 17). The present intensified confrontation
with the supposed decadent culture of the West seems to provoke the Indian
middle class, resulting in a reinforcement of traditional values. Hindu
fundamentalism is especially strong among the middle class, when they strive for
Hindutva, pure Hinduism.

    Hindutva, which contains a strong gender ideology, is also expressed in
growing religious tensions. In 1992 and in 2002 there were fierce clashes between
Hindus and Muslims in which thousands of people were killed. Hindus turn
themselves not only against Muslims, but occasionally also against Christians and
dalits, former outcasts and therefore non-Hindus. Corbridge and Harris (2000)
suggested that the ideology of *Hindutva* has turned to an imagined past.

> The ideology of *Hindutva* contrives to combine a revitalized moral vision of
> domestic and sexual norms that promises to restore the comforts of old sociabilities
> and familial solidarities (2000, p. 190).

In the ideology of *Hindutva*, worshipping of Hindu gods, like Rama and Sita, has a
prominent place. According to the psychoanalyst, Sudhir Kakar, it is Sita who
plays a crucial role in the construction of present-day Indian female identity:

> The ideal of womanhood, represented by Sita is one of chastity, purity, gentle
> tenderness and a singular faithfulness (1981, p. 66).

According to teacher and publisher Madhu Kishwar the image of Sita, wife of Ram, has different aspects. She suggests that the image of Sita should be reinterpreted. She has found that, among her female students at Delhi University, Sita invariably crops up as their notion of the ideal woman. These modern, educated young women give a new interpretation to Sita. They interpret Sita's steadfastness and loyalty in her love for Rama, who mistrusted her, as a sign of emotional strength and not of slavery or docility. They point out that Sita refused to forsake her *dharma*, her duty, even though Ram forsook his *dharma* as a husband. These students perceive Sita as a person 'whose sense of *dharma* is superior to and more awe inspiring than that of Ram' (Kishwar, 1997a, p. 3). She agrees with Kakar, who says that Rama's personality is as ambiguous as that of Sita:

> Rama may have all the traits of a god-like hero, yet he is fragile, mistrustful and jealous, and very much of a conformist, both to his parent's wishes and to social opinion (Kakar, 1981, p. 66).

After redefining the image of Sita and Rama, Kishwar (1997b) also wants to redefine Indian marriage and dowry. These institutions, Kishwar says, have been judged more negatively than they deserve. When she compares Hindu marriages with marriages in the West, she sees many advantages for women in the Hindu system that provides the safety net of the extended family network. Hindu marriage is sacramental. It does not allow divorce. She stresses that in Hindu marriages women are respected as mothers and as sisters, and that they can exercise a great deal of power and influence in their households as they grow older. Kishwar states that dowry in itself is not necessarily bad, because it secures a marriage, and it gives property to women. The only thing is that the dowry should really be women's property, as it is supposed to be for pure Hindus, not subject to greed and merchandise before or after the wedding.

With her defence of Indian marriage and dowry, Kishwar (1997b) brings existing ambiguities to the surface. The institution of Indian arranged marriages finds support among all sections of Indian society. Other forms of marriage, especially Western marriages, with their implicit message of freedom of choice, individuality and personal achievement, are seen as unwanted, or even threatening. Marriage, as long as it is associated with the *kanydan*, serves as a building block in the construction of Hindu identity, as does dowry. Dowry should not be abolished, Kishwar says, but it should be brought back to its pure Hindu form.

The ideology of pure Hinduism can be interpreted as a process of empowerment because it strengthens national identity. In terms of Hannerz' ideas, this empowerment can be interpreted as being able to talk back. However, I hesitate to say if there is actually such a process; except for Indians in the Diaspora, nobody seems to be interested in the message.

Many-Faced Dowries

In present-day India, dowry is embedded in the political and religious context of Hinduism, as well as in the context of economic and monetary developments. Newly available luxury items on the market provoke Indian consumers to use dowry as a means of obtaining these goods. Young men feel that they have a right to ask for dowry, when age-old traditions of son-preference intertwine with modern market values. A leftist, highly educated economist from Kerala once told me that he certainly wanted dowry because, after all, his family had invested in his education, and all these expenses should be met by his future father-in-law.

In her discussion of the social and economic transformations in South India, Kapadia argues that globalization ensured the triumph of capitalist consumerism and that 'dowry embodies this consumerist modernity' (2002, p. 172). She states that dowry is part of a modern world of self-made men, rather than part of the old world of ascribed status. Besides, the modern system of dowry widens the gap between male and female status:

> Through 'dowry', men are able to generate both new wealth and a new social superiority for themselves vis-à-vis women, because 'dowry' generates a new class hierarchy between the sexes as well as a sex-based status hierarchy (2002, p. 173).

The nature of modern dowry in India is ambiguous. Although greed and consumerism play important roles in the rise and spread of dowry, dowry has never lost its sacred character completely. Among new and old castes and classes, one can find a kaleidoscopic range of overt and secret motives for paying dowry.

One of the reasons that it is so difficult to eradicate the custom, or even implement the laws that forbid it, lies in the fact that, for a variety of reasons, both men and women gain from dowry – or at least hope to gain from it. The AIDWA study concludes that:

> ...dowry is perhaps the only crime that is socially sanctioned among its perpetrators/beneficiaries as much as among its victims/losers (AIDWA, 2003).

Fathers and mothers generally want their daughters to live securely and happily, even when marrying them off is considered a burden. A father may want to pay dowry because the marriage of his daughter links his family with a family of higher status, as Van der Veen (1979) observed, or because he wants to impress his *jati*, sub caste, as Srinivas (1996) has argued, or because he feels that it is the duty of a Hindu to sacrifice a daughter, or because he hopes that his daughter will live happily and be treated well.

A woman may want dowry because she associates it with treasured traditions, or because it might give her respect, as the *dalit* girl recounted, or because she recalls that it is a safety net, as Oldenburg (2002) remembers, or because it gives her access to property, as Kishwar (1997b) argues.

Precisely because dowry has many faces, it is difficult to implement the law that forbids it. When dowry itself is forbidden but gifts offered out of love and affection are allowed, then who decides what is love and what is greed? Present-day dowry, the so-called monstrosity, is indeed an evil custom that creates greed and consumerism, and generates violence against women, but it also still encompasses *stridhan*, female property, and *dakshina*, the gift to the groom. Greed is only one face of modern dowry, *dharma*, plight, is another. One more face is formed by *izzat*, honour, and yet another by gendered property and inheritance rights.

In terms of Hannerz' ideas about creolization, the development of dowry in India can be considered a process of creolization when we look at the foreign influence from the centre that interacted with the local culture. British rule, educational reforms, and monetization of the Indian economy initiated the process of commercialization of dowry. The development of the consumer markets pushed the growth of dowry, but there never was a thorough process of cultural domination, as British marriage traditions never became popular in India.

When we look at the spread of dowry, we find a process of cultural dominance in which all local traditions are overruled by the growing importance of high-caste Hindu culture. The ideology of *Hindutva*, recently gaining in strength, is an attempt to restore the sexual and familial moral norms of the past. This process reinforces national Hindu identity, which might be interpreted as a process of empowerment. However, this form of empowerment is based on regression, on turning to the past, not on the progressive processes of creolization that Hannerz had in mind.

Hannerz' ideas sounded attractive to me, because I found a kind of underlying optimism in them: globalization would not necessarily lead to suppression of other cultures because these cultures in the periphery could absorb, change, grow and react. After looking to dowry with Hannerz' ideas in mind, I find that his ideas only explain what happens in India to a limited extent. When it comes to dowry, there is not much to be found that could be called creolization and even less – even with some optimism – that could be called talking back.

References

All India Democratic Women's Association (AIDWA) (2003), 'The Dowry Scourge', *Communalism Combat*, Vol. 9, www.sabrang.com/cc/archive/2003/febr03/gender.html.

Alexander, K.C. (1968), *Social Mobility in Kerala*, Deccan College, Poona.

Altekar, A. (1978), *The Position of Women in Hindu Civilization*, Motilal Banarsidass, Delhi.

Collier, Paul and David Dollar (2001), *Globalization, Growth and Poverty: Building an Inclusive World Economy*, Oxford University Press, Oxford.

Corbridge, Stuart and John Harris, (2000), *Reinventing India*, Polity Press and Blackwell, Cambridge and Oxford.

Dumont, Louis (1972), *Homo Hierarchicus. The Caste System and its Implications*, Paladin Press, London.

Gaulin, Steven J.C. and James Boster (1990), 'Dowry as Female Competition', *American Anthropologist*, Vol. 92, pp. 994-1006.

George, Alex (1990), *The Militant Phase of Pulaya Movement of South Travancore: 1884-1914*, CASA, Working Document nr 22, Amsterdam.

Goody J. and S.J. Tambiah (1973), *Bridewealth and Dowry*, Cambridge, Cambridge University Press.

Hannerz, Ulf (1996), *Cultural Complexity: Studies in the Social Organization of Meaning*, Colombia University Press, New York.

Kakar, Sudhir (1978), *The Inner World: A Psychoanalytic Study of Childhood and Society in India*, Oxford University Press, Oxford.

Kapadia, Karin (ed) (2002), *The Violence of Development: The Politics of Identity, Gender and Social Inequalities in India*, Zed Books, London and New York.

Kishwar, Madhu, (1997a), 'Yes to Sita, No to Ram! The Continuing Popularity of Sita in India', *Manushi: A Journal about Women and Society*, Issue 98, January-February.

Kishwar, Madhu, (1997b), 'Women, Sex and Marriage: Restraint as a Female Strategy', *Manushi: A Journal about Women and Society*, Issue 98, March-April.

Krishnamurthy, S. (1981), *The Dowry Problem: A Legal and Social Perspective*, IBH Prakashana, Bangalore.

Madan, Paul C. (1986), *Dowry and the Position of Woman in India: A Study of Delhi Metropolis*, New Delhi: Inter-India Publications.

Mazumdar, Sucheta (1992), 'Moving Away from a Secular Vision?' in Moghadam, V.M. (ed.) (1992) *Identity Politics and Women: Cultural Reassertions and Feminisms in International Perspective*, Westview Press, Boulder, pp. 243-270.

Menon, Leela (2003), 'Literacy does not improve status of women', *The Hindu*, Sunday Jan 05.

Menski, Werner (ed.) (1998), *South Asians and the Dowry Problem*, Westview House, London.

Miller, Barbara (1997), *The Endangered Sex: Neglect of Female Children in Rural North India*, Cambridge University Press, Cambridge.

Oldenburg, Veena (2002), *Dowry Murder: The Imperial Origins of a Cultural Crime*, Oxford University Press, Oxford.

Reddy, Shravati (2002), *Ancient Practice of Dowry Perpetuates Violence Against Women in India*, Digital Freedom Network, www.dfn.org/news/india/dowry.htm

Rajaram, T. (1983), 'Economics of Bride-Price and Dowry', *Economic and Political Weekly*, Vol. 28, pp. 275-279.

Randeria, S., and L. Visaria (1984), 'Sociology of Bride-Price and Dowry', *Economic and Political Weekly*, Vol. 29, pp. 648-652.

Saradamoni, K. (1991), 'Women, Kerala and Some Development Issues', *Economic and Political Weekly*, February 26th, pp. 501-510.

Seghel, Rashme (2003), 'Dowry Spreads its Tentacles Across India', *Infochange News and Features*, September 2003, www.infochangeindia.org.

Srinivas, M.N. (1956), 'A Note on Sanskritisation and Westernisation', *Far Eastern Economic Review*, Vol. 15, pp. 481-496.

Srinivas, M.N. (1996), *Village, Caste, Gender and Method: Essays in Indian Social Anthropology*, Oxford University Press, Delhi/Oxford.

Upadhya, Carol Boyack (1990), 'Dowry and Women's Property in Coastal Andhra Pradesh', *Contributions to Indian Sociology*, Vol. 24, pp.29-60.

Uyl, Marion den (1995), *Gender, Caste and Kinship in a Southern Indian Village*, International Books, Utrecht.

Veen, Klaas van der (1972), *I Give Thee my Daughter: A Study of Marriage and Hierarchy Among the Anavil Brahmins of South Gujarat*, Van Gorcum, Assen.

Chapter 10

On Globalization, Gender and the Nation-State: Muslim Masculinity and the Urban Middle-Class Family in Islamist Sudan

Karin Willemse

Introduction

In current discussions on globalization it is emphasized that we live in 'a world of flows (…) of 'objects in motion', which 'include ideas and ideologies, people and goods, images and messages, technologies and techniques (Appadurai 2000a, p. 5)'. Though gender is part of these 'ideas and ideologies', the concept has not been very prominent in studies on processes of globalization except in debates on the so-called global resurgence of religious fundamentalisms.

Although there are studies on Hindu, Jewish and Sikh fundamentalisms, most studies on the global resurgence of religious movements focus on the so-called 'world religions' like Islam and Christianity, as these are considered to be global phenomena in and of themselves. Variably, religious fundamentalisms are seen as the effects of globalization, a reaction to it, or both. In any case fundamentalism is a modern phenomenon intricately related to processes of globalization as 'fundamentalism itself has become a global category, part of the global repertoire of collective action available to discontented groups, but also a symbol in a global discourse about the shape of the world' (Lechner 1993, pp. 27-32). Thus, religion plays an important role in the way agents 'attempt to "fix the flow" and mark boundaries in the ongoing flux of globalization processes' (Meyer and Geschiere, 1999, p. 7).

It is precisely in the quest for authenticity of religious fundamentalist discourses that women loom large: as symptoms and causes of the downfall of society, as well as guardians of 'tradition' and guides of the next generation of believers (Tohidi and Bayes, 2001, pp. 37-42; Hawley and Proudfoot, 1994, pp. 25-29; Van Santen and Willemse, f.c). In popular as well as academic debates, Islamic fundamentalists supposedly oppress women because they are Islamic fundamentalists. This is a tautological argument and the question I take up in this article is *why* women are so central in Islamic fundamentalist, which I call here

Islamist, discourses. As these discourses are often central to political projects to transform society and capture the post-colonial nation-state, the answer might be found precisely in the historical relation between gender, politics and power. I will start from the research I conducted as an anthropologist in Darfur, West Sudan, in the period 1990-1992 and a short visit in 1995.[1] The relation between gender and Islamism was prevalent in my research, as the Sudan at that time had just been taken over by an Islamist regime. As the propagated Islamist family ideal was so recognizably 'Western', this made me consider whether this ideal is indeed authentically Islamist, or 'in fact' the result of the globalization of a Western bourgeois ideal. Let me first give more details about this family ideal before considering this question.

The Bourgeois Family Ideal in the Islamist Discourse in the Sudan

In 1989, Lt. Omar Al-Bashir put an end to the four-year-young democratic government of the Sudan, and installed a military junta that allied itself with the National Islamic Front of Hassan Al-Turabi (Bob, 1990, pp. 201-221). The main goal of the new government was to make the Sudan an Islamic nation based on the *shari'a*,[2] and therefore instigated what it called *al-mashru'al-hadari* or 'The Islamist Civilization Project'. This project aimed at 'purifying' Islamic beliefs and practices in the Sudan, and focused mainly on the conduct and appearance of women in public life (Al-Ahmadi, 2003, p. 28). Therefore, the government created separate bus compartments, for example, subsided 'new' modes of veiling and engaged, directly or indirectly, in the harassment of women, both from high and low-class backgrounds, whenever they appeared in public life in an 'un-Islamic' way. In some cases, working women were even removed from public life: low-class women selling food and drinks in the street were rounded-up, while professional women were sent on sick leave, early retirement or were dismissed outright. This policy was legitimized by an Islamist moral discourse that articulated the ideal gender role for Sudanese Muslim women as mothers and housewives within the walls of their houses, while men should be the providers and protectors of their families. In order to boost this gender ideal, mass-weddings were not only propagated but also subsidized by the new government (Al-Ahmadi, 2003; Hale, 1997, pp. 180-230; Simone, 1994, pp. 68-69; Willemse, 2001, pp. 303-323).

This Islamist morality is in fact related to a family ideal based on a breadwinner-cum-housewife ideal[3] that is prevalent in other Islamist discourses, such as that of the Islamist state of Iran where women were deemed most vulnerable to '*gharbzadegi*' or 'Westoxication', and also cast primarily as mothers in need of protection by men. As in Sudan, marriage was 'relentlessly advocated' (Sanasarian, 1992, p. 61), while 'the "family" and "family values" were revived as the cornerstone of a new and proper Islamic society' (Sullivan, 1996, p. 233; *cf.* Haeri, 2000, p. 353). Similar perspectives were articulated by the general secretary for the women's division of the Islamist party in Pakistan (Haeri, 2000, p. 351). In Egypt, Islamists maintain that 'women's main and indeed only role – "(…) firstly, secondly and thirdly" – is to be a good mother and wife' (Zaynab Al-Ghazali quoted in Karam, 1998, p. 215).

The similarities in the Islamist gender discourses seem indeed to indicate a global 'resurgence' of Islam. The bourgeois family ideal, with the domesticity of women and the construction of men as protectors and providers, thereby constitutes a common denominator. There is, however, another debate on this breadwinner-cum-housewife ideal. For, despite the fact that Islamists propagate these gender roles by referring to Islam, these are not specifically Islamist, or even Islamic, as Abu-Lughod (1998b) states with respect to Egypt:

> (…) [T]he assertion of the proper role of a woman as wife and mother, with the assumption of a happy nuclear family (…) is now (…) couched in an Islamic religious idiom that gives it a pedigree. The duty of the mother is to raise good Muslim children (…). But I would argue that this vision of family and women's proper relation to husband and children is profoundly modern and its sources are entwined with the West (Abu-Lughod 1998b, p. 255).

Both Abu-Lughod (1998a, pp. 7-18; 1998b, pp. 255-264) and Ahmed (1992, pp. 150-168) point to the influence of British colonial discourse on the Egyptian urban elite's notions of femininity and masculinity, which have become the core of the current urban middle class family ideal, among liberals, conservatives and Islamists alike. In this colonial discourse, which can be located at the beginning of the 20th century, education of women was propagated in order to make women good housewives and mothers. In other words, the contemporary Islamist family ideal indeed bears strong similarities to the Western bourgeois breadwinner-cum-housewife ideal that might have been taken to the colonies by the colonial powers.

Thus, when analyzing the Islamist notions of gender roles that are central in the Islamist debate in the Sudan and elsewhere in the Islamic world, I am confronted with two alternative perspectives. Either the breadwinner-cum-housewife ideal of current Islamist movements can be traced to European colonial contact that engendered 'Euro-colonial worlds' (Appadurai, 2000b, p. 323) – in other words, these idealized gender-roles are the result of a globalized bourgeois family ideal with a gender regime that has travelled from the root-area, Europe, to the colonies – or these notions of gender are part of a global resurgence of Islam and form an intrinsic part of the way that globalization triggers responses in Islamic, and Islamist, communities that, by reconstructing 'an idealized past (…), reshape the present along the same lines' (Hawley and Proudfoot, 1996, p. 32). In this perspective, globalization triggers a particular re-invention of an Islamic tradition whereby gender fulfils a similar role.

However, I do not want to get stuck in a search for authenticity in having to choose between deciding whether the family ideal propagated in Islamist discourses is 'truly Islamic' or 'really European'? These exclusionary positions entail a search for 'roots' of the bourgeois family ideal. This would mean that I would consider processes of globalization as one-dimensional, one-way processes: in both propositions the role of gender in Islamist discourses is taken to be the result of contact with the Western world. Moreover, such a perspective means that

I would engage in a fundamentalist discourse and its quest for authenticity, considering gender as essential, fixed and bounded. I would rather refer to gender as part of the strategy to 'fix the flow', with flexibility, permeability and performativity as central notions of the way gendered identities are constructed and re-constructed in the context of transformations (*cf.* Butler 1990). I therefore prefer to rephrase the issue along the lines suggested by Kandiyoti (1998): 'The influence of the West was (…) mediated through multiple and varying levels of "othering" that must have had an impact on women's positionality, daily lives, and apprehensions of the "modern"' (1998, p. 275). It means that I will look for diversity in the ways that notions of family and gender intersect as a result of the dynamics of colonial contact and local constructions of belonging and selfhood. It is in fact a search for alternative modernities: modernity does not necessarily mean 'Westernization' but is rather 'a metaphor of new means and ends, of new materialities and meanings' referring, almost everywhere, to 'transformations, indeed, that have made the very idea of the "global" thinkable' (Comaroff and Comaroff, 1992, p. xiii).

In order to envisage such an alternative modernity, I will need to look at 'key-shifts' (Mills, 1997, p. 26; Willemse, 2001, p. 25, *see also Davids this volume*) in the history of constructions of gender and family ideals in a particular location, in this case Sudan. By analyzing the dynamics of the emergence of the bourgeois family ideal in the Sudan as part of a multi-dimensional, long-term process, I hope to understand the intricacies of local transformations in relation to colonial encounters. The focus on transformations in local discourses on gender and family ideals entails an analysis of the perspectives of the actors involved. I will therefore start my search in Kebkabiya, a small town in Darfur, West Sudan, where I conducted my research as an anthropologist.

The Emergence of an Urban Middle Class in Darfur, West Sudan

In 1916 Darfur became part of the Anglo-Egyptian Condominium[4] of Sudan. The introduction of taxation in cash by the new colonial government and the creation of other cash needs caused men to migrate, most often to one of the major towns or cotton-schemes in Central Sudan, while women took over most of the agricultural tasks. These changes fitted well into existing gender roles: women literally fed their families, while men engaged in trading activities and provided 'luxury' items such as shoes and clothing. At the same time, the new colonial rule brought to the few towns in Darfur a new middle class of 'Sudanese' government officials that had a profound influence on local gender relations.

In Kebkabiya, I lived on the compound of Hajja, an elderly woman who had been part of the former sultanic elite by parentage, but who also became a member of the new colonial, professional elite through her training as a medical midwife, and as the wife of one of the main traders. She was therefore squarely located in the shifts that took place in the town of Kebkabiya at the beginning of the 20th century. She was inclined to judge the old or the new regime, favourably or unfavourably, since she gained from both. Hajja was quite specific about the changes in daily life, such as the introduction of taxation in money, the new tastes of beautification, dishes, and fashions. One of the new items was the *tobe*, a six-metre length of cloth that is wrapped around the body:

> (...) The first man who brought *tobes* from al-Fasher was my husband. It was 'Bitt al-Basha', he took them from a British trader in al-Fasher (...) The first woman who wore a tobe here in Kebkabiya was the District Commissioner's wife. He came from al-Fasher, sent by the government. The rich people bought the tobes (...)

Interestingly, despite the fact that the *tobe* was purchased from a British trader, its name means 'daughter of the Pasha', after the first elite woman who wore it. 'Pasha' was a title for government officials of the Turkish-Egyptian government, or *Turkiyya*, ruling in Central Sudan in the period 1821-1885, but which had hardly touched Darfur.

Before the British captured Darfur in 1916, the sultanate of Darfur had never been ruled from Central Sudan. Only under Anglo-Egyptian rule did Darfur become part of the larger Sudan. However, though British colonial rule introduced a new bureaucratic system, it was the new administrative class that settled in the towns of Darfur that was instrumental in the transformation of the position of women, especially in the urban areas in Darfur. This new colonial administrative class came from the Nile Valley in Central Sudan, where the capital Khartoum and seat of the colonial government were located. While most British officers remained in the capital, the Sudanese 'junior administrators' were sent to outlying districts, such as Darfur, to administrate the country for the British.

In Darfur, therefore, the members of this new colonial administrative elite were considered foreigners who replaced or incorporated the old sultanic elite into its own ranks of administrators, policemen, soldiers and traders. In structuring themselves as a new ruling elite, the administrators and traders coming in from Central Sudan used aspects from their Nile Valley culture to distinguish themselves from the local, sultanic elite. They thus introduced a new life-style in the townships of Darfur, with alternative ideas about beauty and housekeeping, and new norms about the rights and duties, tasks and desires of women and men. Slowly, those indigenous social groups that aspired social mobility – and could afford it – took over the same norms, values and life-style. Domesticity, as well as seclusion and segregation of women, became standard practice in the townships. Some groups, like the Fur, even started circumcizing their daughters in order to live up to the new ideas about beauty and chastity and, at the same time, facilitating upward mobility by marrying their girls into the new elite families (Kapteijns, 1985, pp. 57-58, 66-67; Niblock, 1987, pp. 160-203; Willemse, 2001, pp. 241-242). In the context of this chapter, the question is whether the life-style of this new urban elite coming from the Nile Valley in Central Sudan, in particular their notion of gender and family relations, can indeed be traced to the influence of the British colonial rule in Central Sudan, as seems to have been the case in neighbouring Egypt.

The processes of change in Darfur, in the far west of the new Anglo-Egyptian Condominium, took place during the same period as those recorded for Egypt. Authors like Ahmed (1992, p. 158-163), Abu-Lughod (1998a, p.11 and 1998b, pp. 255-262) and Shakry (1998, pp. 131-138, 148-150) point specifically to the influence in Egypt and in other colonies in the Middle East, of the ideas articulated by the lawyer Qasim Amin in his books *The Liberation of Women* (1899) and *The New Woman* (1900) at the turn of the century. He was in particular promoting education for women in order for them to fulfil their duties as housewives and mothers caring for their children 'physically, mentally and morally' (quoted in Ahmed, 1992, pp. 159), thereby explicitly referring to the British as an example. In the same period in England, a pronounced shift in the perceptions of femininity took place, from supporting wives to educated mothers, who were deemed to raise the next generation of citizens for a strong nation (Davin, 1997, pp. 90-108).

Central Sudan, where the new elite that settled in Darfur hailed from, had already come under Anglo-Egyptian rule in 1899 and Egyptian discourses on women, like those instigated by Qasim Amin, might have influenced Central Sudanese society. Indeed, as a document of 1906 on a petition demanding girls' education in the Sudan stated, 'The majority of the signatures were no doubt Egyptian officials anxious that means of education for their daughters should be brought within their reach (...)', whereby Egypt is referred to explicitly as an example for (Central) Sudan (Starkey, 1992, p. 416). In Central Sudan a discourse on the need of educating women similar to the one in Egypt had come up during that period. Sheikh Babikr Bedri, who later started working as an Educational Officer of the Anglo-Egyptian Condominium, opened the first Girls' School in 1907. He promoted schooling of girls, as 'a modern educated young man would be attracted to an educated young woman for a wife' (Beasley, 1992, pp. 24-25). Other middle class Sudanese considered the education of women a means to 'give us better wives and mothers' (Beasley, 1992, pp. 24-25).

However, it seems highly unlikely that Badri was simply echoing the thought of Qasim Amin as, apart from similarities, there were also some marked differences. Not only had girls' education already been introduced in Egypt in the early 19th century, Badri and his contemporaries did not propagate conjugal love, companionate marriage, nuclear families and de-veiling, as Qasim Amin had done, nor did Sudanese spokesmen refer as explicitly as in the Egyptian discourse to the superior culture of the Europeans (Abu-Lughod, 1998, pp. 11-13; Ahmed, 1992, pp. 143, 158-163; Beasley, 1992, pp. 24-25). An indication of this different attitude towards Western innovation is to be found in the fact that Sudanese women who were trained to serve in the government, predominantly as nurses, midwives and teachers, did not dress in British uniforms. Instead, they started wearing a white *tobe*, which was one of the privileges of these government-trained women: entering the public sphere without a chaperone.[5]

Moreover, the principle of 'indirect rule' meant that British officers took up the few central positions in the government structure, while Sudanese nationals were trained to rule the vast country for them. Those Sudanese who were recruited for British colonial administration came predominantly from the vicinity of the capital Khartoum in the Nile Valley. As British officers were not allowed to bring their wives to the colony until after World War I, there were few opportunities for the Nile Valley elite to copy European lifestyles (Frost, 1984, p. 81).

More important, however, was the fact that the new middle class elite and the Darfur host society perceived the new lifestyle as more Islamic – and therefore better. The transformation of the Darfur elite into an urban middle class was also locally experienced as a process of (re-)Islamization rather than Westernization. In order to understand this local perception, I will have to turn to the genesis of the new elite in the Nile-Valley in Central Sudan.

The Genesis of the Riverain 'Bourgeois' Class in Sudan

The genesis of a new bureaucratic bourgeois class in Central Sudan had started at least a century before they arrived in Darfur under British colonial rule. In 1821, Turkish-Egyptian forces captured Sinnar in central Northern-Sudan on behalf of Muhammad Ali, the Ottoman ruler of Egypt. This colonial power facilitated a consolidation of the political and social transformation of this Nile Valley society that had already taken place in the 17th and 18th centuries: 'The forms of rule established by the Turks encouraged the transformation of society in Sinnar (…), giving an intensified stimulus to the spread of bourgeoisie institutions' (Spaulding, 1985, p. xx). It led to a process of urbanization and class differentiation, even before Turkish colonization, that obliterated the former sultanate and transformed its economy into one of mercantile capitalism.[6] Not only did the newly-risen towns attract religious leaders, labourers and traders in goods and slaves, but they also attracted their families (Kapteijns, 1985, pp. 66-67; Spaulding, 1985, pp. 150, pp. 178-198, p. 238). This transformation process in Central Sudan facilitated the emergence of an indigenous middle class that 'claimed Arab identity, practiced patrilineal descent, employed coin currencies, and bound itself in its dealings by the standards of Islamic law' (Spaulding, 1985, pp. xviii-xix).

Although there had been contacts with the Western world before British colonial rule took hold of the Sudan in 1898, the new indigenous elite that emerged in the towns in the Nile Valley in the early 19th century did not pose as a Westernized elite. It turned to a more orthodox Islam in order to distinguish itself from the localized forms of Islam and to undermine the power of local Muslim leaders (Spaulding, 1985, p. 143). In the towns, this more orthodox interpretation of Islam not only influenced commercial dealings, but also social life. Moreover, the increased use of slaves meant that middle class women, in particular, gradually abandoned their productive roles and some of their household tasks, such as grinding grain and fetching water. One of the most visible markers of this new status of women from the newly established middle class was 'their adoption of the modern *tob* (sic), an enveloping robe which covered not only the lower body but also the torso and head, a strikingly beautiful garment, but expensive and awkward, rendering most forms of physical labor impossible' (Spaulding, 1985, pp. 192-193).

In other words, in Central Sudan the emergence of an urban bourgeoisie had not just taken place in the late 19th and early 20th centuries after contact with British colonizers. The ideal of the domesticity of middle class women in Central Sudan developed in the course of the 17th and 18th centuries, and gained dominance in the 19th century. It was the result of the articulation of an Ottoman social economy with an indigenous process of change. It was therefore not a Western bourgeois ideal that the new Nile Valley middle class wanted to live up to, as seems to have been the case in Egypt, but a Nile Valley urban life-style based on a new Islamic moral code. The increasing 'embourgeoisement' (Lewis, 1991, pp. 5, 9) of women was therefore not a result of British colonial discourse that evaluated the position of Sudanese women negatively. Rather, this should be seen as a result of longer-term socio-economic developments, which were justified with reference to a new, more orthodox, interpretation of Islam. This analysis fits with the 'finding that there had already been a pronounced shift toward nuclear families before Turkish reformers boldly denounced the extended patriarchal family as outmoded' (Abu-Lughod, 1998, p. 11).

The formation of a Riverain 'bourgeois' elite class under the Turkish-Egyptian reign at the beginning of the 19th century is, therefore, the result of a pre-colonial process of transformation. During that period the growing power of the professional administrative middle class, which replaced and partly incorporated the sultanic elite, meant that a position in the administration and the new urban life-style became the markers of elite identity, rather than wealth or possession. Both the higher and middle classes aspired to membership in this new bourgeois class and tried to keep out the lower classes. When the Anglo-Egyptian Condominium was established in Sudan at the end of the 19th century, an indigenous administrative class already existed in the Nile Valley. It did not emerge as a result of British colonial rule. It simply provided a good basis for the colonial bureaucratic needs, which in turn boosted the administrative and cultural power of this indigenous bourgeois class (Willemse, 2001, pp. 239-242; *cf.* Beck, 1985, pp. 254-279).

In other words, in Darfur, the population perceived the new colonial administrative elite that settled in its towns in the early 20th century as a foreign Islamic ruling class coming from the Nile Valley in Central Sudan. It was a class that was considered – and that considered itself – to be a setter of standards of how to be a good Muslim person, one addressed by the Turkish titles of address that this class had acquired in its formative period, such as 'bey' and 'pasha'. While the British colonial government facilitated the arrival of this administrative elite class in Darfur, which transformed and partly incorporated the local sultanic and trading elite, colonial discourse did not cause its inception.

Therefore, I consider the new elite class that settled in Darfur at the beginning of the 20th century the result of a process of creolization of an indigenous Nile Valley, or 'Riverain', urban middle class culture and British colonial culture. A position in the government's administration was, as before, a marker of elite identity. However, this position under the new colonial rule was related to formal British education, which formed the basis of the Anglo-Egyptian administration. This conclusion does not necessarily negate the arguments of authors suggesting the constitutive influence of British colonial discourse on the development of a bourgeois family ideal and the domesticity of women at the beginning of the 20th century. However, British colonial dominance in the different locations of Egypt and neighbouring Sudan had different consequences for the construction of an urban elite. Though British colonial rule had a profound impact on both local societies, I maintain that the resulting cultural mix represented by the urban middle class in Sudan could hardly be seen as 'Euro-colonial' in nature. The genesis of a Nile Valley urban middle class from the 17th century onwards points at different, alternative, processes of modernization (see introduction, Davids and van Driel, this volume).

In short, the new urban middle class in Sudan and its notion of the domesticity of women is neither identifiable as a 'Western' bourgeois class nor as an intrinsic Islamic response to processes of globalization, even though the population in Darfur did perceive the transformation under British colonial rule as instigated by an Islamic Nile Valley class. The question then is how to interpret the current resurgence of Islamic fundamentalism with gender in relation to a bourgeois family ideal at the heart of both its globalizing and revitalizing discourses? Why are women that are in religious moral discourses allotted comparable subject positions in the construction of an 'authentic' cultural identity? As I stated in the introduction, the answer is to be found in the relation between gender, politics and power. I will therefore return to the context of the contemporary Islamist discourse in the Sudan and its relation to nation building.

Sudanization, Contested Masculinity and the Nation-State

While in the Sudanese Islamist discourse women in general were addressed in their capacity as wives and mothers, in practice the implementation of Islamist policy towards women differed according to the class backgrounds of the women involved. Though poor women were harassed in public when acting as petty traders, and beer houses were destroyed, most efforts of the government, like demoting, sending on leave, or outright dismissal of professional women in high positions, checking on their dress and behaviour and subsidizing veils and weddings, were directed at elite women rather than non-elite ones. The Islamist government obviously felt that women of the administrative elite needed to be guided in living up to their notions of providers, mothers and housewives. This constitutes a paradox, as the Islamist notion of 'correct' Muslimhood was based on those of the administrative elite. The Islamist government referred to the so-called educated elite women as the model of the Muslim woman. A closer look at this paradox, whereby ideal-typical female Muslims are the most targeted subjects, might offer a clue as to why the moral discourse was so important to the Islamist government.

As I stated in the introduction, Islamist discourses and their policy with respect to working women should not to be understood as a logical outcome of the supposed misogynist nature of Islam. Explicit references by governments to gender relations have to be analyzed as part of the politics and power game in which the post-colonial nation-state is involved. Hawley and Proudfoot (1994, pp. 27-29), for example, point out that in fundamentalist discourses women are singled out because of the idea that only when women would take up their symbolic roles in real life are men able to take up theirs. How, then, can one understand this discursive strategy of the Islamist government, which refers to women as points of reference for men to construct their gender identities?

In Sudan, as I described above, formal education gave members of the indigenous administrative elite[7] access to positions within the colonial government. Also, after independence in 1956, education remained one of the main avenues of upward mobility, especially for ambitious young men. These came from different parts of the new post-colonial state, and also from rural areas where Islamization and Arabization had not been very influential, to join government service. They were expected to engage in a process of 'Sudanization': to denounce their local, ethnic, religious and kinship loyalties in favour of a Sudanese identity related to a national 'imagined community' (Anderson, 1991). These potential new administrators were therefore not only taught lessons, but also the correct conduct and lifestyle befitting a member of the administrative bourgeois elite, as it had developed over the last centuries in Central Sudan.

In other words, this national identity was not as 'national' as the label 'Sudanese' suggested. In fact, general citizenship for all Sudanese subjects was never part of the quest for a national identity. The established Riverain urban elite referred to their 'core culture' (Harir, 1994, p. 49) in defining this general 'Sudanese' identity. These former Nile Valley elites, who were prominent and early members of the new 'Sudanese' national elite, used its specific history of Islamization and Arabization to legitimize their exclusivist claims to political power as 'the legitimate sons of the land' (Beck, 1998, p. 267; Harir, 1994, pp. 27-33). To be a Sudanese national, one was required to have a lifestyle that was based on that of the old administrative ruling elite, which had taken over colonial rule and combined its indigenous lifestyle with new, 'Western' immaterial and material items to mark their elite identity, such as sophisticated food-dishes, imported cloth, the use of cutlery and porcelain, furniture and brick walls that allowed for separate living arrangements for men and women, the responsibility of men to buy all the necessities of his household with money; in short, a life-style based on the salaries earned by elite members in government administration. One of the most important distinguishing aspects was the fact that this money came from a white-collar job, not from trade or agriculture (Doornbos, 1988, pp. 99-102; *cf.* Beck, 1998, p. 258; Willemse, 2001, pp. 242-248).

The 'new', post-colonial Sudanese administrative class mainly comprised members of the established Nile Valley elite. This 'old' elite simply added British formal education as one of the assets for safeguarding its privileged position as administrators and, thus, as a ruling national class. However, this strategy of exclusion is inherently contingent. Not only is a national identity by definition accessible to all nationals, education is also part of a process of inclusion and upward mobility that allows boys, including those from non-Arabized rural areas, to become elite members. This contingency forms the basis of the Islamist discursive strategy with respect to gender.

In the 1970s, President Nimeiri (1969-1985) based his military rule on socialist ideology. His liberalization of education meant the establishment of primary schools in remote areas and an increase of secondary high schools in regional capitals. This facilitated access to education for rural children, both boys and girls, and at the same time made a stay in boarding houses less necessary. Pupils maintained relations with their kin and local culture. This prevented the early and intense socialization of prospective elite members into the Nile Valley elite culture, as had been the case before. This process was accelerated by the economic crisis in the 1970s, which led to increasing migration of educated men to the oil-states or to the West (Brown, 1990).

The subsequent demand for educated white-collar workers not only allowed women into government service but also accelerated the inclusion of secondary-school dropouts into the government ranks. As these junior administrators, teachers, et cetera, were not trained sufficiently, they had to make do with lower qualifications, salaries and social status than their predecessors. As a result, since the 1970s, this younger generation of educated men has increasingly had difficulties paying for the upkeep of nuclear families of their own, and have thus failed to be the 'good fathers and husbands' their own class propagated. Apart from the fact that they could hardly pay for the high bride prices and other wedding-costs, young educated employees simply could not afford the expenses that accompanied an elite lifestyle for keeping up an elite status. This means that the current economic crisis stimulates the new generation of elite members to stay in contact with their families in local areas, even after they enter government service.

Although their elite identity stipulates a denial of kinship ties and emphasizes the conjugal relationship within a nuclear family, the family's coping strategies dictate the opposite. Consequently, the educated elite has grown in numbers, but has thereby lost control over its 'core culture'. It has had to admit educated men and women as members to its ranks, despite the fact that these new members retain characteristics of 'other', non-elite classes, which goes against the construction of a national identity intended to escape local, parochial identities (Willemse, 2001, pp. 303-325).

In other words, recent processes of economic, social and cultural change have led to a contestation of the dominant Sudanese identity and its middle class notion of the ideal family from within its own ranks. Though the national ruling elite had to construct boundaries to differentiate themselves from the 'non-elite' in order to safeguard its privileged position, it is this heterogeneity within the elite itself that poses the largest threat to the moral and political dominance of the government. Young middle class members of the administrative elite have not been 'properly Sudanized'. It is this generation of discontent, young, educated males that the Islamist government targets in its moral offensive. These young men are important to the Islamist party, as they constitute a potential and powerful constituency; while at the same time these young administrators are pivotal in implementing the government decrees. More importantly, however, dissatisfied young professional men, in particular those living in the capital, have to be pacified, since they might endanger the current government as they did in the past.[8] Hence, the Islamist moral discourse in Sudan that focused on women was meant to distract the attention of the population, in particular of the young urban elite, from economic and social problems and to relieve the insecurity and anxiety of the current generation of young urban middle class men about their status.

The construction of women as mothers was thus a discursive strategy by the new Islamist government to claim political viability and maintain its position of power in the face of deteriorating economic and social circumstances. Women in general were constructed as a threat to social stability and the moral order if they did not keep to their symbolic roles as mothers and wives, as propagated by the male members of their own class. Women, in particular educated elite women, were used to marking the boundary between 'us' – the educated administrative ruling elite – and 'them' – the non-elite aspiring to an elite status – while it also held out the promise that men would be restored in their rightful positions, as the ones in control. In principle, as educated, professional women were sent home in order to take up their roles as housewives and mothers within the confines of their homes, this at least allowed men to take over the positions of these women. Once the society was organised 'properly' – in other words, was Islamic – a better, wealthier, life would be possible and men would be able to fulfil their 'proper' roles as breadwinners, the only legitimate providers of their families. This discursive strategy triggered the Sudanese imagination about wealth and images of a 'good life', as exemplified by (orthodox) Muslim oil countries such as Saudi Arabia (Bernal, 1992, p. 10; Hawley and Proudfoot, 1996, pp. 25-9; Willemse, 2001).

The moral discourse of the Islamist government was thus a strategy to redress the permeability of the boundaries of its national elite, an attempt at re-masculinization, which often occurs after traumatic 'un-masculinizing' events (Benyon, 2002, pp. 90-91). Women are central to this re-masculinization, as they constitute a common denominator that goes beyond economic and political differences. As symbols, they are able to get the male insiders to close their ranks. Whatever the differences among men, they are bound to agree on the need to protect their women, control their conduct and thus safeguard public order (Stoler, 1991, pp. 64-72). As Charlton, Everett, and Staudt (1989) point out, for nation-state building also in Europe and elsewhere in colonial Africa:

> state elites have discovered that promoting male domination contributes to the maintenance of social order in a period of state formation. A common solution involved offering a bargain to (some) men: in return for ceding control over political power and social resources to the state, they gain increased control over their families. Not only does this solution promote male domination, but it also establishes or strengthens a distinction between public and private spheres, and subordinates the private sphere to the public (1989, p. 180).

As gender is not an identity in and of itself, re-masculinization by the current Islamist government in Sudan also refers to a re-defining of Sudanese national identity. However, the government poses its discourse as genuinely Islamic and a break with the past. Since the post-colonial administrative elite was based on the indigenous 'Nile Valley' Islamic culture, the Islamist government was actually referring to a global Islamist discourse on gender in order to construct a new 'modern' political identity, while reconstructing the boundaries of the new *modern* Sudanese ruling elite. As a marker of this new élan, the government denounced the 'real Sudanese' *tobe* that had become an important marker of post-colonial elite identity as 'un-Islamic'. The new Islamist government proposed an alternative, 'correct Islamic dress' for women, fashioned after those worn by women in cities in Iran, Egypt and Palestine. For centuries in Sudan, the dress of women has been the material marker *par exellence* of cultural change, used in subsequent 'key-shifts' of Sudanese political history. The mercantile administrative class that populated the towns in the Nile Valley in the 19th century marked its new status by having women wear the '*tobe*', while releasing her from most household chores. Under colonial rule the cloth of the *tobe* was imported from India (another British colony) and had to be bought in the marketplace, as Hajja recollected; while professional women working for the colonial government started to wear the white *tobe*. At the end of the 20th century, this 'real Sudanese' *tobe* was considered a sign of a parochial identity and thus had to be replaced to mark the new modern, global Islamic identity of the Sudanese ruling class. Women in general thus carry '"the burden of representation" as they are constructed as the symbolic bearers of the collectivity's identity and honour' (Yuval-Davis, 1998, p. 29). In other words, the Islamist discourse on gender in Sudan is instrumental in representing a new political course that, at the same time, constructs a national identity based on a shared cultural aspect, Islam. The Islamist discourse thus propagates a 'bourgeois' notion of gender and family relations as part of a project of modernizing politics in relation to a 'global' Islam. This discourse on gender uses the symbolic construction of the Muslim woman as a means of offering educated young men an alternative, attractive future. How does this relate to Islamism as a global phenomenon?

Gender, Family Ideals and the Nation-State

Interestingly, the ideal of the Islamist 'bourgeois' nuclear family is not unique to Sudan, or to Islamist movements. In non-Islamic towns like Yaoundé, Dar es-Salaam, Nairobi and Mexico, the emphasis on marriage, domestication of women and men as providers is central to the ideal of urban family life. Moreover, male members of these urban middle class elites, express similar feelings of frustration and failure as urban males in Khartoum did (*cf.* Gutman, 1996, p. 221; Guzmán Stein, 2001, pp. 130-132; Niger-Thomas, 2000; Silberschmidt, 2001, pp. 661-667). There is apparently more commonality among urban elites elsewhere in the world than the focus on religious fundamentalisms would suggest. As Wilford (1998) states:

> What matters here is not whether fundamentalist interpretation of Islam, Hinduism, Judaism, or, for that matter, Christianity (...) is more or less oppressive to women,

but the role(s) women are assigned as cultural markers of national identity and property. The compulsory veiling of women by nationalist movements in Sudan, Iran or Afghanistan, whether they are seeking to shore-up existing regimes or fashion new ones, is but a graphic representation of women's subordination that elsewhere may assume more subtle forms but which are, nevertheless, integral to the processes of defining a national identity (Wilford, 1998, pp. 5-6).

It is not religious fundamentalism that is the common, global, aspect but the vulnerability of the nation-state. In other words, the relation between globalization, gender and religion is to be found in the construction of national identity:

> [N]ationality and citizenship, like race and ethnicity, are unstable categories and contested identities. They are all gendered identities and the construction of 'women', inside and outside their borders, are part of the processes of identity formation (Pettman, 1996, quoted in Wilford, 1998, p. 16).

As all post-colonial nation-states are confronted with the effect of processes of globalization and modernity, the contingency of the national identity is related to processes within as well as beyond state boundaries. Boundaries of national elites are contested as their lifestyles and positions of power are aspired to and problematized by members of lower classes who have gained access to education and government positions in the last decades. Attempts at re-masculinization are therefore merely attempts to address this contingency by reconstructing the dominance of its national elites. As Gutman (1996) states for Mexico:

> (…) the fate of machismo as an archetype of masculinity has always been closely tied to Mexican cultural nationalism (240)

while:

> Mexican masculinity has been at the heart of defining a Mexican nation in terms of both its past and its future (241).

What's more, the alliance between nationalism and bourgeois respectability is not a coincidence:

> Nationalism and respectability assigned everyone his place in life, man and woman (…) Woman as national symbol was the guardian of the continuity and immutability of the nation, the embodiment of its respectability (Mosse, 1985, quoted in Wilford, 1998, p. 14).

In other words, attempts at reconstructing a dominant masculinity such as in the Sudan (and elsewhere in the world) is related to this contingency of national identities. On the one hand, nation-states are themselves part of the globalization process resulting from contact with colonial powers. On the other hand, the legitimacy of national identities to claim political power and an exclusive elite identity are contested in current processes of transformation, due to recent processes of economic, political and cultural globalization. This in turn problematizes dominant masculinities. A generalized notion of the ideal woman as a mother serves to redress the permeability of the boundaries of ethnic, religious and nationalist groups and thus looms large in strategies of inclusion as well as exclusion. Outsiders are kept out while insiders are pressured to close ranks around a similarly homogeneous conception of masculinity that relates to a dominant notion of femininity (Anthias and Yuval-Davis, 1989, pp. 1-14; Kandiyoti, 1991, pp. 9-10; Stoler, 1991, pp. 51-101).

Concluding Remarks: Contingent National Identity and Contested Masculinity

As I have analyzed above, in the Sudan gender has been prominent in the recent re-construction, or re-masculinization, of an urban educated ruling class, which was constructed in a period before the establishment of British colonial rule. Though it is evident that 'Europe was a crucial context for its historical development and its political and cultural life' (Abu-Lughod, 1998, p. 18), it is not self-evident that the current national elite's discourse and culture in the Sudan is itself the result of a process of globalization, extrapolating from Europe. Abu-Lughod (1998) states that 'one may argue that there persisted alternative "traditions" within which argumentation took place, and thus that intellectual life was not only, as earlier intellectual historians of the Middle East have suggested, reactive to Europe' (1998, p. 19). It is precisely such an 'alternative tradition' and its effect on urban society that I have analyzed.

The current modern administrative elite, with its particular lifestyle and notions of gender and family in the Sudan, is not a direct result of colonial contact, or of an indigenous 'authentic' Islamic process of change, but constructed in the dynamics of both local and global processes of change and consolidation. The genesis of this urban 'bourgeois' class and its particular moral discourse on gender points to the existence of an alternative modernity that is related to the local history of mercantilism, nation-building and Islam: alternative in the sense that this modernity is not similar to Westernization or merely a reaction to Western contact or control.

In general, ethnicity and/or religion can be considered the 'mobilizing force of nationalism' (Wilford, 1998, p. 10). As education in Sudan and elsewhere in the post-colonial world has led to integration of culturally diverse citizens into the elite, the boundaries of the elite have become fuzzy, which problematizes the authority of this elite to rule. Therefore, governments of post-colonial nation-states need a unifying discourse to address their citizens and legitimize their power in an era of globalization that questions the capability of the nation-state to cater for the needs of its citizens. In Sudan, Islam is such a unifying discourse. It 'provides a stable identity in a rapidly changing society' (Moghadam, 1994, p. 11 quoted in Al-Ahmadi, 2003, p. 100), both in a local and a global context. It forms a basis for re-constructing a specific 'Sudanese' national identity in times of change and insecurity, while it has a global, modernizing aspect for the Sudanese, who relate political power and prosperity to Muslim oil-countries such as Saudi Arabia.

Religion is thereby not globalized, but mediates processes of globalization and localization. The reference to women as markers of the boundaries of national elites is a common theme in post-colonial nation-states. However, as gender is related to these historically specific ethnic and religious elites, it is not a gender regime in itself that has been globalized. Gender serves comparable purposes as boundary markers in discourses of inclusion and exclusion in historically and culturally diverse settings. It seems to me that the study of 'contested masculinities' in relation to nationalism offers a most promising avenue for a better understanding of this relation between processes of globalization and gender.

Notes

1   This chapter is based on a total of 16 months of field research (1990-92; 1995) I conducted for my PhD thesis, which was funded by the Research School for African, Asian and Latin-American Studies (LU) as well as the Scientific Foundation for Research in the Tropics (WOTRO), whom I would like to thank for their financial support. I also thank WOTRO for a 'fringe grant' in the project 'Globalization and the Construction of Communal Identities' (1999-2000; *cf.* Meyer and Geschiere, 1999, n. 8) as well as the Erasmus University for financially supporting this pilot study.

2   The *shari'a*, the Islamic law, was officially introduced as the Penal Code on the first of February 1991, and implemented on the 22nd of March 1991.

3   See Mies (1982), who coined the concept of 'housewifization' (1982, p. 180), a process concomitant to capitalist relations of production.

4   Sudan was formally not a British colony, but an area governed by Egyptian and British administration. The British, however, were dominant in the governing of the Sudan (Woodward, 1979). Although both Darfur and Central Sudan are officially located in North Sudan, their colonial histories differ considerably.

5   Personal communication with Sitt Yvonne, one of the first female teachers in el-Obeid, Kordofan: see the pictures of pioneering Sudanese women in education in Beasley (1992, pp. 344-345).

6   Although the term mercantile capitalism used for this new economy suggests a relation to European-based capitalism, this is not necessarily the case. The term refers to the dominance of a monetary exchange market economy, which does not necessarily mean a capitalist economy.

7   The highest positions one could attain via education were in the government administration, as private businesses hardly existed in Sudan.

8   Nimeiri, the military dictator who ruled the Sudan from 1969 to 1985, was ousted after the so-called bread riots in major cities, led by members of the educated middle-class (Harir et al, 1994, p. 267).

References

Abu-Lughod, Lila (1998) 'Introduction: Feminist Longings and Post-Colonial Conditions', in Lila Abu-Lughod (ed.), *Remaking Women: Feminism and Modernity in the Middle East*, Princeton University Press, New Jersey, pp. 3-33.

Abu-Lughod, Lila (1998), 'The Marriage of Feminism and Islamism in Egypt: Selective Repudiation as a Dynamic of Postcolonial Cultural Politics', in Lila Abu-Lughod (ed.), *Remaking Women: Feminism and Modernity in the Middle East*, Princeton University Press, New Jersey, pp. 243-270.

Ahmed, Leila (1992), *Women and Gender in Islam: Historical Roots of a Modern Debate*, Yale University Press, London.

Ahmadi, Hala, al (2003), *Globalisations, Islamisms and Gender: Women's Political Organisations in the Sudan*, Dissertation Catholic University of Nijmegen, Nijmegen.

Anderson, Benedict (1991) [1983], *Imagined Communities: Reflections on the Origin and Spread of Nationalism*, Verso, London.

Anthias, Floya and Nira Yuval-Davis (1989), 'Introduction', in Nira Yuval-Davis and Floya Anthias (eds.), *Woman-Nation-State*, MacMillan, London, pp. 1-15.

Appadurai (2000a), 'Grassroots Globalization and the Research Imagination', *Public Culture*, vol. 12, no.1, pp. 1-19.

Appadurai (2000b), 'Disjuncture and Difference in the Global Cultural Economy', in Frank J. Lechner and John Boli (eds.), *The Globalization Reader*, Blackwell Publishers, Oxford, pp. 322-331.

Bayes, Jane H. and Nayereh Tohidi (2001), 'Introduction', in Nayereh Tohidi and Jane H. Bayes, *Globalization, Gender and Religion: The Politics of Women's Rights in Catholic and Muslim Contexts*, Palgrave, New York, pp. 1-17.

Beck, Kurt (1998), 'Tribesmen, Townsmen and the struggle over a proper lifestyle in Northern Kordofan', in Endre Stiansen and Michael Kevane (eds.) *Kordofan Invaded: Peripheral Incorporation and Social Transformation in Islamic Africa*, Brill, Leiden, pp. 254-279.

Beynon, John (2002), *Masculinities and Culture*, Buckingham, Philadelphia, Open University Press.

Beasley, Ina (1992), *Before the Wind Changed: People, Places and Education in the Sudan*, edited and annotated by Janet Starkey for the British Academy, Oxford University Press, New York.

Bob, Ali. (1990). 'Islam, the State and Politics in the Sudan', *Northeast African Studies*, vol. 12, no.2-3, pp. 201-219.

Brown, Richard (1990), *Sudan's Other Economy: Migrants' Remittances, Capital Flight and their Policy Implications*, ISS Working Paper, Sub-Series on Money and Finance and Development, No.31, Institute of Social Studies, The Hague.

Butler, Judith (1990), 'Performative Acts and Gender Constitution. An Essay in Phenomenology and Feminist Theory', in S. Case (ed.) *Performing Feminisms*, The Johns Hopkins University Press, Baltimore, pp. 270-282.

Charlton, Sue Ellen, Jana Everett and Kathleen Staudt (1989), *Women, the State and Development*, State University of New York Press, Albany.

Comaroff, John and Jean Comaroff (1992), *Ethnography and the Historical Imagination*, Westview Press, Boulder.

Davin, Anna (1997), 'Imperialism and Motherhood', in Fredrick Cooper and Ann Laura Stoler (eds.), *Tensions of Empire: Colonial Cultures in a Bourgeois World*, University of California Press, Berkeley, pp. 87-151.

Doornbos, Paul (1988), 'On Becoming Sudanese', in T. Barnett and A. Abdelkarim (eds.), *Sudan, State, Capital and Transformation*, Croom Helm, London, pp. 99-120.

Frost, John W. (1984), 'Memories of the Sudan Civil Service', in Robert O. Collins and Francis M. Deng (eds.), *The British in the Sudan 1898-1956*, Hoover Institution Press, Stanford University, Stanford, pp. 65-105.

Gutmann, Matthew G. (1996), *The Meanings of Macho: Being a Man in Mexico City*, University of California Press, Berkeley.

Guzman Stein, Laura (2001), 'The Politics of Implementing Women's Rights in Catholic Countries of Latin America', in Nayereh Tohidi and Jane H. Bayes (eds.), *Globalization, Gender and Religion: The Politics of Women's Rights in Catholic and Muslim Contexts*, Palgrave, New York, pp. 127-157.

Haeri, Shahla (2000), 'Obedience Versus Autonomy: Women and Fundamentalism in Iran and Pakistan', in Frank J. Lechner and John Boli (eds.) *The Globalization Reader*, Blackwell Publishers, Oxford, pp. 350-59.

Hale, Sondra (1997), *Gender Politics in the Sudan: Islamism, Socialism, and the State*, Westview Press, Boulder, Colorado.

Harir, Sharif (1994) 'Recycling the Past in the Sudan. An Overview of Political Decay', in Sharif Harir and Terje Tvedt (eds.), *Short-Cut to Decay: The Case of the Sudan*, Nordiska Afrikainstitutet, Uppsala, pp. 10-68.

Harir, Sharif, Kjell Hødnebø and Terje Tvedt (1994), 'A Chronology of the Sudan 1972-1992', in Sharif Harir and Terje Tvedt (eds.), *Short-Cut to Decay: The Case of the Sudan*, Nordiska Afrikainstitutet, Uppsala, pp. 259-274.

Hawley, John S. and Wayne Proudfoot (Ed.) (1994), 'Introduction', in John Hawley (ed.), *Fundamentalism and Gender*, Oxford University Press, Oxford, pp. 3-44.

Kandiyoti, Deniz (1998), 'Some Awkward Questions on Women and Modernity in Turkey', in Lila Abu-Lughod (ed.), *Remaking Women: Feminism and Modernity in the Middle East*, Princeton University Press, New Jersey, pp. 270-289.

Kapteijns, Lidwien (1985), 'Islamic Rationales for the Changing Social Roles of Women in the Western Sudan', in Martin W. Daly (ed.), *Modernization in the Sudan*, Lilian Barber Press, New York, pp. 57-72.

Karam, Azza M. (1998), *Women, Islamisms and the State: Contemporary Feminisms in Egypt*, MacMillan Press Ltd, New York.

Lechner, Frank J. (1993), 'Global Fundamentalisms', in William H. Swatos (ed.), *A Future for Religion?*, Sage Publications, London, pp. 27-32.

Lewis, I.M. (1991), 'Introduction', in I.M. Lewis, Ahmed al-Safi and Sayyid Hurreiz (eds.), *Women's Medicine: The Zar-bori Cult in Africa and Beyond*, Edinburgh University Press, Edinburgh, pp. 1-14.

Meyer, Birgit and Peter Geschiere (1999), 'Introduction', in Birgit Meyer and Peter Geschiere (eds.), *Globalization and Identity: Dialectics of Flow and Closure*, Blackwell Publishers, Oxford, pp. 1-17.

Niger-Thomas, Margareth (2000), *'Buying Futures': The Upsurge of Female Entrepreneurship: Crossing the Formal and Informal Divide in Southwest Cameroon*, Research School of Asian, African, and Amerindian Studies, Leiden University, Leiden.

Niblock, Tim (1987), *Class and Power in Sudan: The Dynamics of Sudanese Politics, 1898-1985*, Macmillan Press, Hampshire.

O'Fahey, Rex, S. (1980), *State and Society in Darfur*, Hurst, London.

Sanasarian, E. (1992), 'The Politics of Gender and Development in the Islamic Republic of Iran', in Joseph G. Jabbra and Nancy W. Jabbra (eds.), *Women and Development in the Middle East and North Africa*, Brill, Leiden.

Santen, José, van and Karin Willemse, f.c. 'The issue of "Islamic Fundamentalisms", Masculinities and Femininities: A Joint Introduction', in Wim van Binsbergen, Anneke Breedveld, and José van Santen (eds.) *Transformations of Islam in Africa*, Brill, Leiden.

Shakry, Omnia (1998), 'Schooled Mothers and Structured Play: Child Rearing in Turn-of-the-Century Egypt', in Lila Abu-Lughod (Ed.), *Remaking Women: Feminism and Modernity in the Middle East*, Princeton University Press, New Jersey, pp. 126-171.

Silberschmidt, Margarethe (2001), 'Disempowerment of Men in Rural and Urban East Africa: Implications for Male Identity and Sexual Behaviour', *World Development*, vol. 29, no. 4, pp. 657-71.

Simone, T. Abdou Maliqalim (1994), *In Whose Image? Political Islam and Urban Practices in Sudan*, University of Chicago Press, Chicago.

Spaulding, Jay (1985), *The Heroic Age in Sinnar*, Ethiopian Series Monograph no. 15, Michigan State University, Michigan.

Stoler, Ann, L. (1991), 'Carnal Knowledge and Imperial Power: Gender, Race, and Morality in Colonial Asia', in Micaela di Leonardo (ed.), *Gender at the Crossroads of Knowledge: Feminist Anthropology in the Postmodern Era*, University of California Press, Berkeley, pp. 51-101.

Sullivan, Zohreh T. (1998), 'Eluding the Feminist, Overthrowing the Modern? Transformations in Twentieth-Century Iran', in Lila Abu-Lughod (ed.), *Remaking Women: Feminism and Modernity in the Middle East*, Princeton University Press, New Jersey, pp. 215-243.

Tohidi, Nayereh and Jane H. Bayes (2001), 'Women Redefining Modernity and Religion in the Globalized Context', in Nayereh Tohidi and Jane H. Bayes (eds.), *Globalization, Gender and Religion: The Politics of Women's Rights in Catholic and Muslim Contexts*, Palgrave, New York, pp. 17-61.

Willemse, Karin (2001), *'One Foot in Heaven': Narratives on Gender and Islam in Darfur, West-Sudan*, Dissertation Leiden University, Leiden.

Willemse, Karin f.c., '"A Room for One's Own": Single Female Teachers Negotiating Alternative Gender Roles', Special Issue on Women in the Horn of Africa, *Northeast African Studies*, vol. VIII, no. 3 (2001).

Woodward, Peter (1979), *Condominium and Sudanese Nationalism*, Rex Collings, London.

Chapter 11

Political Representation and the Ambiguity of Mexican Motherhood

Tine Davids[1]

> The world can survive without professional women but not without mothers.

Introduction

These are the words of a former female Member of Parliament (MP)[2] of the PAN (Partido Acción Nacional) during a round table discussion organized by a reporter of one of Mexico's national newspapers, El Nacional[3], on women's participation in politics. This discussion was held during the presidency of Salinas de Gortari, a period in which the NAFTA (North American Free Trade Agreement, ratified on 1 January 1994) was in the making and Mexico's president was investing heavily in the neo-liberal restructuring of Mexico's revolutionary political and economic heritage. What struck me at the time was that in this period of modernization a well-respected female MP still felt obliged to account for women's public and political participation on the basis of such a seemingly traditional notion of femininity, 'motherhood', while being herself a single woman without children. Why this need to pinpoint women in their roles as mothers? Departing from a perspective that takes women's agency seriously, as explained in the introduction of this book, this question needs to be addressed by taking a closer look at what this image means for women participating in politics.

In the daily dealings of female politicians, promoting this image of motherhood can be part of a strategy to deal with mainstream hegemonic political discourses. Women can negotiate with these discourses to create room to manoeuvre for themselves within the political arena. At the same time, at a national level, the image of motherhood as articulated by political parties could be intended to keep women in their 'places', inside as well as outside the political realm. At the level of political subjectivity, it could signify a strategy of emancipation for individual women. The boundary of this strategy is determined elsewhere, though, and lies within the power of the political discourse, enabling and inhibiting women's political participation.

This brings us to other related questions. How is this image related to the fact that women are still largely absent from political power in Mexico? Why, at this particular moment in time, does this image of motherhood surface and how is it connected both to modernity and to tradition? In short, how is this image entangled with Mexico's national political modernization project? To answer these questions, the analysis has to be broadened from individual political participation and women's agency to party politics – and to national and cultural politics.

Here, it concerns an ideal image of motherhood that is based on the religious image of La Virgen de Guadalupe, the Mexican dark version of the Virgin Mary. It forms part of Mexico's cultural heritage as a country where Catholicism is still dominant, a country where the relation between the church and the state can still be very problematic[4]. The image of motherhood figures prominently in this relation between the state and the church in Mexico's political history and is paramount in Mexico's national imagery (Brading, 2001). It is in relation to that heritage that this image gets loaded with all kinds of moral connotations such as responsibility, sensibility, decency and purity within the public and political realm and in the formulation of a national identity, as I will argue in this chapter.

The politicization of this image is not unique for Mexico, though. Chaney (1979, 1998), based on her research in Chile and Peru, refers to it as the image of the 'supermadre' (super mother), meaning the extrapolation of motherhood from the private to the public and political realm. Chaney indicates that women make use of this image mainly to legitimize their entry into the public and political realms. My argument is that the ambiguity of this image enables it to figure equally successfully within political discourses that wish to exclude women from politics and public spaces (see also Pateman, 1992; Massolo, 1994, p. 19). This is where globalization comes in. I understand globalization to be processes that, through the workings of modernization, connect places and people in complex relations, crossing boundaries of space, time and culture, as described in the introduction of this book. Political democratization, as part of nation building, is such a process, one that connects Mexico with other Latin American countries and with the rest of the world.

Democratization is also a highly gendered process. The way in which the ideal of motherhood as part of Latin American's heritage figures in these processes of modernization and democratization, of exclusion and inclusion of women into politics, results in similar patterns among these countries. Motherhood figures as a marker in the creation of what Appadurai has called 'alternative modernities' in his attempt to disrupt the dichotomies between the West and non-West, colonizer and colonized, modernity and tradition (Appadurai, 1991). Based on research in Nigeria, Larkin turns this term into 'parallel modernities', arguing that modernity, parallel to the West, changes the basis of social life. However, at the same time, these changes are firmly rooted in conservative cultural values (Larkin, 1997, p. 410). In this chapter I will argue that Mexico forms such a parallel modernity with other Latin American countries through the cultural repertoire of gender; i.e. the image of motherhood that tends to become dominant in national politics and in the creation of a national identity at moments of democratic transition.

In order to do so, I will take a closer look at two such crucial moments of transition in Mexico's political history, moments of key shifts[5]: the struggle for suffrage at the beginning of the last century and the more recent democratization process. I will not do this in chronological order, since the history of female political participation in Mexico is not one of seamless evolution and progress. Taking Foucault's notion of archaeology, it is not continuity but repetition that is recovered within this historical struggle (Foucault, 1972, p. 138; Perréz, 1999, p. 219). My analysis starts during the period of the more recent democratic opening of the regime of Salinas de Gortari[6]. Starting from the perspective of women's agency, in particular women of the PAN, it was their *negotiation* with this image (because it is in their *struggle* and daily dealing with this image) that I discovered this sense of historical *repetition*. Illuminating this process of *repetition*, *struggle* and *negotiation* of the 'supermadre' ideal first requires an explanation of the context in which these women were operating, or, to use the metaphor of this book – to give a general overview of the local landscape from which this process evolved.

Setting the Stage: Modernization at the End of the 20th Century

A key shift occurred in Mexico's history at the turn of the 21st century. This particular moment in time was one in which Mexico's ruling party, the PRI (Partido Revolucionario Institutional), showed signs of its dynasty starting to crack for the first time in more than 70 years of ruling the country. Since the beginning of its rule, the PRI was described as an enlightened one-party dictatorship. While often considered as one of the most politically stable countries of Latin America, Mexico's regime can be characterized by corporatism, populism, authoritarianism, personalism and electoral fraud. The political momentum referred to here is the regime of Salinas de Gortari. Salinas de Gortari (1988-1994) won the elections with just a small majority of votes. For the first time in its history, the PRI acknowledged the small percentage of votes on which this electoral victory was based. The then political context in Mexico was one of the gradual but steady growth of opposition forces, on the leftwing as well as on the rightwing (PAN). On the left, the opposition formed a coalition of different parties on a broad front, the PRD (Partido de la Revolución Democratica). On the right, the PAN was gaining strength by winning governorships in the northern states.

The democratic tendencies emerging in this period culminated in 2000 in the electoral victory of President Vicente Fox of the PAN. These democratic tendencies have to be considered as the outcome of a complex mixture of national and international liberalization processes. Free trade was a permanent part of the political and economic agenda. Former president Salinas's strategy was, among others, to create international confidence in Mexico's economy and remove most restrictions on foreign ownership. Salinas tried to modernize the political bureaucracy to a certain degree and to destabilize the power traditionally held by labour unions in Mexico. As such, it was a moment of political transition, part of a broader process of democratization and modernization that had taken place in states controlled by the military and in civilian regimes in Latin America, since the late 1970s (Craske, 2003)[7].

The activism of women's movements all over Latin America has contributed substantially to the accomplishment of these processes of democratization and women's increased political participation. Consequently, Latin American states have adapted feminist and gender issues in their legislative programmes. But this cannot be considered only as the result of women's political mobilization. As Craske (2003) describes, the transition to democracy has to be understood as part of the states' need to prove their commitment to modernity, democracy and internationalism. The pressure to grant women political and civil rights as part of a modern democratic state was reinforced by the United Nations conferences and conventions during the 1980s and the 1990s, which started with the first 1975 World Conference on Women in Mexico City. The international agreements concerning women's rights since then have been an important part of the democratization process, along with women's participation in democratization struggles (Craske, 2003).

In Mexico, this process of democratization became tangible at the end of the 20th century during the regime of Salinas, with the first signs of the cracking of the PRI dynasty. It was also a political moment coloured by the struggle and mobilization of women, for example with the initiative called 'from A to Z' (de la A a la Z), an initiative to bridge the distance between politics and gender issues. On both the left and right wings of the PRI, the opposition was able to mobilize large groups of women. The left formed a large platform, Women for Democracy (Mujeres por la Democracia). But the right, in particular the PAN, also succeeded in mobilizing women. At the same time, it was a moment in which political leaders tried to construct a democratic image by achieving greater integration of women in politics. According to Marta Lamas, a well-known Mexican feminist, Salinas negated conveniently feminist issues such as the struggle to legalize abortion for this purpose (Lamas, 1989). It was clear that the PRI felt pressured to modernize and, as has been more often the case, women's liberation and political participation were considered part of that process – or an easy route to get there.

From the first struggles for suffrage on the continent – for Mexico dating back as far as 1916 – until the more recent democratization of Latin American states, international processes of modernization and democratization have shaped the outcome of the struggle for women's rights at the national political level. The ideal image of motherhood resurfaces in this opening up of democratic processes, as happened at the beginning of the 20th century in establishing a Modern Mexican state, where suffrage became an issue. Both moments reflect that women's citizenship was considered a vital part of the creation of modern Mexico, with its image of democracy, progressiveness and economic stability (Craske, 2005).

At moments like this, moments of crisis, political upheaval or transition, it is the ideal image of motherhood that seems to become a dominant representation of femininity in national political discourses. This image is used and evoked by different parties involved in the process of women's political participation. This ideal image of motherhood is not only presented as a point of reference and identification for women but also as a powerful metaphor, which is convocated to come to the rescue of men in particular and the nation in general, making the transition possible (see also Martin, 1990; Mattelart, 1980).

Motherhood is certainly not the only image available with which women can identify in legitimating their political participation. Feminist movements and women's movements in Mexico have flourished at different levels in society and have inspired women's collective action as well as individual female politicians. Leftwing opposition parties, for example, have known successful female MPs as protagonists of feminist movements. Still, the political representation of women's movements and feminist ideals has always been problematic within Mexico's political parties. This applies equally to the PRI as to the present ruling party, the PAN. It is precisely this image or metaphor of motherhood that, in my opinion, is central to the problematic relation between the political representation of women and the way in which these representations influence women's political participation. In the next section I would like to explore precisely how this works.

Motherhood Politicized and Political Subjectivity

During the presidency of Salinas de Gortari, it was the women of the opposition party, the PAN, who were most articulate in propagating an image of women as being mothers foremost. They did so by emphasizing the importance of the family, their own roles within it and the family atmosphere within the party. The family served as a metaphor in representing the party and the way in which women's participation in the party was organized.

One could even sense this atmosphere in the way people dealt with each other during visits to the party's head office in Mexico City. The PAN phrase 'we are one big family here' seemed to be taken very seriously and literally. Gatherings were organized in such a way that they resembled real family get-togethers. For some female active party members who lacked a family of their own, the party was a substitute for the family (see also Barrera, 1994; Venegas, 1994). On the other hand, women, especially those active in the middle and higher ranks of the party, often became involved in politics via their families (e.g. belonging to families with a long politically active tradition) or via their husbands, following them in their political carriers (see also Rodríguez, 2003). Illustrative of this pattern of female enrolment in the party is what the director of Promoción Femenina (the women's section of the party) replied when I asked her how she got involved in the party:

> Well, I came into this because of my husband. To the extent that I became aware of the situation of the country, and therefore the motivations started to be more personal. Nevertheless, I think I am here in Mexico City because of my husband. If my husband hadn't become national director (*of the PAN, TD*), I would be in Chihuahua exercising my profession.

This rather informal pattern of female enrolment received support at a more formal and organizational level through a special women's section called Promoción Femenina. Organized to attract and integrate more women in the party ranks, women received training and were then supposed to move on and take up positions or perform tasks within the party. Promoción Femenina was not a place where they could stand still.

This was a successful strategy. The PAN had the highest number of women in the higher party ranks compared to other parties. One way in which the PAN created this was by presenting its politics and political events as close to the private and domestic sphere. This contrasted sharply with the political culture and rhetoric of the then ruling party, the PRI, where private life was displaced by public issues (Barrera, 1994, p. 89; Massolo, 1994; Venegas, 1994). The PAN promoted this image so much that even one of its political leaders, in an attempt to reach out to women, once claimed that women could 'do politics from behind the kitchen sink'. It was this style of doing politics that was a key to their success in co-opting large sections of the female population of popular 'barrios' (neighbourhoods) into the party, sections traditionally belonging to the parties left of the PAN (Barrera, 1994, p. 89; Massolo, 1994; Venegas, 1994).

Entering politics as wives and mothers allowed women to participate in politics without necessarily having political controversies in their families. Significantly, according to several of the women interviewed, having a political career often meant paying the personal price of divorce. This is particularly true of higher-ranking women, substantially more so for those belonging to the PRI and leftwing parties than for those of the PAN. The PAN seemed to solve these kinds of problems by offering women a subject position that integrated the family in women's political roles.

The controversy that a lot of women have to deal with in their daily lives between being professional women, such as having political careers, and good mothers is 'smoothed over' at a discursive level into an alliance of roles – being mothers and politicians at the same time: being a 'super mother' (supermadre) (see Chaney, 1979, 1998). In ascribing the super to the mother, the PAN creates an ideal motherhood that is both professionally and politically modern, as well as traditional. It is an image of femininity that women can identify with and that legitimizes their political activism. Not surprisingly, women articulate this image as part of their political subjectivity, as the words of the female MP cited at the top of this chapter, shows. This does not mean, however, that women merely reproduce their parties' discourses. To take the MP cited at the beginning of this chapter as an example, there are several things that immediately catch the eye in the way she represents this party ideal of motherhood:

> The evolution (*of humankind, TD*) exists of maintaining what's worthwhile and changing what's inherited without questioning its value. It is impossible to think of progress while ignoring the essence itself of being a woman, her motherhood.

I encountered a constant idealization of motherhood, as if women possessed a certain kind of femininity that, when geared towards politics, would outperform men's approach to politics. In one of the interviews I had with her, she even literally said that she thought women were less corrupt than men.

Although this seems a rather essentialist notion of femininity, there is more to it then reproducing a stereotypical image of women as mothers. In telling her life story, she constantly spoke of her own political participation and that of other women as something that came naturally, albeit as if they were to the manner born. At the same time, in analyzing her story as a text, it became clear that she created a subtext in her story. Through all kinds of controversies in her text and slips of the tongue, she acknowledged the fact that this naturalness was not something all women were born with, but something one decided or wanted to be. The creation of this image of morally superior women was a discursive strategy. The emergence of such a discursive strategy can be found in the pressure or the need to present women as being less corrupt then men and, to some extent, morally superior to men.

This MP did not construct an ideal image of motherhood as an essentialist notion but as a moral notion. As such, she opened the possibility for all women, whether mothers or not, of becoming moral mothers[8]. Simultaneously, based on this moral notion of motherhood, she was able to create the room to manoeuvre as a professional, modern and very ambitious single, childless woman in politics. In this way she did not risk losing her femininity and, even more importantly, her decency. She was not the only woman who did this. More women from the PRI displayed this need to prove that they did not lose their femininity or their decency even though they operated within a pre-constructed masculine domain, which politics still is.

The women of the PAN were far more outspoken than their PRI sisters in defending their decency by way of evoking an ideal notion of motherhood. Nevertheless, this notion was not altogether absent within the ranks of the PRI.

As described above, the pressure on the PRI to modernize its organization as a party was internal and external in its origin. An internal commission for modernization was called into being to effectuate this change. Salinas' goal was to overcome the authoritarianism that had dominated the party for so long, organized along corporatist lines (Rodriguez, 2003: 116; Cockcroft, 1983). Organizing women in a special women's section, based on traditional notions of women as caretakers and the reproductive roles as women, was part of such corporatist tendencies. Although women participated in the party, the way in which the party organized its female participants did not stimulate a further integration of women into all party ranks, especially not the higher ranks.

There was also resistance to this way of organizing women. One former female MP in particular understood that organizing women along separatist lines within the party was part of a discursive practice in politics in which women still got 'othered' on the basis of their femininity[9]. Women were ascribed traditional roles as caretakers and the educators of Mexico's next generation. Although women's economic participation in society was acknowledged and stimulated, this did not alter women's reproductive roles and the traditional subtext articulated with them. She portrayed these special women's sections rather cynically as female playgrounds. 'While men were occupying themselves with real politics, women were allowed to play. As long as women would stay in their play ground why should men bother?' In the opinion of this woman, the PRI was not able to reach out to large groups of women outside the party and mobilize them. She attributed part of that incapacity to the way in which the party organized its own women.

A democratic opening up of the party for women was necessary in her eyes. She proposed that the modernization commission should abolish the special women's section of the party. Despite the seemingly encouraging circumstances of a party in need of modernization and democratization, this proposal did not make it. It aroused too much protest, in particular from the members of this women's section themselves. They were furious. The proposal engendered heated discussions, debates and protest. The then president of the party did not want to cause too much disturbance and upheaval among the party ranks and turned the proposal down. This particular incident shows the ambiguity of the traditional notion of femininity articulated by the party. On the one hand, it enabled women's cooptation within the corporatist ranks of the party, resulting in a certain degree of political participation for the happy few. Hence the furious protest of the members of the women's section against its abolishment. On the other hand, it stood in the way of overcoming women's traditional roles and enhancing further emancipation and political participation.

Within leftwing opposition parties, the notion of motherhood was nearly absent. Particularly among higher-ranking female politicians such as MP's, it was the ideal of feminism that inspired their political careers. In the history of the leftwing parties, in particular the socialist party, it was not so much a traditional notion of femininity that stood in the way of women's liberation but the submission of women's liberation to the broader goal of socialist reform. Nevertheless, in the figure of Rosario Ibarra de Piedra, who ran as candidate for the presidency for the PRT (Partido de los Trabajadores, Mexican Party of Workers, which became part of the leftwing party alliance, PRD (Partido de la Revolución Democratica; Party of the Democratic Revolution), the image of motherhood was evoked. She told me that her political involvement originated from 'the sorrow and pain of a mother over the loss of her son'. Rosario's political activism was spurred by the political disappearance of her son. As a mother, she fought for the right to know what happened to her son and for accountability for his disappearance, which she made part of her political struggle.

Although originating from a totally different context, this way of politicizing motherhood resembles the way in which the mothers of the Plaza de Mayo politicize motherhood in their political struggle. It also resembles the way in which Molyneux describes the politicization of motherhood through the idealization of the mothers of the martyrs as part of the revolutionary movement of the Sandinistas in Nicaragua (Molyneux, 1985). Women became acknowledged and active by extending their roles as mothers within the private sphere to the more public sphere of the Sandinista movement.

Thus, at a political level, the articulation of this ideal notion of motherhood could be considered part of a strategy to make women's political participation possible and acceptable, or as part of a strategy to be modern working women, pursuing careers in politics. Although women's agency cannot be ignored, at the level of the national political discourses still other connotations of this ideal of motherhood were at stake. This particularly applies to the women of the PAN. I would now like to take a closer look at the PAN's strategy for making the limits of the discursive strategy of individual women tangible.

The Discourse of the PAN and Nationalism

At the time, the PAN promoted itself as the party that guaranteed change. It thereby propagated a new nationalism according to a more modern and civilized society. It profiled itself as a movement against governmental corruption of the PRI and a protector of civil rights. In the eyes of the PAN, the family was – and still is – considered the breeding ground for the moral principles necessary to enable this change. Women are addressed in their roles as wives and mothers, the ideal fighters for democracy and against corruption. Within this discourse, they became pillars of morality and defenders of democratic rights.

It is this ascribed capacity of women as mothers to mediate in a corrupt world that guarantees democracy. Mothers as defenders of the family are at the same time considered to be defenders of the well-being of society as a whole, as if the former were an intrinsic part of the latter (Davids, 1993). Democratic characteristics are attributed to women, as if women by nature were more democratic then men because they defend the general interest of the family. Through the extrapolation of this role to the public and political realm, the general interest of the nation is defended at the same time. Not only does femininity get narrowed down and represented as motherhood, the nation also becomes a symbol of family.

This lies at the heart of nationalist aspirations: a nationalist identity that women should secure for the country and the party's sake. Motherhood then becomes a political morality. By articulating the 'super' with the 'madre', motherhood not only gets politicized but also modernized to the extent that it symbolizes new democratic values, as opposed to the old authoritarian system of the PRI. The PAN does not promote itself overly by advocating its neo-liberalism or anti-populist measures; it promotes itself by presenting a nationalist image of an anti-corruption movement, protector of civil and political rights (see also Barrara, 1994; Venegas, 1994).

In propagating a new nationalism, the PAN opposes the old nationalism of the PRI. By constituting a new moral order, the PAN promises that, once in power, a change from the old system would be guaranteed. The slogan 'unite for change' (únete al cambio) symbolizes that change. It works both ways: articulating women's roles within the family serves to create a moral order, as opposed to the immoral political order of the PRI. At the same time, it serves as a role model for women, making it possible for them to be modern, professional women without losing track of their predisposed destinies as mothers. Motherhood as such becomes a rhetorical trope for women of the PAN in talking about their political participation – a rhetorical trope, meaning a culture text in the sense of one of the rhetorical structures within which cultural (and political) power has been organized (Crenshaw, 1992, p. 403). This rhetorical trope is not exclusive to the PAN though, and not exclusive to rightwing discourse or even Mexico. It made the PAN relatively successful in mobilizing women and integrating them into the party. As a national discourse, it is at the same time exclusive to women who propagate other identities than this ideal of motherhood, such as a feminist identity. Thus, as described above, although the strategy of articulating the ideal of motherhood by individual women could be a strategy to be included in politics, at the level of the PAN, it was simultaneously a strategy to exclude feminist women.

The urge felt by the PAN to propagate its new nationalism, as articulate as it was, has to be understood within the context of the political momentum, as explained above. At the same time there is a familiar historical ring to it. It is not so surprising that, in the discussion organized by the newspaper El National and cited at the beginning of this chapter, women themselves, in addressing the issue of women's political participation, reproduce these images of women as moral keepers, or make reference to it. For all participants, explaining the lack of women's political participation by referring to past images of women as too conservative, too closely tied to the clergy, as a consequence of their caring and reproductive roles as mothers, was a recurring theme. In the next section I will take a closer look at these images and this repetition in the struggle for women's political participation.

History and Repetition

The representation of women as moral superiors surfaces during the struggle for suffrage in Mexico. This became particularly clear at two moments in the history of that struggle: during the first feminist congresses of 1916 held in Yucatán and in a later phase of active women's participation during the regime of president Cárdenas (president from 1934-40). More or less against the odds, it was General Salvador Alvarado, as governor of the southern state of Yucatán in 1915, who tried to create a platform for granting women a role in the Mexican revolution. Alvarado was a moderate socialist. Education was the driving force of his political career.

He wanted modernization for Yucatán, following the North American example. Women's education and participation in society were prerequisite for this modernization process. Insisting on women's legal equality and advocating that women were capable of participating in political life, he initiated two feminist congresses in 1916. He also planned to create an electorate in favour of his reforms. He therefore turned to the female teachers of the region. Women were considered the best educators of children and should be prepared for this task. Emma Pérez (1999) states that the Mexican revolutionaries essentially expected women to be the moral guides of the nation. No matter how progressive Alvarado's views may have been, they did not move beyond the context of revolutionary discourse regarding women's education.

Although the two feminist congresses of 1916 can be seen as landmarks in the development of feminist consciousness concerning women's political and civil rights in modern Mexico, this new political space was profoundly orchestrated by the revolutionary rhetoric on femininity. The congresses also made clear that few Yucatecan women strived for active political involvement and that the majority subscribed to the moral and traditional connotations of the revolutionary rhetoric on femininity. It was a sort of enlightened traditionalism that these women advocated in their roles as educators of the nation.

It seemed that granting women political rights was not yet considered a serious option. Although the constitution of 1917 did not exclude women from civil rights, the electoral law of 1918 restricted the vote to men only. Opponents to women's suffrage ventilated arguments such as 'politics was a man's business' and that it would only corrupt women and make them impure. Besides, women were considered to be too emotional and capricious to vote sensibly.

In a later phase of this struggle – and as the outcome of five feminist congresses organized by and for women from different classes and groups – the 'El Frente Unico pro Derechos de la Mujer' (the sole front for women's rights) was formed in 1935. Although starting out as an autonomous movement, the then ruling president Cárdenas co-opted a major part of the front as part of his populist regime, filling his ranks with more women. In exchange, Cárdenas communicated to the nation that granting women their full political rights was a deed of intrinsic justice that could no longer be postponed. On 23 November 1937, the secretary of state of internal affairs sent a proposal to the senate to reform article 34 of the constitution by simply adding the words 'hombres y mujeres', considering this sufficient to grant women their full political rights. By May 1939, all states of the Republic had ratified the amendment. The only thing left for the congress was to declare formally that all states had amended the proposal. This would take until 1953 to happen.

Cárdenas succeeded in co-opting large sections of the population, men as well as women, at a time of fierce divisions between the right and the left, mainly over the anti-clerical attitude of the left. Cárdenas was in favour of women's suffrage but also afraid that, in exercising this right, women might create anti-revolutionary conflicts in the already tense relations between state and church, since the post-revolutionary, modern nation of Mexico was deeply anti-clerical (Farías Mackey, 1988). The right wing general Almazán took advantage of this polarization and campaigned effectively, unsettling the official party. The broad alliance of women's organizations became fragmented again and, from a federal deputation, declared that:

> ...women's suffrage could not be approved because the spiritual values represented by feminine virtues would be lost. Besides, women have not embraced enthusiastically the idea of participating in the political life of Mexico (Ríos Cárdenas in Ramos Escandón, 1998, p. 98).

Women figured as feminist, socialist and communist front fighters, as well as mothers, in the Mexican struggle for suffrage. Despite the radical positions and feminist identities that women represented in the new political spaces, it was the same image that Alvarado propagated at the beginning of the suffrage struggle on behalf of modernity. It was women's moral superiority that was turned into a conservative image, which became central in denying women their full political rights.

Within the context of the antagonism between church and state, women's moral superiority became the single representation of femininity that excluded them from their rights. Modernity, thus, could be articulated as a process in need of women's political participation. At the same time, the separation of church and state, as part of modernity, positioned women as 'the other' of men, being defined as a binary opposition between conservative women and revolutionary men. As such, women's conservatism played a functional role in the creation of revolutionary men.

Needless to say, achieving their political and civil rights in the end meant access to the political arena for women. For the ruling party, this also meant that women were organized in a special women's section of the party. In later years, this image of women as morally superior to men was part of the political discourse, organizing women in a separate section. We can therefore read the following in the preambles of the PRI:

> The party needs the collaboration of women, with their sensibility, their decency and their emphasis on spiritual values, to fight against dishonest practices and corruption (ANFER, 1984).

The image of motherhood giving ground to both women's entrance into politics, as well as women's exclusion from politics, is not unique for Mexico. During the struggle for suffrage in Chile, for example, a comparable 'wave' took place. There, too, the ascribed moral purity of women played a crucial role in women's access to the political arena. A variety of women's movements came into being in Chile, which collapsed once they entered the political stage. According to Kirkwood, this was largely the effect of the moralistic policy of one of the women's parties that had made it into politics. Failures were unforgivable (Kirkwood, 1986). Women, so to speak, walked into the pitfall of their own purity ideal.

Similarly, in other Latin American countries, such as Colombia, Peru, Bolivia and the Dominican Republic, the ascribed conservatism and the image of women as mothers got articulated in the struggle for suffrage and in granting women their civil and political rights (Pinzon de Lewin, 1975; Mota, 1980). Mota, for example, studying feminist struggles for suffrage in the Dominican Republic, writes:

> The woman in politics is the mother who soothes in difficult moments, which tranquillises a tumultuous world, and above all, who serves as a permanent example of the moral principles which are the basis of our Christian traditions (Mota, 1980, p. 272).

These struggles for suffrage are moments of 'key shift' in Latin American political history. History shows that women's liberation was not only a genuine struggle of women fighting for their rights, but also a potential tool in the hands of national leaders for establishing modernization and democratization. Although the inclusion of women in politics up to a certain degree was the result of modernity, the historical repetition shows that the ideal notion of women as mothers, articulated in the name of modernity, served simultaneously in including and excluding women from the political arena. Furthermore, in the cases of Mexico and Chile at least, there seems to be evidence of another type of repetition: women organizing themselves, forming broad alliances, eventually partly getting co-opted within the system and then silenced again.

This collapse is connected to the trends of national regimes – to essentialize the notion of motherhood. This lies at the core of the problematic relation between feminism and nationalism. As Cockborn states:

> Essentialism is not merely an interesting theoretical concept. It is a dangerous political force, designed to shore up differences and inequalities, to sustain dominations. It operates through stereotypes that fix identity in eternal dualisms: women victim, male warrior: trusty compatriot, denigrate foreigner (Cockburn, 1998, p. 13).

This history repeated itself within the more recent transitions in Mexico, to which I will now turn and discuss the limited power and troublesome nature of this metaphor of motherhood.

Interpretations and Reflections: Motherhood and Parallel Modernities

The questions that need to be addressed are: why motherhood and why is this troublesome? To start with the question of motherhood, there are several possible reasons. As has become clear from the historical repetitions and particularly within the discourse of the PAN in the period of transition, the ambiguity of the image of motherhood makes it suitable to be articulated with modernization and democratization, as well as with nationalism and tradition. In extending the super to the mother, the traditional idealization of motherhood of providing family care and nursing gets articulated with the modern, the super: working and participating in politics simultaneously. In extending the super to the mother, the national, in the sense of the Mexican mother nursing 'la Mexicaneidad' (Mexicanness), also gets articulated with the international in the sense of democratization and liberal labour participation. The way in which this image of gender figures in these processes is thus as much a reinvention of modernity as it is of tradition.

This is particularly clear in deconstructing this image as merely traditional at a subjective dimension. There, this image seems less essentialist. It leaves room for individual women to be professionals and politicians without entering into the controversy between being mothers (private sphere), workers or politicians (public sphere), or without running the risk of losing their respect or decency. At a discursive level, this image of motherhood serves nationalist discourses because of its moral connotations. It is this morality within the image of motherhood that is paramount in constructing a national identity (see also Yuval-Davis, 1997). In Mexico, the image of the mother as an image of decency and moral purity is connected to the image of the Mexican Virgin Mary, La Virgen de Guadalupe, representing self-sacrifice and moral purification through suffering. Therefore, it is the mother that becomes the representation of femininity at the national level – a femininity that suggests closeness in the sense of the asexuality and decency of the

Mother Virgin and is not opposed to masculinity (Melhuus, 1996, p. 224; Yuval Davis, 1997).

Furthermore, the image of motherhood represents the particular, specific Mexican and the general, albeit universal, at the same time. As part of the imagery of nation building, it forms a constitutive element in the complex connections among Latin American states, belonging simultaneously to international processes of globalization, nation building and processes of democratization and modernization and to the specific ethnic-cultural repertoire of local history and colonial heritages, rendering Latin American nations as parallel modernities. Gender thus figures as a marker in the creation of parallel modernities. This parallelism is also found in the way this ambiguity of motherhood leaves room to articulate women's inclusion in – as well as exclusion from – politics.

When these cultural values of motherhood are targeted with a turn to the right and towards conservatism, as the PAN momentarily shows, the relationship between feminism and the state will become even more problematic. When PAN took over in 2002, history repeated itself. On the leftwing of the PRI, the broad front of women for democracy collapsed with the victory of the PAN. Many traditional voters from the left voted for the alliance represented by Vicente Fox: a vote for Fox was a vote for change and thus a vote to finally kick the PRI off its throne. So far, most analysts agree that Fox has yet to make that promise a reality. Once in power, the PAN took a further turn to the right as far as women were concerned. At present, there are fewer women in high-ranking political positions in parliament and the senate than before (Rodriguez, 2003). The PAN turned to the right, however, not only in numbers.

Based on a religious worldview, their conservatism brought back the old controversy between the state and the church. In a speech for International Women's Day, the Secretary of Labour took a strong position against feminism, blaming feminists for several social ills. Inspired by the pope, the Secretary of Labour made it very clear that a woman's position should be in the home:

> A woman must recognize, love, and give herself fully to the profession of mother and heart of the home [and] must recognize the superiority of this mission above any other (Abascal, in Rodriguez, 2003, p. 253).

Although many women from the PAN, including Vicente Fox, distanced themselves from what they considered to be the personal opinion of the Secretary of Labour, personal views, as is often the case in Mexico, as part of populist tendencies, do shape public policy. Besides, the disapproval PAN women emphasized of this personal opinion had to be balanced with party loyalty and, as such, was not convincing (Rodriguez, 2003). The PAN's 'new moral order' was not only supposed to defeat the old order of the PRI, but also targeted leftist movements, including the feminist movement.

Women of the PAN claim to be modern women, emancipated and professional, but they do not identify with women's movements or feminism. What happens at a subject dimension (i.e., de-essentializing the image of motherhood) is the reverse of what happens at a discursive level: essentializing the image of motherhood. It is this trend to essentialize the image of women as mothers that lies at the core of the problematic relationship between feminism and nationalism, which makes this image so troublesome and an easy tool for excluding women from the political arena. Also, the fact that in the election of 2000 the wives of two state senators, with different party backgrounds, tried to alter their positions and run for governor of the state themselves, indicates this pattern and the difficulty women face in crossing the divide between public and private sphere.

It would be worthwhile investigating just how global this conservative turn of the motherhood ideal is. In contemporary Argentina and Chile, such conservative shifts to the right also seem to come more to the forefront. In Argentina, the clergy participates openly in policy decisions and, in Chile, divorce has yet to be legalized (Rodriguez, 2003, p. 253). Bacchetta and Power (2002) point out that rightwing female activism in state building and agenda setting is growing around the world and that motherhood is part of their strategy in relating to – and resisting – feminism. The extent to which this conservative trend is global also requires additional investigation, since the imagery of motherhood as a gender marker of national or regional identity is also connected to the specific emergence of neo-liberal discourse. In her work on the NAFTA agreement in relation to neo-liberal restructuring, Marianne Marchand (2000), for example, describes how the image of women as wives and mothers is being used as a marker in redefining the borders between the United States and Mexico.

Invited to reconsider the question of whether the imagery of the super mother could imply a source of women's power, Elsa Chaney replied in her article 'supermadre revisited', why not, if this is the reality for so many women in Latin America (Chaney, 1998)? Why not depart from this reality, as it is impossible to deny its persistence? Although I do not want to negate the potential of this image for women, I consider it to be a hazardous standpoint. I am less optimistic about this potential, for the reasons I have given above. However, much will depend on the women themselves and the direction that feminist and women's movements take.

Notes

1   With special thanks for their comments and support to Nikki Craske, Francien van Driel, Marta Lamas, Ana Lau Jaiven, Nienke van der Veen and Karin Willemse.

2   As Mexico does not have a parliamentary system but a republican styled after the US it would be better to use representatives and House of Representatives or congress. But a political representative is a rather undefined term and can also refer to political positions in a party. Therefore I use the term Member of Parliament.

3   Held on 9 May, 1989, El Nacional published an article based on these discussions: El Nacional, suplemento politico, Thursday 18 May. Present were another female politician of at that time the ruling party, the PRI (Partido Revolucionario Institucional) and the female head of the National University (UNAM) trade union and myself.

194   *The Gender Question in Globalization*

4   Mexico's Revolution of 1910 was deeply anti-clerical but experienced a clerically inspired counter-revolution in 1926 called La Cristiada, which was finally overcome in 1929, but the suspicion of the church's political influence still lingers on.
5   See for a discussion on the meaning of key shifts Mills (1997) and an application of this notion in the study of Willemse (2001) on Sudan.
6   Thanks to a grant of WOTRO (Scientific Research in Tropical Countries), I was able to carry out research in Mexico during the period of the regime of president Salinas.
7   There is a lively debate going on, centred on the question whether this transition really signifies democratic political and societal democratization of Mexico. This is beyond the scope of this article. For further discussion, see some of the literature on this subject, for example, Barbara Hogenboom (2003).
8   Willemse (2001) describes a similar construction of moral motherhood as a strategy exercized by women in the Islamic context of Sudan.
9   Within the PRI, women were organized in the ANFER, which was succeeded by the (CEM) Consejo pare la Integración de la Mujer.

References

ANFER (Alianza Nacional Femenil Revolucionaria), (1984), *Participación Política de la Mujer en México, Siglo XX*, ANFER, México, D.F.
Appadurai, Arjun (1990), 'Global Ethnoscapes: Notes and Queries for a Transnational Anthropology', in Richard Fox (ed.) *Recapturing Anthropology: Working in the Present*, SAR Press, Santa Fe, Cal., pp. 191-210.
Bacchetta, Paola, and Margaret Power (eds.), (2002), *Right-Wing Women: From Conservatives to Extremists Around the World*, Routledge, New York.
Barrera, Dalia Bassols (1994), 'Ser Panista: Mujeres de las Colonias Populares de Ciudad Juárez, Chihuahua', in Alejandro Massolo (ed.) *Los Medios y los Modos, Particpación Política y Acción Colectiva de las Mujeres*, El Colegio de Mexico, Mexico D.F., pp. 81-118.
Brading, David A (2001) *Mexican Phoenix, Our Lady of Guadalupe: Image and Tradition Across Five Centuries*, Cambridge University Press, Cambridge.
Chaney, Elsa M (1979), *Supermadre: Women in Politics in Latin America*, University of Texas Press, Austin.
Chaney, Elsa M (1998), 'Supermadre Revisited' in Victoria Rodriguez (ed.) *Women's Participation in Mexican Political Life*, Westview Press, Oxford (USA), pp. 78-87.
Cockburn, Cynthia (1998), *The Space Between Us: Negotiating Gender and National Identities in Conflict*, Zed Books, London and New York.
Cockcroft, James D (1983), *Mexico: Class Formation, Capital Accumulation, and the State*, Monthly Review Press, New York.
Craske, Nikki (2003), 'Gender, Politics and Legislation', in Sylvia Chant and Nikki Craske, *Gender in Latin America*, Latin America Bureau, London, pp. 19-46.
Craske, Nikki (2005), 'Ambiguities and Ambivalences in Making the Nation: Women and Politics in 20th-century Mexico', *Feminist Review*, no. 79, pp. 116-133.
Crenshaw, Kimberlé (1992), 'Whose Story is it Anyway? Feminist and Antiracist Appropriations of Anita Hill', in Clarence México Thomas (ed.) *Racing Justice, Engendering Power: Essays on Anita Hill*, Pantheon Books, New York, pp. 402-440.
Davids, Tine (1993), 'Identidad Femenina Representación Política: Algunas Consideraciones Teóricas', in María Luisa Tarrés (ed.) *La Voluntad de Ser, Mujeres en los Noventa*, El Colegio de México, México, D.F., pp. 213-241.

Foucault, Michel (1972), *The Archeology of Knowledge*, Pantheon, New York.
Hogenboom, Barbara (2003), 'Mexico in Transition', *European Review of Latin American and Caribbean Studies*, No.75, October 2003, pp. 137-143.
Kirkwood, Julieta (1990), *Ser Politica en Chile: Nudos de Sabiduría Feminista*, Editorial Cuarto Propio, Chile.
Lamas, Marta (1989) 'Las Mujeres y las Políticas Públicas', *FEM*, Vol.14, No. 86, pp. 7-14.
Larkin, Brian (1997), 'Indian Films and Nigerian Lovers: Media and the Creation of Parallel Modernities', *Africa*, Vol.67, No. 3, pp. 406-440.
Mackey, Ma. Emilia Farías (1988), 'La Participación de la Mujer en la Política', in *México 75 Años de Revolución*, Fondo de Cultura Económica, México. pp. 693-817.
Marchand, Marianne H. and Runyan, Anne Sisson (2000), 'Introduction, Feminist Insights of Global Restructuring: Conceptualizations and Reconceptualizations', in M. Marchand and A.S. Runyan (eds.) *Gender and Global Restructuring, Sightings, Sites and Resistances*, Routledge, London, pp. 1-22.
Martin, Joann (1990), 'Motherhood and Power: The Production of a Women's Culture of Politics in a Mexican Community', *American Ethnologist*, Vol.17, Nr. 3, pp. 470-490.
Massolo, Alejandro (1994) 'Introducción. Política y Mujeres: una Peculiar Relación', in Alejandro Massolo (ed.) *Los Medios y los Modos: Particpación Política y Acción Colectiva de las Mujeres*, El Colegio de Mexico, Mexico D.F., pp. 13-40.
Mattelart, Michele, (1980) 'The Feminine Version of the Coup d'Etat', in June Nash and Helen Safa (eds.) *Sex and Class*, Bergin and Garvey Publishers, Inc., Massachusets., pp. 279-302.
Melhuus, Marit (1996), 'Power, Value and the Ambiguous Meanings of Gender', in Marit Melhuus and Kristi Anne Stølen (eds.) *Machos, Mistresses, Madonnas: Contesting the Power of Latin American Gender Imagery*, Verso, London and New York, pp. 207-230.
Mills, Sara (1997), *Discourse*, Routledge, London and New York.
Molyneux, Maxime (1985), 'Mobilisation without Emancipation? Women's Interests, the State, and Revolution in Nicaragua', *Feminist Studies*, Vol.11, Nr 2, pp. 227-254.
Mota, Vivian M (1980), 'Politics and Feminism in the Dominican Republic: 1931-1945 and 1966-1974', in June Nash and Helen Safa (eds.) *Sex and Class*, Bergin and Garvey Publishers, Inc., Massachusets., pp. 265-279.
Pateman, Carole (1992), 'Equality, Difference, Subordination: The Politics of Motherhood and Women's Citizenship', in Gisela Bock and Susan James (eds.) *Beyond Equality and Difference*, Routledge, New York.
Pérez, Emma (1999), 'Feminism-in-Nationalism: The Gendered Subaltern at the Yucatán Feminist Congresses of 1916', in Caren Kaplan, Norma Alarcón, and Minoo Moallem (eds.) *Between Woman and Nation*, Duke University Press, Durham and London, pp. 219-243.
Pinzon, de Lewin (1975), 'Women the Vote, and the Party in the Politics of the Colombian National Front', *Journal of Inter American Studies*, Vol.17, No. 4.
Ramos, Carmen Escadón (1998), 'Women and Power in Mexico: The Forgotten Heritage, 1880-1954', in Victoria Rodriguez (ed.) *Women's Participation in Mexican Political Life*, Westview Press, Oxford (USA), pp. 87-103.
Rodríguez, Victoria (2003) *Women in Contemporary Mexican Politics*, University of Texas Press, Austin.
Venegas, Lilia Aguilera (1994), 'Mujeres en la Militancia Blanquiazul', in Alejandra Massolo (ed.) *Los Medios y los Modos: Particpación Política y Acción Colectiva de las Mujeres*, El Colegio de Mexico, Mexico D.F., pp. 45-78.

Willemse, Karin (2001), *'One Foot in Heaven': Narratives on Gender and Islam in Darfur, West-Sudan*, Dissertation Leiden University, Leiden.
Yuval-Davis, Nira (1997), *Gender and Nation*, Sage Publications, London, Thousand Oaks, New Delhi.

Chapter 12

Layered Meanings of Community: Experiences of Iranian Women Exiles in 'Irangeles'

Halleh Ghorashi

Introduction

By the end of 20th century, the impact of globalization was especially visible in the emergence of new forms of identifications. Hall (1992, p. 297), for example, says that 'modern nations are all cultural hybrids'. Young believes that 'heterogeneity, cultural interchange and diversity have now become the self-conscious identity of modern society' (Young, 1995, p. 4). The era of globalization has created strong bedding for the emergence of newly constructed local and/or transnational imagined cultural communities. In this chapter I will focus on the emergence of an Iranian community – 'Irangeles' – in Southern California, in the United States of America, and its impact on the lives of a group of Iranian women living in the area. The data presented in this chapter are the result of nine months of fieldwork in California in 1997 and another two months in 1998. During this period, I used the method of participant observation, by being actively present at Iranian gatherings and ceremonies. Also, I listened to the life stories of 20 Iranian women who were politically active in leftist organizations in Iran during and after the revolution of 1979. These women had to leave Iran because of their political involvement and went into exile in the USA in the 1980s. In the first section of this chapter I present the background of these women in Iran and their experiences of the revolution. I then describe the context of California where these women live at present. After that, I explore different, somewhat contradictory meanings that 'Irangeles' has for the women of this study. I argue that cultural communities in a new country can contribute to a sense of belonging for immigrants. However, when tradition is reinvented in these communities, it also means that traditional gender roles are reintroduced. The central point in this chapter is to explore how the women of this study deal with these somewhat contradictory aspects of their new community, through which multiple identities intersect.

The Impact of the Revolution

The involvement of women in the Iranian revolution of 1979 took place at many different levels. Their most intense participation was during the two years after the overthrow of the Pahlavi regime (1926–1979). During 1979–1981, which was called 'the spring of freedom', a number of political groups came into existence, which at that time were permitted by law. These groups advanced a wide range of ideologies, including forms of Marxism, Islamism, liberalism and women's rights. Both the extent of the freedom enjoyed during these years and the opportunity for political involvement gave Iranian women a chance to become part of political change in their country on an extensive level for the first time. Nahid, thirty-eight, mentions the following:

> I can say that those years were the better years of my life. I think that I never in my life enjoyed life like that. I gained a lot of personal freedom at that time and socially all those restrictions were not there anymore. You could go wherever you wanted to go, you could do whatever you wanted to do. It was really a safe environment and a democratic one. It was friendly and everything was good. It was as if it was paradise – it was my paradise anyway. Those were the best years of my life.

I listened to the stories of women between the ages of 30 and 50, those who had lived in the United States for more than ten years. These women were involved with various Marxist organizations. Although they came from different social, religious and economic backgrounds, what they all had in common was that their political involvement in leftist organizations made it possible for them to transgress the limitation of their background, to some extent. As Nahid mentions, those years opened a door for them to 'feel free to do whatever they wanted to do'. This meant that being politically active, even for a short time, changed the lives of these women drastically.

The 'spring of freedom' did not last. Confrontations had been growing between secular/leftist political groups and the Islamists in power from the first days after the revolution. Those confrontations took a turn for the worse on 18 June 1981. From that date on, the streets of Tehran and other Iranian cities bore witness to terrible violence. Islamists began institutionalizing their absolute power. All other political groups were declared illegal and the majority of their followers arrested, tortured or killed. Neda, forty-five, is a highly educated woman who began her education in Iran and continued it in the United States. She describes those years of suppression as follows:

> It was a period full of waiting and a period in which I lost a lot. I was questioning what had happened: was everything finished, would I not see these people anymore? [...] All that excitement, all those hopes and relations, all those were lost. I left the university; I divorced my husband. In the group I found my first love, then I lost it, and I was losing more and more. It was a very bad period for me. It was a period of waiting to see what happens next and I felt many losses. I probably was depressed then. When I remember that I become very sad. [...] The most difficult thing was the loss of ideals or dreams. So much enthusiasm and excitement and then there was

emptiness. [...] When I look at it now I realize that it was very complicated. You gave yourself a kind of value by being inside political activism. You gave yourself a kind of meaning. Doing this and that and this gave you a social meaning, a meaning between your friends and a status for yourself, not only a social status but also a psychological status. Then there was only a big emptiness.

Revolution changed the lives of these activists. Their souls were filled with dreams and ideals, and they were suddenly punished because of those ideals. They suffered during those years of suppression, either being arrested themselves or living in fear of being arrested day by day, or seeing their loved ones arrested, tortured, or killed. Those were the memories that made the women of this study – and many others – feel like exiles in their own country. Those who had a chance left the country and found themselves in exile outside Iran. A new start in a new country went together with the memories of a lost home and an insecure future. In the next section I first explore the Californian context where these women settled, and then describe their experiences in this new context.

Iranians in Los Angeles, 'Irangeles'

A sizeable community of Iranians lives in the United States, especially in Southern California, mainly in Los Angeles. Los Angeles is one of the most multicultural cities in the country, with one-third of its current population having been born in other countries (Kelly and Friedlander, 1993, p. xi). Los Angeles, called 'Irangeles' by Iranians and some Americans[1], has the largest number of Iranians outside of Iran, although estimates vary as to the actual number of Iranians in the city. The census of 1990 estimated the number of Iranians (including Iranian-born Armenians) in the United States at 285,000, of which 100,000 lived in the Los Angeles area (Bozorgmehr et al., 1996, p. 376, note 15). According to Iranian media, the number is much higher.

A Los Angeles Iranian magazine recently reported that, according to the 1990 Census, there are 1.8 million Iranians in the United States, a third of whom live in Southern California (Bozorgmehr et al., 1993, p. 73).

Time magazine reported the number of Iranians in Los Angeles by the early 1980s as 200,000 (Kelly and Friedlander, 1993, p. xii), and Iranian media sources estimated the number in the mid-1980s at between 200,000 and 300,000 (Bozorgmehr et al., 1993, p. 70). Blair estimates the number of Iranians between 250,000 and 400,000, based on the claim that no official statistics are available (Blair, 1991, p. 157). There are various explanations for the difference in the numbers. Bozorgmehr argues that the exaggeration of numbers by the Iranian media is based on political motives aimed at winning the support of politicians (Bozorgmehr et al., 1993, p. 70). Another possible reason is that a large number of Iranians living in the Los Angeles region are not legally registered, since they lack official legal documents. The census does not cover this group. Taking this aspect into account, an estimate of the number of Iranians in Los Angeles is somewhere between the official data and the lowest numbers released by the media, around 200,000.

Sabagh and Bozorgmehr distinguish between two waves of emigration from Iran to the United States (1987, p. 77). The first wave arrived between 1950 and 1977, comprised of students who could be considered temporary immigrants, as well as other immigrants. The second wave came between 1977 and 1986, the years before and after the revolution of 1979. People in this second group are considered political refugees and exiles, whereas people in the first group are seen as immigrants.

The second wave, Iranians who left Iran as a result of the Iranian revolution, can generally be divided into two groups. The first group, those from the higher classes associated with the previous regime in Iran, left Iran with their extensive, accumulated capital when the political situation became uncertain. They came mainly to Southern California and settled in the better areas of Los Angeles, such as Beverly Hills. They used their capital to start cultural and political activities. Among them were politicians, famous singers, actors and radio and television personalities, who continued their activities abroad. They used their experiences in Iran to build new communication networks and cultural activities in LA. The second group, which was the largest Iranian emigration to the United States, did not leave Iran until 1980. These newcomers, who left Iran because of the hardship of the years after the revolution, included many who departed because of their political convictions or religious backgrounds. Much more heterogeneous than the first group, the second one varies in class, education and political ideas.

Iranians in Los Angeles are considered by many to be a successful community with good educations and high incomes (Bozorgmehr and Sabagh, 1988, p. 25). Unlike many other immigrants in LA, Iranians do not live in a single ethnic area but are spread throughout the city, mainly in the more prestigious neighbourhoods (Naficy, 1993b, p. 4). In spite of this, Iranians still form a rather tight community, through diverse activities organized by and for Iranians. Based on my observation, I can conclude that up to 80 percent of informal connections of Iranians in Los Angeles are with other Iranians. Religious beliefs and ceremonies as diverse as Islamic, Armenian, Judaist are practised by Iranians in LA[2]. There are various political convictions, from monarchists to leftist activists. Activities organized in LA vary from religious and cultural to political. During the 1980s, there were various Iranian political activities in this area. From the early 1990s, there was a shift in concern from political activities to cultural activities (Naficy, 1993b, p. 27).

My interest was mainly in the organizations in which the women I interviewed were active. Most of these women, who used to be leftist activists, are now strong defenders of women's rights. Some founded women's groups and others are active participants in these groups. *Jamiyat-e zanan-e Irani in Los Angeles* (Society of Iranian Women in Los Angeles) is the only registered women's group among the three whose activities I followed. The group began in 1987 with the name *Jamiyat-e mostaghel-e zanan* (Independent Women's Association). A number of women activists were initiators of this group. In 1997, they registered the group with its new name as a non-profit organization. In 1998, they started a monthly newsletter named *taswir-e zan* (Image of Woman). The group organizes public lectures on women's issues and raises funds for humanitarian causes. *Gorouh-e motaleati-e zanan-e Orange County* (Women's Study Group in Orange County) started its work in 1992. This group has informal monthly gatherings at members' homes. They discuss books in the group or invite guest speakers for informal lectures. They also organize public events and gatherings in order to raise funds. This group was the main organizer of the celebration of International Women's Day on 7 March 1999 at UCI (University of California at Irvine). Other groups involved were the Society of Iranian Women in Los Angeles and the Organization of Iranian Students of UCI. *Anjoman-e farhangi-ye zanan* (Cultural Society of Women) is another informal group that mainly concentrates on the experiences of womanhood on a personal level. They organize study sessions and lectures. Next to these women-orientated gatherings, other Iranian group activities were popular in the areas in which they were organized (for more on this, see Ghorashi, 2003a). All these activities are mainly in Persian and the guests invited are also mainly Iranian diaspora from all over the world. During my own stay in LA, I was invited to give lectures at some of these organizations.

In addition to these organizations, Iranians in California have access to a 24-hour Iranian radio station, which not only functions as an important medium among them but also between Iranians and American society. For example, different professional programmes present information about medical and legal issues. The latest changes in various legislation, for example, immigration bills, green cards, etc., are discussed and Iranians get a chance to call and talk to advisors in their own native language. In this way, an Iranian medium serves as a bridge for Iranians to interact within and stay updated about the American context. In addition to the radio station, there are also various Iranian television programmes: '...although relative newcomers, Iranians have been one of the most prolific ethnic minorities in this country in producing television programmes' (Naficy, 1993a, p. 327). Naficy reports that from 1981, of 62 regularly scheduled programmes broadcasted, many have disappeared and have been replaced by others (1993b, p. 64). What almost all of the TV programmes have in common is an overdose of commercials, which made them less popular than the radio programmes. Through these activities in Los Angeles, Iranians have claimed space for their cultural identity within America and, by doing so, they have added an Iranian flavour to the American context. In this way, a new piece of mosaic has been added to an already multicultural LA – which means a little Iran next to little Mexico, Korea or China, to name a few.

'Irangeles': Home Away from Iran

In many ways, the Iranian community[3] in Los Angeles is a re-creation of the years before the revolution, an Iran outside of Iran. For many Iranians who were brought up during the reign of the Shah, 'Irangeles' feels more like Iran than the Islamic Iran after the revolution. A passage from my field notes in LA shows this re-creation of the homeland, which in many ways is replacing the 'real homeland':

> This morning I was listening to California-based Iranian radio. During the programme an old woman called and she said that she had taken out a subscription for six months and that she was going to Iran for a while. She said that she would miss the radio terribly while staying in Iran. One of the things that would make her happy to come back to the US would be the continued existence of the radio. What I found interesting was that an elderly Iranian lady would miss the Iranian radio programme abroad while going back to visit Iran. This shows how one can feel at home when a concept is separated from its original place and is re-created in a new home. Iranians who were brought up during the time of the Shah would hear the music from their childhood. The old lifestyle is much closer in LA than in Iran after the revolution. Iran consistently has other elements that would attract Iranians, especially emotionally. But the fact that Los Angeles can in many ways replace Iran as a homeland creates a familiar environment for Iranians to deal with their new lives in a new context and in a less-conflicting way (field notes of 23 July 1997).

Los Angeles had the same impact on me, as a person who had left Iran about eleven years before and who was in search of her roots, while living in the Netherlands. I soon felt at home in Los Angeles in many ways. I could relive so many similar images of my childhood, the ones that I had already lost when I was still in Iran. The whole setting of Iran outside of Iran, or 'Irangeles', serves as a familiar environment for many, similar to the places where they grew up. As a result of globalizing processes, a selected form of Iranian culture has been detached from its 'original' physical space and time and reinvented within a new space. 'Irangeles' clearly concerns Iranian cultural space that has moved from Iran and taken root in California. The fact that Iranians in America select and promote their old pre-Islamic culture in America is due in part to their own upbringing before the Islamic revolution; but it also has to do with the message they wish to bring to the American community by distancing themselves from Iranian-Islamic government. In this way, this process of de-territorialization and re-territorialization is about hybridity. In this case, hybridity is about the creation and promotion of a kind of Iranian cultural identity that makes possible a link to American national identity. In this way, along with other communities in the US, Iranians contribute to a diversity of ways of being American. For this reason, Hall's quotation at the beginning of this chapter ('modern nations are all cultural hybrids') is probably even truer for America than it is for other nations.

The existence of 'Irangeles' could stimulate Iranians' sense of belonging in California. Feeling at home is not merely a reflection of the conscious choices that people make, but also of the surroundings where they could feel at ease: familiar surroundings to the embodied history in the form of cultural/social *habitus* (Bourdieu, 1990, p. 56, for more on this, see Ghorashi, 2003b). The existence of the past in present-day Los Angeles, or the continuation of the cultural/social *habitus*, has partly contributed to the fact that Iranian women in this study see themselves as part of American society. But, as mentioned before, this link to

American society is a connection of one's own cultural identity to the American national identity. In this way, American national identity serves as a rather thin umbrella that covers a diversity of cultures (for more on this, see Ghorashi, 2003a, 2003b, 2004). Women living in California also have conflicting ideas about 'there' and 'here', combined with the emotional bond to Iran; but these multiple feelings do not keep them from feeling at home in LA.

In 18 interviews, life in LA is mentioned in a positive sense. Many consider Iran outside of Iran even more positive than Iran itself. When the women talk about Iran, there is still an emotional attachment, but the explicit, rational choice is for their lives in LA. When the interviews reveal a conflict between past and present, between rational and emotional choices for 'there' and 'here', the final choice is often LA.

When I asked, 'Do you consider yourself a stranger in this society?' Shadi, an artist of 45, who has lived for more than ten years in the United States, answered, 'Not now'.

Then I asked, 'Has this become your home in a way?' She said:

Yes, I don't like to think of going back to Iran. [...] It is possible that I would go back later, and would stay there, but not now in my present situation. I like the kind of life that I have here. A life in Iran has nothing for me. I have expectations from life that I can fulfil here. At least I think this now. Another point is that I have better possibilities on my own here in comparison to Iran. My wishes can be fulfilled here.

When I asked, 'Could you give me some examples?' she replied:

Take for example my work in music [she composes classical music – HG]. By making music I can give my past a place. You do it through anthropology, I do it through music. There are also my social activities on women's questions. [...] Sometimes when I think of Iran, I become emotional. I feel like crying, despite the fact that my whole family is here. However, there is something from my past, which is there, [...] I miss my friends. I miss the cities and the people, the streets, all those things. When I am melancholic, I become emotional and feel like crying. Even now, when I say that I do not want to live in Iran, I still become emotional.

When I asked in what ways she misses Iran, Sadaf, an artist of 35, who came to the United States about fifteen years ago, responded: 'The memories. I know that when I go back to Iran many things will shock me. [...] Before, I missed Iran more, but not now'.

[HG] This has become your home, in some way?

'Yes, I feel that.'

[HG] You told me that you don't feel a stranger here.

I don't feel like a stranger in my daily life, but there are incidents at my work and my school [this refers to some discriminatory acts she had faced – HG] when I feel like a stranger, but in general I am very happy and do not feel like a foreigner. I spoke to a friend who lived in Germany and she told me that there you feel like a foreigner all the time and you have no feeling of belonging. They look at you as a foreigner. This feeling is very weak in me, it is possible that this is somewhere inside me but it is not something I think of very often. [...] It is not like that at all here. When I came here, I thought that I had entered paradise. I wrote to my aunt that it is paradise here.

When I asked 45-year-old Jaleh, who has lived for more than ten years in the United States, the question, 'Do you feel at home here?' she answered, 'Yes, I do'.

[HG] Do you feel like a stranger here?

No, I feel that I have become part of this society, in some ways. Maybe I feel like this because my husband is American. However, this feeling is not always present. Even in Iran, I felt that I did not belong to anywhere, but to everywhere.

The majority of the women in this study, 18 out of 20, felt as if they were part of the new society. For these women, being Iranian and living in the United States are not mutually exclusive forms of identification. They have been able to combine their Iranian cultural identity with their present lives in the United States. Some of them call themselves Iranian-American, which means that these two identities are not defined in an exclusive way. Iranian women feel a sense of belonging in the new context and are able to position themselves in a diversity of practices. Sometimes this diversity could mean a combination of different cultures in a ceremony, for example, celebrating Thanksgiving in an Iranian way. But feeling at home in the USA. means mainly being Iranian in an American way, or having an Iranian cultural identity that relates to and fits in with American national identity. The claim of Iranian-American identity certainly has to do with the thinness of American identity (2003). This thinness is partly related to fact that American identity is rather 'a design through ideological means' instead of 'cultural means' (Stratton and Ang, 1999, p. 141). Being an American is about respecting the universal, abstract idealist terms and values such as democracy and freedom. This results in a thinness of identity on the national level, which creates space for a diversity of cultures related to American culture. This, in turn, makes American identity culturally heterogeneous. It may not be too far fetched to claim that being American is about being culturally different.

Yet, it is necessary to add that hybridity here is not only about the ways that Iranian culture has been changed to meet the American context. It is also about the ways that the presence of Iranian culture has added a new element to American identity. It shows that, for this group of Iranians, home does not necessarily have to coincide with the national borders of 'the country of origin'. In this way, the often taken-for-granted linking of home to 'the country of origin' is de-territorialized (see Appadurai, 1988; Malkki, 1992). Home outside of Iran is linked to the newly constructed space, 'Irangeles', located in the USA. In this way, the existence of 'Irangeles' is an example of a constructed form of de-territorialized local, cultural community through which past and present, tradition and modernity intersect. This intersection is the result of immigration as a consequence of globalization. This new space called home has contributed to the sense of belonging of this study of Iranian women in Los Angeles. However, there have been other factors, such as structural similarities, history of and discourses on immigration, that have contributed to this sense of belonging as well (see Ghorashi, 2003a).

When There is Home, There is Tradition

One of the reasons Iranians imagine that community contributes to a sense of belonging of Iranians in LA is that it can serve as a strong social resource, safety net and network for Iranian people of various backgrounds and interests. The Iranian network provides information for all Iranians living in California. Wherever people are, if they have legal or health-related financial problems, the Iranian network operates efficiently to help them. The following is an example. On 27 October 1997, the Metro section of the *Los Angeles Times* reported the following: 'Tragedy: Woman who was holding her 4-year-old daughter survived jump from a hotel roof, but the girl died. Now the mother faces murder charges while her husband and her relatives feud'. The American media reported the accident extensively and public opinion saw the mother as the murderer of her child. The court was also strongly in favour of the father of the child, the defendant. But the Iranian community actively participated in making clear to the court that the woman, abused by her husband and emotionally very unstable, did not act on purpose. Some Iranian lawyers helped her with the case, and many gatherings were organized to discuss the issue. Different Iranian cultural and religious organizations collected money and sent her letters of support. When I went back for my second fieldwork in 1998, I heard that she had won the case, mainly due to the support of the Iranian community.

For Iranians in California and especially in Los Angeles, the existence of diverse groups, different activities, and other considerable resources are essential to their feeling of being socially included in the new society in an Iranian way. The Iranian social resources available to Iranians in LA for internal communication enable a tightly knit network among its members. In this way, the Iranian community in Los Angeles serves as a safety net for its members, even when Iranians select their own activities and contacts within their own community. This safety net creates a sense of continuity for Iranians with past experiences in Iran, where they had their own networks of families and friends. However, the existence of an extended Iranian community in the new country has a less attractive side in terms of gender. The re-creation of Iranian networks and the revival of Iranian culture in the United States means that some traditional ideas related to expectations of women remain intact. One of the obvious manifestations of the reinvention of tradition through Iranian networks is the reproduction of traditional ideas through gossip in daily life. During my stay in Los Angeles I have heard amazing things about myself, based on rumours that I was both married and divorced during the nine months I stayed there. The funniest thing was when, in a gathering, a woman approached me when she heard I was from Holland, assuming I was a tourist, and started to tell me stories about an Iranian woman anthropologist from Holland, not knowing that I was that woman. The power of gossip in 'Irangeles' is especially limiting for women who want to transcend the boundaries of traditional gender relations and roles, and therefore have less space to do so. This is especially important for women in this study who were activists in the revolution.

What Makes These Women Different?

The experience of political activism in Iran had a great impact of the ways that the women of this study considered gender relations. Those highly politicized years had a complex influence on gender relations. On the social level, those years gave women in general greatly increased social possibilities and mobility. Women from various strata of society participated in social and political events. Regardless of the extended space created in those years, public participation was not new for all women. For the first time in decades, women from all levels of society were present in public. The impact of those years of activism was such that most of the women I interviewed were very aware of their limitations as women in Iran because of the traditional ideas. During the years of suppression, they faced those limitations on a daily basis (see Ghorashi, 2003a for more details). Those revolutionary years made these women fighters and achievers, who were no longer limited by traditional ideas. These experiences of the past changed these women in four significant ways.

Firstly, political revolutionary training made these women fighters. They learned that they could not expect anything without fighting for it. This fighting attitude towards life created an important driving force for these women to settle in a new country. Also, they learned not to take anything for granted. Disappointments after years of suppression resulted in them trusting no one but themselves. They could no longer be 'made' happy by the life offered to them, either by society, their families or their husbands. They were resolved to take life into their own hands.

Secondly, they could no longer be satisfied with a simple life bereft of higher ideals. One woman said, 'There is no way back. When you have experienced the complexities in life and had higher ideals, you cannot go back and accept a simple life by just having a beautiful house, cooking, and raising children'. Many new ideals have replaced old political ideals. What almost all of them have in common is the wish to make at least a small contribution to changing the world. This aspect of changing the world is expressed in various ways. Some do it by their choices of study. As one of them told me:

> What I do now and my plans for the future are influenced by my past. I am not a member of the organization now but my life is formed by my past: I still have ideals, but new ones. Take for example my choice of study, psychology. This choice is unconsciously or maybe consciously influenced by the past: I want to help people.

Others seek to contribute by voluntary involvement in various human and women's rights organizations. Most of the women in Los Angeles with a leftist background are involved in women's organizations. Some women present their ideals through their work as artists and filmmakers. Others are involved in human rights, such as Amnesty International or Human Rights Watch, or leftist political organizations of the new country, like the American Green Party. The most visible example of a woman who had a shared background with the women of this study is Ms Sara Amir. Ms Amir was the Green Party candidate for Lieutenant Governor of California in 1998, receiving a quarter of a million votes. The following quotation from her website shows the link with the past: 'Her background as an immigrant from a repressive regime fuels her appreciation of freedom and democracy and links her sympathies to emerging constituencies'[4].

Thirdly, the women's views of internationalism reflect the impact of old socialist ideas. Women active in leftist organizations, who were focused on internationalist ideals, criticize nationalist notions of homeland. They were focused on internationalist ideals. However the political issues related to internationalism have changed for many. The impact of seeing 'the world as the homeland' has not vanished completely. Some even mentioned the term, when I asked them about their homeland. This view also can contribute to the openness toward a new start in a new country.

Fourthly, revolutionary training in self-critique sessions, in addition to the painful experiences of the past, made these women rather self-critical. They do not automatically take their cultural backgrounds as something that should be preserved. They are open to change, and they are relatively more open to reflection on their social backgrounds than the average Iranian. For this reason, these women are relatively more open towards change in general, which eases interactions with the new culture.

The above-mentioned characteristics of female Iranian political activists make them different from Iranian women migrants in general. The main difference between female Iranian political activists and other Iranian women is that these female activists question patriarchal ideas regarding women's roles in the family in Iran. This process began before their exile; they had already begun to re-evaluate their gender-based positions in Iran. However, legal limitations in Iran did not leave much room for them to act on their gender awareness to change their living conditions[5]. Once in exile, they acquired this room, so they grasped the opportunity. This can be seen by the diverse activities of these women on the issues of human, women and children's rights, besides other activities inside and outside of the Iranian community. Many of the women's organisations organize diverse programmes and lectures in Persian to inform Iranian women about their rights, their opportunities and their sexuality. The new space in exile leads to an explosion of the accumulated awareness of these women regarding their gender. This is not the case for all Iranian women who migrate. Many of them believe in traditional gender roles in the families. This does not mean that this group does not fight for their rights. Their fight, however, is a different fight, which is not the focus of this study.

As mentioned above, the existence of a large Iranian community in Los Angeles contributes in different ways to the sense of belonging of Iranians living in the area. However, 'home' has different meanings for various groups of Iranians in Los Angeles. During my participation in different gatherings and my conversation with Iranians, I realized that for many Iranians the recreation of the old rituals and ceremonies is very important. For others, the existence of an Iran outside Iran with a similar diversity has become the reason for a sense of belonging. A large and diverse Iranian community in Los Angeles makes it possible for these women 'to find their kind of people' as they told me. For the women of this study, the notion of home is much more layered and somewhat contradictory. The same community that contributes to their sense of belonging could also limit their actions as women because of reinforcement of traditional gender ideas. Besides this, the political background of these women makes them sceptical if not resentful of cultural activities with connections to the previous regime in Iran. In fact, most of the women remain aloof from those cultural activities. Most of them did not watch or listen to Iranian television and radio. The ones who did were very selective in doing so. They listened mostly to the news about Iran and Iranian gatherings in California. But what these women praised the most was the possibility of activism within different Iranian intellectual and women's organizations. For these women, the variety of choices in LA seemed to be more essential than the known environment of pre-revolutionary Iran. Nevertheless, this same environment, given implicit and indirect approval, helps them to feel a sense of belonging on a latent level. The whole setting of Iran outside of Iran, the 'embodied history' called 'Irangeles', could serve as a familiar environment, similar to the places where they grew up and could stimulate their sense of belonging in the new context. Also, it seems that the diversity that 'Irangeles' offers the women make it possible for them to transcend the limitations they face from the community. Besides, the fact that the community is based in California and not in Iran makes it possible for these women to see 'Irangeles' as one of the available social resources, but not the only one. The following narratives make these points clear.

From Sahar's story it is clear that she remained aloof from aspects that dominate the Iranian community, but that her ideas changed when she was able to find people she enjoyed being in contact with. She is 43 years old, and has lived in the United States with her husband and children for about 11 years.

In the beginning I saw Iranians driving their cars and being busy with their own jobs. When I entered any group they just talked about work and money, as if there was nothing else to talk about except of being successful and having more money. This was really shocking for me. [How do you think now? – HG] I do not think like this at all. And also I have been able to find the people I like to have contact with [She refers here to her Iranian contacts – HG]. Now, I like it here very much. [Do you see this place as your home at this moment? – HG] Yes, but I miss Iran, also. [What do you miss? – HG] I do not know, I miss my family and my friends, the part of my life that has been there. The best part of my life has been there. For years I saw things as temporary, and I thought that this was not the place that I wanted to live. But now I do not have this feeling at all. Now I think that now I am living here and I like it here very much. I enjoy my possibilities. [Do not you feel a stranger in this society? –

HG] Not at all. [Do you enjoy Iranian activities and programmes here? HG] No, I do not watch television and I feel that I do not belong to the Iranian community in general. The Iranian community here is somewhat traditional, it is the same as in Iran; you have traditional people there as well. From the beginning I was in search of people that I like. All my life I was interested in my contacts [she means here Iranian contacts – HG], and the first years in which I did not have them it was difficult, but now that I've found them I feel great.

Sahar's story shows perfectly how she resents some elements of the dominant Iranian, reinvented culture in Los Angeles (such as displays of wealth and success), besides the recreated traditional elements. She even mentions that she sometimes feels that she does not belong to this Iranian recreated culture. However, the same recreated little Iran has enabled her to find Iranians whom she likes and with whom she feels comfortable. Thus, having the space in LA to make her own selection within the recreated Iranian culture makes it possible for Sahar to feel at home in Los Angeles, a feeling that has been grown with the passing of time. The same kind of resentment is present in Sadaf's story when she talks about the Iranian community in Los Angeles:

The Iranian community is very mixed here. The majority is traditional and businesslike with a merchant mentality. Iranian radio and television make me so tired that I do not listen to or watch them. [Did you watch in the beginning? – HG] No. I think I never was interested. Those media remind me of the traditional ideas in Iran. No I never liked it. But the advantage of Los Angeles is that you kind of find your own type. When I came to Los Angeles, an Iranian women's organization helped me a lot. I found out that I am not that different. In the beginning I felt so different from the rest of Iranians here. A friend always told me: 'You do not fit in any category.' I thought to myself, why am I like this? I felt that I had a kind of problem and felt very lonely. When I went to that women's organization, I liked it so much, that meeting gave me so much energy that I cannot forget. The meetings gave me bonding with some of the members of that organization.

The diversity of Iranians in Los Angeles makes it possible for these women to find the kind of Iranian people they feel comfortable with. Thus, the existence of an extensive Iranian community in itself is not enough for their sense of belonging. The diversity of the group, which would include intellectuals, leftist, human rights activists along side monarchists, traditional and commercial Iranians, for example, is more important in finding people with whom one feels a sense of belonging. What remains is that the traditional ideas regarding women are persistent in Los Angeles, as is the strong social control within the community. However, the impact of patriarchal ideas on the lives of the women of this study is different, compared to the impact of the same ideas in Iran. This is because, in Los Angeles, they have at least two multiple spaces to interact with, the Iranian and the American one, each with its own diversities. For these women, the availability of these two types of multiple social resources offers opportunities, and they can use both spaces interchangeably. This makes life in the new country more favourable than in Iran. Also, the existence of Iranian traditional culture in Los Angeles influences the ways the past is constructed. It is almost impossible for the women living in Los Angeles to be too selective about their memories because the past in many ways is recreated in the present. This helps them remember the shortcomings of their own culture. The constant presence of the past does not allow for unrealistic nostalgia. Yet, in some ways they can be selective in the way they position themselves in this recreated past in the present 'Irangeles'. The presence of both the positive and the negative aspects of the past in Los Angeles give the women a chance to remember what the past meant for them, as women. This 'past in the present' gives these women an opportunity to explore new opportunities and to feel secure in life instead of developing strong nostalgic feelings towards the past by creating the past in their minds.

Conclusion

The emergence of 'Irangeles' in California is a perfect example of how the intersection of the past and the present results in a newly constructed space called home. The sense of belonging to this new space contributes to hybrid positioning of being both Iranian and American at the same time. This form of hybridity is not so much about the mixture of cultures as shown above but about linking the Iranian cultural identity to the American national identity. In the process of making this link of culture to nation, both Iranian culture and American identity transform through which a space is created for a new hyphenated identity and a hybrid positioning within an American context: Iranian-American identity. This hybrid positioning also goes beyond the assumed exclusive link of the Iranian culture with the national border of Iran as 'the country of origin'. The little Iran in California thus exemplifies a re-territorialized locality and, for that matter, a hybrid, cultural community as the consequence of immigration and globalization. Previously, I quoted Hall (1992) in seeing modern nations as cultural hybrids and Young (1995) in considering heterogeneity and diversity as the identity of modern society. Through my research findings, I have shown how both utterances are true in the case of the United States, especially in California. The United States, as an immigration country in general and California as a strong heterogeneous state in particular, provides a perfect context for the Iranian community to flourish. However, it is through the interplay of the context with the specific background of certain groups of immigrants that newly constructed local spaces are reinvented, in which hybrid positioning emerges. In this way, 'Irangeles' is one of many newly created spaces by immigrants that could be considered as a localized reaction to the processes of globalization. It is in this space that global movements and local needs coincide and it is this process that makes modern nations diverse, heterogeneous and hybrid.

It was in Los Angeles that a little Iran is recreated, an Iran that is different from the homeland Iran that Iranians left behind coming to the United States. 'Irangeles' is different from present Iran because it is constructed on the memories of the Iran before the revolution. In this chapter I have explored the various meanings that, even though contradictory, this new space called home has for the Iranian women whom I interviewed. These women were activists in the Iranian revolution of 1979 and, because of their past experiences, very aware of their rights as women. The existence of a home abroad contributes to the sense of inclusion of these women in the new society. 'Irangeles' works as a safety net that replaces old networks and offers Iranians support in their lives in California. Also, the re-creation of the past in the present creates a familiar environment for these women, which indirectly could contribute to their sense of belonging. However, the other side of the coin is that the re-creation of the past in the present also means the re-creation of traditional ideas on gender roles in 'Irangeles'. This negative re-creation of the past influences the life of Iranian women of this study, but not that significantly. They are able to transcend the impact of these traditional ideas in some ways. Firstly, by emphasizing that 'Irangeles' offers diversity through which they can find people they like. Secondly, contrary to Iran, 'Irangeles' is one of the available social resources they have in California. This means that they have the space to distance themselves from 'Irangeles' when they feel limited by it. The re-creation of Iran in Los Angeles also means 'the presence of the past' in the new context, with all its positive and negative impacts. This 'past in the present' makes it easier for these women to let go of strong feelings of nostalgia common among exiles. They are then able to focus on their present achievements and the opportunities offered by that new context. This emphasis on the present instead of the past makes it also possible to consider their new country as 'home', by including the elements of the past in the present, by calling themselves Iranian-Americans or being American in an Iranian way.

Notes

1   See, for example, the title of the book edited by R. Kelly and J. Friedlander in 1993, *Irangeles: Iranians in Los Angeles*.

2   For detailed information on the religious diversity and ceremonies of Iranians in LA, see Kelly and Friedlander, 1993.

3   The term community refers mainly to collective activities organized by Iranians in LA. I am aware that community, especially in the case of ethnic minorities, is a contested concept. It leads to equation of community with culture, through which culture becomes reified (Baumann, 1996, p. 10).

4   For more information, see the following website: http://www.saraamir.org/bio.html.

5   For further studies on women's position after the revolution, see the following: on compulsory veiling, Gerami, 1994; V.M. Moghadam, 1993; on legal rights, Afshar, 1987; Nashat, 1983; Reeves, 1989; Tabari, 1982; Sanaserian, 1982.

References

Afshar, Haleh (1987) 'Women, Marriage and the State in Iran', in H. Afshar (ed.), *Women, State and Ideology*, The Macmillan Press, Houndmills, pp. 70-86.

Appadurai, Arjun (1988) 'Putting Hierarchy in its Place', *Cultural Anthropology*, 3, 1, pp. 36-49.

Baumann, Gerd (1996) *Contesting Culture: Discourses of Identity in Multi-Ethnic London*, Cambridge University Press, Cambridge.

Blair, Betty A. (1991) 'Personal Name Changes Among Iranian Immigrants in the USA', in A. Fathi (ed.), *Iranian Refugees and Exiles since Khomeini*, Mazda Publishers, Costa Mesa, pp. 145-160.

Bourdieu, Pierre (1990) *The Logic of Practice*, Stanford University Press, Stanford.

Bozorgmehr, Mehdi, and Georges Sabagh (1988) 'High Status Immigrants: A Statistical Profile of Iranians in the United States', *Iranian Studies*, 21, pp. 5-36.

Bozorgmehr, Mehdi, Georges Sabagh, and Claudia Der-Martirosian (1993) 'Beyond Nationality: Religio-Ethnic Diversity', in R. Kelly and J. Friedlander (eds.), *Irangeles: Iranians in Los Angeles*, University of California Press, Berkeley, pp. 59-79.

Bozorgmehr, Mehdi, Claudia Der-Martirosian, and Georges Sabagh (1996) 'Middle Easterners: A New Kind of Immigrant', in R. Waldinger and M. Bozorgmehr (eds.), *Ethnic Los Angeles*, Russell Sage Foundation, New York, pp. 345-378.

Gerami, Shahin (1994) 'The Role, Place, and Power of Middle-Class Women in the Islamic Republic', in V.M. Moghadam (eds.), *Identity Politics and Women*, Westview Press, Oxford and Colorado, pp. 329-347.

Ghorashi, Halleh (2003a), *Ways to Survive, Battles to Win: Iranian Women Exiles in the Netherlands and the United States*, Nova Science Publishers, New York.

Ghorashi, Halleh (2003b), 'Multiple Identities between Continuity and Change: The Narratives of Iranian women in Exile', *Focaal: European Journal of Anthropology*, 42, pp. 63-75.

Ghorashi, Halleh (2004) 'How Dual is Transnational Identity? A Debate on Duality of Transnational Immigrant Organizations', *Culture and Organization*, 10, 4, pp. 329-340.

Hall, Stuart (1992), 'The Question of Cultural Identity', in S. Hall, D. Held, and T. McGrew (eds.), *Modernity and its Futures*, Polity Press, Cambridge, pp. 273-316.

Kelly, Ron, and Jonathan Friedlander (1993) 'Introduction', in R. Kelly and J. Friedlander (eds.), *Irangeles: Iranians in Los Angeles*, University of California Press, Berkeley, pp. xi-xiv.

Malkki, Liisa (1992) 'National Geographic: The Rooting of Peoples and the Territorialization of National Identity Among Scholars and Refugees', *Cultural Anthropology*, 7, 1, pp. 24-44.

Moghadam, Valentine M. (1993) *Modernizing Women: Gender and Social Change in the Middle East*, Lynne Rienner Publishers, Boulder.

Naficy, Hamid (1993a) 'Popular Culture of Iranian Exiles in Los Angeles', in R. Kelly and J. Friedlander (ed.), *Irangeles: Iranians in Los Angeles*, University of California Press, Berkeley, pp. 325-67.

Naficy, Hamid (1993b) *The Making of Exile Cultures: Iranian Television in Los Angeles*, University of Minnesota Press, Minneapolis.

Nashat, Guity (1983) 'Women in the Ideology of the Islamic Republic', in G. Nashat (ed.), *Women and Revolution in Iran*, Westview Press, Boulder and Colorado, pp. 195-217.

Reeves, Minou (1989) *Female Warriors of Allah: Women and the Islamic Revolution*, E.P. Dutton, New York.

Sabagh, Georges, and Mehdi Bozorgmehr (1987) 'Are the Characteristics of Exiles Different from Immigrants? The Case of Iranians in Los Angeles', *Sociology and Social Research*, 71, pp. 77-84.

Sanasarian, Eliz (1982) *The Women's Rights Movement in Iran: Mutiny, Appeasement and Repression from 1900 to Khomeini*, Praeger, New York.

Stratton, Jon, and Ien Ang (1998) 'Multicultural Imagined Communities: Cultural Difference and National Identity in the USA and Australia', in D. Bennett (eds.), *Multicultural States: Rethinking Difference and Identity*, Routledge, London/New York, pp. 135-163.

Tabari, Azar (1982) 'Islam and the Struggle for Emancipation of Iranian Women', in A. Tabari and N. Yeganeh (eds.), *In the Shadow of Islam: The Women's Movement in Iran*, Zed Press, London, pp. 5-26.

Young, Robert J.C. (1995) *Colonial Desire: Hybridity in Theory, Culture and Race*, Routledge, London.

CONCLUSION

Chapter 13

Gender and Globalization: An Analytical Alliance

Tine Davids and Francien van Driel

Introduction: Multiple Connections and Practices

What has gender to do with globalization? This is the question that led us to write this book. We began our search for a possible answer on this question in the opening chapter with the metaphor of the landscape, and identification with the different stories and storytellers who observe the globalization landscape. If, as we stated in the introduction, this landscape is simultaneously shaped through structures as well as through flows, in this concluding chapter we want to reflect on the question of how gender figures in this process of flow and fixing.

What we have seen in this book is that globalization is about complex connections that link people, places, artefacts and ideas in unpredictable ways. It is not only tangible elements that get deterritorialized and are travelling, such as people, companies or artefacts, ideas and images also travel. These ideas and images are connected to tangible objects, but they can also travel on their own. In the different chapters we have seen people migrating (Halleh Ghorashi and Annelou Ypeij), a book on a world trip (Kathy Davis) and industries on the move (Fenneke Reysoo). Images and ideas are travelling, such as on masculinity (Anouka van Eerdewijk), on labour arrangements (Lineke Stobbe and Lorainne Nencel), on family ideals and nationality (Karin Willemse, Tine Davids and Marion den Uyl) and on conflict intervention (Dorothea Hilhorst and Mathijs van Leeuwen). However, we also have seen that people are the intermediaries in converting these elements.

Looking through our gender lens we see that what is fixed in the analyses in the different chapters only acquires meaning in a specific landscape (locality), be it a book, exiles in an 'imagined' community, the position of single migrant women, or the sexual behaviour of a young man. These specific localities all represent contradictory ideas and ideals. In practice, the subjects living in these localities have to deal with many choices, contradictions and opportunities. In the end, the connections made are not pre-determined, but unpredictable in their flows and outcomes.

Neo-liberal labour restructuring can lead to feminization of management in one locality and to unreliable and low paid jobs for women in another. Different ideas on women and labour compete at these places with surprising outcomes. The journey of the OBOS book shows that the connection of American feminist ideas and practices with Egyptian feminist practices resulted in a book that the original writers never could have imagined. What all the chapters have in common is that changes in labour relations, in ideas on male sexuality, female peace building, family ideals and so on, have been modified and are re-interpreted by people of flesh and blood. Although sometimes apparently similar changes may occur at the structural and symbolic level, at the subject level the outcomes of these changes are different and varied. They show that globalization is about the production of differences, connecting different localities, cultures and people.

All the connections that have been analyzed in this book offer an illustration of these processes of re-interpretation, reshaping and restyling. Through those connections people, groups and nations are compelled to define and redefine themselves and the world around them. It is precisely the interconnection of subjects, institutions, practices, ideas and images that formed the special perspective on the globalizing landscape in this book.

This landscape does not hold pre-given meanings of gender, even though one is tempted to consider the landscape as familiar and known. It depends on the perspective of the observer, what different and unexpected meanings are attached to gender in the multiple connections and practices that curve and shape the landscape. Depending on the chosen perspective, different power struggles emerge. Those power mechanisms never point in just one direction. In the chapters of this book we have seen that the meaning of gender itself is at stake in these power struggles. Moreover, it is the struggle about the meaning of gender that reflects power mechanisms at work. The outcome of these struggles is as unpredictable as is the meaning of gender. The authors demonstrate how these power struggles are acted out in different practices, structures and institutions in which different actors have to negotiate different meanings, ideas and ideals.

In the concluding part of this book we want to take a closer look at the meanings of gender that are generated in the different parts and chapters and at the related power mechanisms. Here we assess the possibilities of the gender lens as a methodological and analytical tool in studying the link between gender, globalization and locality. In chapter 1 we stated that both the analytical emphasis chosen by the different authors and the locality differ. Here we will follow the same clustering of emphasis and start with assessing the gender lens and its *symbolical, institutional and subjective* dimension. We emphasize the consequences of the perspective chosen by the respective author and the related power mechanisms in the section on local lived realities. In the section on unexpected outcomes we focus on the global orthodoxies and the way the global/local nexus materializes. Thirdly, in the section on globalized gender identities we focus on the tradition-modernity divide and how this divide is problematized by looking through the gender lens. Finally, we return to the feminist agenda and the questions that lie ahead.

Local Lived Realities: Agency Instead of Victimization

This part of the book rejects the global orthodoxy of the victimization of women and dismantles the myth of women as being primarily victims of globalization. On the contrary, women and men contribute actively, whether consciously or unconsciously, to processes of flow and fixation at a local level. The actors in these chapters, be they women or men, secretaries, managers or labourers, are all clearly situated in a specific environment with different local discourses on gender.

In the chapter by Anouka van Eerdewijk, for instance, the young Senegalese boy Malik cannot but relate himself to local representations of masculinity in identifying his own sexual identity. In chapter 3 Lorraine Nencel gives insight into the way in which Peruvian secretaries are embedded in bureaucratic office practices and are struggling with discourses on work and sexuality. In chapter 2 Lineke Stobbe unravels how labourers in different factories in Argentina are affected differently by international neo-liberal management and labour restructuring. The discourses they have to relate to, i.e. the 'nimble fingers' rhetoric and the notion of women as 'agents of change' compete with notions of women not suitable for the kind of labour required in the car industry. These discourses are circulating at a local level but, at the same time, are informed and to a certain extent shaped by international discourses. Hence, globality obviously comes in at a *symbolical dimension* and gender seems to figure centrally in the articulation of this globality by actors within this specific locality.

If we take a closer look at the chapter by Lorraine Nencel, for instance, neo-liberal rhetoric is clearly part of the Peruvian repertoire available to secretaries, next to very outspoken discourses on women as secretaries and their ascribed sexual identities. While the neo-liberal discourse on new professional and rationalized labour relations seems to be a-sexual, according to the author, secretaries identify with this discourse and its representations of professionalism. They do so to counterbalance the constant attempts to sexualize their identity and dealings on the work floor. It is not the international neo-liberal discourse on labour relations that ascribes a certain sexuality to women in their capacities as secretaries, it is the secretaries themselves in an attempt to negotiate both decency and sexuality that give this professionalism its specific local meaning – a meaning (of gender) never envisaged by the designers of neo-liberal management restructuring.

It is via women's ascribed sexuality that these neo-liberal representations of gender get articulated with Peruvian cultural ideals and practices. As Lorraine Nencel describes, women are ideally compelled to repress their feminine sexuality. The sexualization of the secretary reflects a sexualized gendered order. As secretaries are situated close to the 'bad girl' category, masculine control over feminine sexuality in the working place, a public place, gets legitimized. Women do recognize the power of this gender order by defending their decency through an appeal to their professionalism. As such, the neo-liberal discourse figures in defining and redefining – at an *institutional* dimension (labour arrangements) – gendered representations of sexuality that form part of practices in which the public-private divide is renegotiated.

This particular perspective of the author on the articulation of gender, sexuality and professionalism situates power mechanisms, primarily at the subjective dimension. It is the way in which secretaries identify with both these discourses at the same time that generates this specific meaning, demonstrating their agency in globalization processes. The fight for the modernization of their profession involves the risks and insecurity that accompany flexibilization of labour, but it also includes a kind of emancipatory potential in countering Peruvian discourses on sexuality. It at least enables women to uphold, defend or enlarge their room to manoeuvre, which in this particular Peruvian context is restricted by notions of decency.

In this chapter the global/local nexus seems to be coloured by a dynamic in which the global gets articulated at a local level and not so much the other way around. This chapter gives us insight into how gender figures in fixing global flows in a specific context through the agency of a specific group of people. In the chapter by Anouka van Eerdewijk a different dynamic seems to shape the global/local nexus. What is ascribed as a typically African and traditional way of dealing with sexuality, namely polygamy and promiscuity, is identified in international discourses on reproductive health as one of the causes for the spread of HIV/AIDS, which should be resolved by the modernization of such traditional sexual practices. It is, again, through sexuality that global representations of gender are articulated in the Senegalese context. However, this articulation works both ways. Where Peruvian discourses do not seem to appear in global discourses on labour restructuring, African traditions, or what are considered to be African traditions, are part of the international discourses at a *symbolical* dimension. At the same time, these international discourses inform local African discourses in such a way that a renewed search for tradition seeks to counterbalance the loose morals of modernity. From an emic point of view, these loose morals are considered to be responsible for the spread of HIV/AIDS. This search forms a local answer to these international allegations.

At a *symbolical* dimension, there seems to be a dynamic of mutual influence between global and local discourses. Contrary to what Connel describes as a global trend, this dynamic does not result in the fixation of one hegemonic notion of masculinity, but in the existence of different, even contradicting notions of masculinity. Anouka van Eerdewijk analyzes how the Senegalese boy Malick is struggling with these contradicting expectations and ideals of masculinity. Conflicting requirements of virility and virginity are troubled by messages of safe sex and condom use in the HIV/AIDS era. These contradicting ingredients provide a paradox that invites trouble. AIDS is associated with urban lifestyles, modern education, the breakdown of social control and moral codes, of prostitution. The local situation propagated is one of returning to tradition. But that so-called tradition in itself is conflicting, requiring sexual experience and abstinence at the same time. Hence, at the subject level, notions of masculinity are prevalent that are inherently contradictory.

Malick may not be very happy or balanced in trying to find his own way and live up to modern as well as traditional notions of masculinity. Yet, in his narrative, there is no evidence of him losing manhood. Where the secretaries of

Peru seem to fixate one particular notion of gender, if they are not to lose their decency and femininity, Malick seems to have more choices available without risking this loss. Hence, he has an escape, more room to manoeuvre than the women, since he can switch positions offered to him at the symbolic dimension. Where female gender in the case of Peru seems to figure in fixing the flow, male gender in this Senegalese case seems to be part of the construction of flows at the *symbolical* as well as at a *subjective* dimension.

The women within the Argentine firms in the car industry that Lineke Stobbe described for us have to face a rather rigid fixation of gender at different levels and dimensions. At the level of the industry, masculinization is the trend. At lower levels, as is the case in Peru, feminization and flexiblization seem to become more and more synonymous. Nevertheless, this chapter shows us that the complex dynamics between women's own agency (the *subjective* dimension) and the way in which gender representations (the *symbolical* dimension) get institutionalized in different practices of firm management (the *institutional* dimension) do not uphold this trend. Lineke Stobbe deconstructs in this way the thesis of the feminization of labour trend as a global orthodoxy, similar to the deconstruction of the feminization of poverty thesis.

In this chapter it becomes clear that women are active participants and can be agents of change in processes of industrial restructuring. Also in this chapter it is clear that *symbolical* representations of gender at the local level are informed both by local as well as international notions of gender. The specific choices concerning firm management and labour arrangements (*institutional* dimension), inspired by the notion of women as agents of change (*symbolic* dimension) lead to very different outcomes for women in different firms, but also for different women within the same firm. The articulation of conflicting ideals at the *symbolical* dimension (flow) and fixation at the *institutional* dimension influence the room to manoeuvre at the subject dimension. The power dynamics are situated primarily along the axes of the *institutional* and *subjective* dimension, as an outcome of women's agency – and women make strategic use of these possibilities. It is the women in the end who choose whether to become managers, proving that they can be real agents of change.

In these three chapters the authors have shown that actors react to changes and create new ones, but that the room to manoeuvre to do so is restricted in a rather diffuse way. Although the restrictions can be informed by conflicting symbolic ideals and institutional practices, the way the actors deal with these challenges is not given in advance. The gender lens forces us to look at the three dimensions simultaneously. The interaction of the three dimensions reveals challenges, contradictions, opportunities and limitations at the subject dimension, rendering women and men not as victims but as active participants in global change. This production of differences becomes even clearer in the second cluster, where the gender lens focuses on persistent global orthodoxies.

Unexpected Outcomes: Globalization and the Production of Difference

That global processes such as neo-liberal industrial restructuring do not produce straight forward and predictable effects locally is also shown in the chapter by Fenneke Reysoo. In her analysis of firm management concerning the reproductive rights of women working in export industries in Morocco and Mexico, Fenneke Reysoo argues that although the global neo-liberal ideology is similar and stems from the same source, firms' policies in the two different countries could vary fundamentally.

When we look at economic restructuring, the most notorious exponent of what is called globalization, we see conflicting and competing ideas about family ideals and women's labour. Multinational firms in Mexico and Morocco hire women based on the idea that they are cheap and docile labourers. But these firms have different policies and practices when their female labourers get pregnant. The context in these two countries differs to such an extent that, in Mexico, national and international labour laws are violated in order to avoid expenses for maternity leave and other reproductive costs; while, in Morocco, women leave the workplace voluntarily once they get pregnant. Moreover, in the Mexican case, women organize themselves in order to address these labour-law violations and other discriminating practices, while, in Morocco, women seek individual solutions by just quitting their jobs. A process of homogenizing economic restructuring cannot explain these differences. Connections in the notions of gender and, thus, on 'proper' and decent behaviour of women mediate the outcome of these processes.

In this case, the differences between Mexican and Moroccan cultures, combined with export management, produces different notions of feminine gender. In the Mexican case, women as workers (young, unmarried) are also seen as sexual beings. By pregnancy testing and dismissing pregnant women, firms make it their business to control and contain not only women's labour power but also their sexuality. In the Moroccan case, unmarried women will leave factories voluntarily when pregnant. Firms therefore do not have to control their sexuality. In this chapter, it is not so much women's agency that produces these different meanings of gender, although not absent, as the Mexican case shows. It is the articulation of a neo-liberal discourse with different cultural discourses on gender that produces these differences. The different outcomes of these processes in the two countries set different limits on the room to manoeuvre for women working in these factories. Although this chapter does not shed considerable light on the actual agency of women in Morocco, it should be clear from the Mexican case that the limits on the room to manoeuvre could inspire other actions than in the Moroccan case. Women in Mexico are seduced to different forms of resistance, according to the power exercised over them, than are their Moroccan sisters.

Where the chapter by Fenneke Reysoo deconstructs the orthodoxy of globalization as a top-down process, the chapter by Kathy Davis deconstructs the orthodoxy of globalization as a one-way process from the West to the rest. The journey of the book *Our Bodies, Ourselves* shows that, due to women's agency, particular practices of re-writing this book took shape, which ultimately changed and altered the very content of the book. Ideas and ideals on sexuality, health and women's bodies in the various versions of the *OBOS* book are connected to ideas on women as active subjects, who organize and direct their own lives.

Via the journey of this book, the West meets the rest and the rest talks back. Women in different countries struggled as much with representations of gender from their own cultures as with representations of gender presented in the book. So these women had to relate to local as well as international (North American) gendered notions of sexuality, health and women's bodies. Out of the dynamic of reworking these gender representations and within the constraints of publishing practices, different and divers books were produced that did not simply mirror North American feminism. In these books, not only does the West meet the rest of the world, modernity also encounters tradition, resulting in surprising mixtures such as the Egyptian version of the book. It was not cultural imperialism that spread on the wings of modernity from the West to the rest, reproducing neo-colonial power relations. The rest was talking back in different voices, as an expression of multiple feminisms.

Not only at the level of exchange of ideas does the rest come back to the West, people also travel from a post-colonial world to live in the West, taking with them lifestyles and ways to survive, as discussed in the chapter by Annelou Ypeij. The differences between the Surinamese, Antillean and Moroccan single mothers in the Netherlands are directly connected to family arrangements and ideals in their countries of origin. Surinamese and Antillean women have been able to migrate as autonomous persons because of the matrifocal value system in their countries of origin.

This opportunity has been facilitated by Dutch immigration policy and the availability of social-security benefits for single mothers. Interestingly, Dutch 'traditional' family ideals and the provision of an institutionalized social safety net for single mothers offer these migrant women autonomous lives. It is much harder for Moroccan women to migrate to the Netherlands as individuals, and most women migrants are married and follow their husbands. Once in the Netherlands, although they can potentially lead independent lives, isolation and stigmatization are lurking around the corner for these women. Hence, the opportunities offered by the Dutch welfare state are interpreted and used very differently by the female migrants. Dutch institutions are being used by Surinamese women to shape their independent matrifocal lives, even though these institutions are based on a reverse notion of disadvantaged motherhood.

Thus, in this chapter we see an example of interaction between the *symbolical, institutional* and *individual* dimension that exceeds the limits of one locality by creating a transnational flow. The articulation between Surinamese, Moroccan, Antillean and Dutch representations of gender situated within the constrains of Dutch practices results in very different and unexpected lifestyles, survival and coping strategies for the different groups of women. The way in which, in particular, Surinamese and Antillean women succeed in surviving in the Netherlands due to this transnational flow, deconstructs the feminization of poverty orthodoxy and alters the very meaning of locality.

In this cluster we have seen that the gender lens forces the authors to problematize and expand the notion of the local. The specific localities that are chosen to study neo-liberal restructuring of industries, feminist knowledge on the move and migration of women demonstrate that global orthodoxies do not hold. Female labourers in two export zones experience different control mechanisms, feminist ideas and people travelling from the West to the rest and the other way around challenge notions of cultural imperialism and the local. The local becomes a locality, where global/local ideas and practices are entangled.

Globalized Gender Identities: Tradition and Modernity Deconstructed

Globalization does alter the meaning of locality, not only because similar processes could have very different local and international effects but also because globalization forces us to alter the way in which we connect localities to modernity and/or tradition. Halleh Ghorashi makes this clear in her chapter on Iranian exiles in the USA.

Among the Iranian community in Los Angeles, 'Irangeles', a very real and lively re-invention of tradition can be found. But what is tradition in this case? Some of the Iranian refugees and migrants identify themselves with traditions from the period of the Shah, while others might consider this time period as modern, since they identify with 'original' Islamic traditions. Others, such as the women studied by Halleh Ghorashi, cherish the revolutionary period after the Shah and seek similar experiences in the USA. This could be described as a reinvention of Iranian modernity rather than of tradition since, for the women involved, the revolutionary past was full of feminist potential in Iran. In this sense, these women not only reinvent tradition but also modernity. This happens by identifying themselves with a certain period and culture in Iran and also by identifying themselves with modern and feminist movements in the United States of America. At the same time, in order to feel at home, these women seem to feel the need to be part of a community in which Iranian tradition is being reinvented. All these identifications, lifestyles and rituals makes 'Irangeles' a locality that is both modern and traditional, both Iranian and American, rendering peoples' identities fundamentally hybrid.

From Halleh Ghorashi's perspective on globalization, we learn that we cannot understand the complex relations that arise from globalization processes within the narrow scope of a dichotomy between modernity and tradition. Understanding the multiple identities that migrants develop as a consequence of their transnational situations puts hybridity on the research agenda. Not only does this hold true for migration and migrants' identities, but also for national identity and nation building. Examples of this can be found in the cases of nation building discussed in chapters 9, 10 and 11. Although the process of nation building is seen as a product of modernity, creating standardization and homogeneity, the meanings given to national identity and the nation at large can be composed out of modern as well as traditional elements. In the end, in this sense, they may even be hybrid. In the contributions on dowry and nation building in India, and on nation building and masculinity in Sudan, 'seemingly' traditional ideals mould women and men in such a way that they are respectively 'true' Indians and Sudanese. These seemingly similar family ideals are not the result of Euro-colonialist influences, but locally created exponents of national identities. These national identities are cherished and defended as authentic Muslim and Hindu. But how authentically Muslim and Hindu are these identities?

For Sudan, Karin Willemse argues that local variations of modern ideas on masculinity and femininity in pre-colonial times lie at the heart of the Islamist family ideal in Sudan, not changes induced by colonization. In this process of modernization, influences from 'the West' and from the rest of the Arabic world serve as models of modernization for the Sudan. This ideal looks 'Western', but seems to be the result of the globalization of a bourgeois ideal that, at a later stage, is transformed and adjusted in such a way that it is considered locally authentic.

In contemporary Sudan, this family ideal that defines women as primarily mothers and seeks to assure their place in the home resurfaces in times of economic crisis. The emphasis in national Islamic discourse on women's chastity and their sacred roles as mothers is not only targeted at women, but serves to define men as primarily breadwinners. This is no coincidence, according to Karin Willemse. The ruling elite seeks to bind young men to their interests, i.e. the formation of a Sudanese state and national identity. This is done by restoring their manhood, which is under attack in these times of economic crisis when it is difficult to provide for their families.

While Karin Willemse sees the Islamist family ideal as a product of a local alternative of modernization, the result of a process of hybridization, Marion den Uyl sees contemporary dowry in India as a process that can be considered both as homogenization and even of regression and hybridization. Marion den Uyl approaches this phenomenon from different perspectives. She wonders whether the former colony (India) is talking back, by expanding a practice such as dowry in order to counteract foreign influences. Dowry develops hand in hand with the increase of capital, the opening of markets, and modern feelings of greed and individualism. The increasing foreign influence in India is experienced as threatening, especially by the Indian middle classes, followed by an emphasis on Hindu traditions.

The result is an institutionalized dowry system that reflects a tendency of homogenization. Dowry as a ritual crosses borders within India from the north to the south and from elite classes to poorer classes. It also results in a wish for homogenization of Indian national identity when looking at the phenomenon from an Indian perspective, which, according to Marion den Uyl, is based on regression, on turning to the past. At the same time, however, it incorporates modernity in the way it commercializes dowry. Looking at the foreign influence, the development of dowry in India can be considered as a process of heterogenization and hybridization. British rule, educational reforms, and monetization of the Indian economy initiated the process of commercialization of dowry, but there never was a thorough process of cultural domination, as British marriage traditions were never popular in India. Hence, what is labelled authentic or traditional is a construction that can consist of modern elements as well as traditional, rendering states such as Sudan and India as alternative modernities, instead of mere copies of Westernized modernities.

According to Tine David's perspective, Mexico is a state that could also be considered an alternative modernity. It is an alternative modernity because it combines trades of Western modernity with local cultural patterns. However, this process shows similar or parallel trades with other Latin American countries and, as such, Tine Davids labels Mexican modernity as a parallel modernity. The ideal of motherhood and the way this ideal figures in processes of democratization, as part of modernization processes, is paramount in this parallelism. The image of the ideal mother suits many political and national purposes. It serves as an ideal in national political discourses, appealing to women's ascribed moral superiority and democratic gifts, in the name of Mexico's democratization, to participate and make use of those characteristics within the political arena. At the same time, this ideal of moral superiority is used to 'safeguard' women from this harsh political world, as motherhood is considered to be the primary task of women, excluding women from the public and political realm. This is not unique for Mexico. It is also recognizable in the democratization processes of other Latin American countries; hence the parallel modernities.

What we see happening from this author's perspective is a hybridization of modernity and tradition, democratization and nationalism, internationalism and Latin cultural patterns. The inherent ambiguity of this ideal of motherhood makes this image central and instrumental to the articulation of all these processes. The same ambiguity, however, allows room for the agency of individual women. Women participating in politics can use different meanings of this ideal of motherhood. For some of these women, this ideal means an opportunity to combine professionalism with motherhood and, as such, to smooth out the contradictions of every day life.

The chapters in this part of the book not only provide insight into the limited scope in which a rigid dichotomy between modernity and tradition imprisons us. If we are to analyze globalization processes, we have to go beyond this rigid dichotomy. It also illuminates the value of looking through the gender lens. Depending on the chosen perspective of the authors, similar processes can be both homogeneous and heterogeneous. Locality can, thus, embrace both modernity and tradition. In addition, the time frame of what is called modern or traditional (and, in the end, globalization) is very elastic and has to be specified for each locality.

The Feminist Agenda: Questions for the Future

What we have seen so far in discussing the different parts of this book is that all authors have their own ways of fixing a certain perspective. The different ways the gender lens is used to observe the landscape also imply a different analytical emphasis on the interaction between the different dimensions of gender. One author highlights the interaction and power mechanisms of the interplay between the subjective and the symbolical dimension, as in questions of agency. Another author mainly highlights the interaction between symbolical and institutional dimensions in analyzing the global/local connection, as in the part on unexpected outcomes of globalization. This does not mean, however, that only the dimensions under scrutiny are at stake. The gender lens suggests a constant dynamic interplay and exercise of power within and between all dimensions of gender simultaneously. Analytically unravelling the knot that these dimensions form in practice illuminates and situates the complex interconnections between globalization, locality and gender.

We have addressed the analytical value of our gender analysis in this book and, in our view, it proves to be a useful methodology for scrutinizing the meaning of gender in globalization processes. The methodology of the multidimensional gender analysis forces us time and again to consider the power dynamics involved in this fixing, which involves all dimensions and, thus, to consider simultaneously the personal and the societal, the local and the global. In sum, what we see when looking through the gender lens is that the interaction within and between the separate different dimensions produces diversities that are no longer connected to a specific place. Nevertheless, these interactions are always situated in specific (power) relations and reworked by people. The gender approach offers us the tools to apprehend those connections, which are tied to a certain locality but, at the same time, surpass the limits of that locality. The symbolic dimension shows that ideas and symbols are, in essence, not authentic, but constructed out of all kinds of regional, local, national, religious and historical notions. Certain dominant discourses might seem universal, such as neo-liberalism. However, in the articulation with the institutional and subject dimensions, these discourses get reworked and altered. In the end, so-called universalism becomes diversified.

What we learn from the different chapters and the different perspectives in this book is that it is not so much the meaning of gender that is constant within globalization processes, it is rather the way in which it functions that offers similarity. From an actor's perspective, gender often figures in the articulation of the global with the local in such a way that it is a border marker in fixing the flow. This could be fixing the flow between modernity and tradition or between culture, nation and class or the fixing of certain discursive elements, e.g. sexuality and professionalism, under Peruvian secretaries (in chapter 3). At the same time, different meanings of gender are created in the global/local nexus that produce flows such as conflicting masculinities in Senegal (chapter 4) or conflicting ideals on feminine managerial capacities and on the inability of women to work in the car industry.

In our view, an alliance between the multidimensional gender approach and discussions of what globalization really encompasses, therefore, offers the prospect of a potential revitalization of the political project of women's studies. The political agenda is not an agenda of endless deconstructing, but a search for alliances – alliances that are context and time-related, which can be formed out of shared interests that may not necessarily include shared identities or positions. A shared methodology, though, without the aspirations of creating a new master narrative, could serve as a meeting point in such alliances, as this books shows. The methodology includes a continuous consciousness of the situatedness of knowledge production. Not only does this force an author to situate the subject being studied, but also to relate this to one's own perspective. Science production is also about politics, as we have seen in this book. Alliances are necessary both at a scientific level as well as on a practical level. This also means that, in practice, as Mohanty argues (cited in the introduction), not all anti-globalization needs to be feminist and vice versa. Some of it needs to be, some does not.

We agree that we see certain trends, such as the pervasive reappearance of the ideal of the nuclear family, with the domesticity of women and the role of provider for men. We also see a trend of feminization of labour as a result of neo-liberal restructuring, along with a trend of feminization of migration. But are these trends really global in the sense that they occur on a world scale causing the same effects everywhere? Does this make women the victims of globalization and globalization inherently suspect and wrong? We do not think so.

This does not mean, however, that we consider the world to be one happy creolization. Obviously we cannot negate the sometimes negative and destructive developments that accompany globalization. Nevertheless, we refuse to go along with generalizing theories that leave no room for differences and diversity among people, which call for resistance. Resistance to what and in which localities? This also means that the meaning of resistance has to be rethought. What is it that we want to resist and who is still the enemy. Resisting globalization and its impact has no meaning when it is not clear what we are talking about. As scientists, we have to have the courage to explore these questions. As policymakers and activists, we might not be able to afford such a luxury. Defending strategically inspired standpoints could go hand in hand with such scientific practice. However, these kinds of standpoints run the risk of becoming scientific truths, such as the different orthodoxies addressed in this book. The two need to be disentangled. Science production and policymaking have to be two critically-allied practices.

Thus, still more research is needed, which shifts away from essentialist stands on the public/private divide and integrates economic perspectives with politics, such as national identity building, or which combines a study on sexuality and ethnic identity. This means that we need more research that is not only interdisciplinary, but that takes into account the centrality of cultural processes in studying the global/local nexus. We are left with challenging questions in an ever-changing landscape, and answers to these complex questions never seem to be conclusive; hence, the analytical alliance.

Index